Lockheed
P-80/F-80
SHOOTING
STAR

A Photo Chronicle

David R. McLaren

Schiffer Military/Aviation History
Atglen, PA

Front cover artwork by Steve Ferguson, Colorado Springs, CO.

TERRORS OF TAEGU

As of June, 1950, the 49th Fighter-Bomber Wing stationed in Japan was one of the first all-jet units in the new U.S. Air Force ready to counter the North Korean offensive. The 7th, 8th, and 9th Squadrons were equipped with the Lockheed F-80, the first operational jet aircraft in USAF service, when they advanced to Taegu, South Korea. The 49ers had gained fame in World War II while flying the Lockheed P-38 Lightning, but the new generation jet was not a comparable air-to-air fighter. The 49ers were relegated to tactical missions and proved the F-80 to be an excellent fighter-bomber, despite its limited range.

The cover depicts 8 FBS "Blacksheep" in a napalm attack on a communications center in the snow dusted highlands of North Korea circa early 1951. Their Shooting Stars carry the notorious "Misawa" tip-tanks which afforded them the range to reach the most distant targets. The 49ers eventually transitioned to the Republic F-84 Thunderjet as the F-80s fell into obsolescence.

Dedicated to Homer D. McLaren
"Ab Origine Fidus"

Book Design by Ian Robertson.

Copyright © 1996 by David R. McLaren.
Library of Congress Catalog Number: 95-72398

Printed in China.
ISBN: 0-88740-907-5

We are interested in hearing from authors with book ideas on related topics.

Published by Schiffer Publishing Ltd.
77 Lower Valley Road
Atglen, PA 19310
Please write for a free catalog.
This book may be purchased from the publisher.
Please include $2.95 postage.
Try your bookstore first.

Contents

Foreword

The Shooting Star was designed from the onset to be the United States Army Air Force's first operational jet fighter. With this in mind, remember that although the F-80 was aesthetically attractive, it was a machine of war, to be maintained and flown by warriors. A fighter aircraft is nothing more than a highly mobile gun platform operated by a skilled combatant. To this end, it may seem, particularly in the portion of this book on the Korean War, that I have placed too much emphasis on detailing the circumstances of those pilots that were lost. Well, this was my intention, as this book is intended to be a tribute to both the aircraft and the pilots that flew it in the "Forgotten War."

One thing that should be mentioned here, also, is that I have used interchangeably the designations of "Field" and "Air Force Base" as well as P-80 and F-80. In September 1947 the signing of the National Security Act that created the United States Air Force also brought about the redesignation of all Air Fields to Air Force Bases. In June 1948 all Air Force fighters were changed from "P," pursuit, to "F," fighter. As the time span covering the history of the Shooting Star jumps back and forth across this period from chapter to chapter so often, I felt it best to just continue with using the dual designations, for continuities sake.

OPPOSITE: The dark stripe above the number 34 contained a simple string that would slew off to the side, indicating to the pilot that the aircraft was yawing. Although new, the grey paint is already beginning to show wear, and it was soon done away with, as it was superfluous to the operation of the aircraft. (USAF)

Chapter I: In The Beginning

Although development of jet propulsion and jet powered aircraft began in the late 1930s, the war clouds and national security of the involved nations obscured the knowledge of most of these programs from the general public. Frank Whittle of Britain was the first to perfect a viable jet engine. Germany was the first to get a jet powered aircraft into the air, on August 27, 1939, with the Heinkel He 178. But the aircraft industry in the United States at this time was concentrating upon developing newer and faster conventionally powered aircraft, along with planning how to gear-up these industries for the anticipated mass production of these aircraft for the foreseeable war.

Then, in 1941 the Bell Aircraft Corporation was awarded a contract for the first American built jet fighter, the XP-59A, their Model 27. This aircraft was equipped with two I-16 engines, based upon Whittle's original design, and were supplied from British sources, At this time the American engine manufactures were still involved with developing conventional engines.

First flown on October 1, 1942, the XP-59A proved to be a disappointment, for many reasons, even though it was on the cutting edge of the new era. Aerodynamically it suffered from 1930s technology and its critical Mach, the maximum attainable speed it could reach, was held back by its very shape and airfoil employed. The British furnished engines were less than sufficiently powerful for the XP-59As weight and inherent drag. Depending on altitude, it was some 50 mph slower than the presently operational fighters, the P-38 and P-40, and 75 mph slower than the early P-47 and P-51 models.

Although the Lockheed Aircraft Corporation, Burbank, CA had indicated in late 1939 that they were interested in becoming involved in a jet propelled aircraft program, this was officially discouraged by the War Department. They wanted Lockheed to concentrate on their P-38 and other programs for the duration.

Finally, in May 1943, their Chief Research Engineer, Clarence "Kelly" Johnson was approached by Army Air Force officials while he was observing some P-38 armament trials at Eglin Field, FL and informed that the Air Force was now interested in seeing a proposal from Lockheed for a new jet propelled fighter. The idea for which had never been far from Johnson's mind to begin with, and on the flight back to California, Johnson roughed out his thoughts on foolscap. Johnson then presented his sketches to Lockheed's Vice

OPPOSITE: The first American attempt at jet propulsion came through the Bell Aircraft Corporation XP-59. This example was a YP-59A-BE, and it was powered by two General Electric I-16 (J31-GE) engines that only provided 1650 pounds of thrust, each. This particular aircraft was assigned to the U.S. Navy as BuAer 63960, thus it was one of the Army Air Force's first jets, and the USN's first jet, too. (Bell Aerospace Textron)

A P-59-BE with an abbreviated serial number, due to a replacement rudder. Nineteen examples of this version of the Airacomet were assigned to the 412th Fighter Group for development of jet fighter procedures and tactics prior to the Group receiving P-80s. (Bell Aerospace Textron)

Clarence "Kelly" Johnson. The master designer whose contributions to American airpower are legendary. (Lockheed)

July 17, 1943 and design work on the XP-80 is underway. The entire engineering section facilities were in temporary facilities attached to Lockheed's main plant in thrown together quarters. Eventually this establishment would be identified as the "Skunk Works." (Lockheed)

Kelly Johnson and Lockheed engineers discuss the placement of internal equipment in the XP-80's nose. (Lockheed)

President and Chief Engineer, Hall L. Hibbard, and other Lockheed representatives, and then with their blessings, he flew to Wright Field, OH later in the month to present a rough draft of what Lockheed had in mind, their Model L-140, to the Air Force.

Based upon this preliminary work, they were again invited back to another conference at Wright Field between June 16-18 to seriously pitch their program, fully identified as Project MX-409. Johnson and a Mr. Meeker from the attached Army Air Force Project Section, presented this proposal to Colonel N. P. Swofford, from Wright's Aircraft Laboratory.

Some comments upon this initial proposal were: The air intake ducts appeared to be too small to meet the engine's demand and capability, the 185 pounds allowed for the installation of radio equipment was not sufficient, the ratio between empty and gross weight, 71% was optimistic. The estimated highest speed attainable was probably conservative, as it was based upon data furnished by the XP-58 Chain

Lightning's wing, which had a greater thickness that the one envisioned. The elevator and rudder controls appeared that they might be marginal, as they were 19% and 27%, respectively, of the total horizontal and vertical tail surfaces. Aileron control appeared that it would be satisfactory. Here was a case where Johnson knew exactly what he was proposing, as he foreseen the need for a hydraulic aileron boost system, whereas Swofford did not believe that it would be necessary. The ailerons in all P-80s and later T-33s would require boosting for ease of controllability. Johnson guaranteed delivery of the first aircraft within 180 days. But again, he knew what he was doing, as he already had jump-started the program in May by gathering a team of engineers and ordering the project to commence.

It was through this jump-starting that another entirely new era began through the creation of the now famous "Skunk Works." The original development team of 128 people for the XP-80 program had to be located in a makeshift area next to Lockheed's wind tunnel in a facility constructed from packing

The hand fabricated mock-up of the XP-80 with a dummy H-1B engine on July 24, 1943. (Lockheed)

The prototype XP-80 under construction on August 4, 1943. A good indication of how the air intakes were incorporated into its fuselage is given. (Lockheed)

Four days later, August 7, and the construction of the leading edge of the wing is underway on a hand built jig. (Lockheed)

August 14, 1943 and the XP-80's fuselage longerons and bulkheads are in place. (Lockheed)

crates and tents, as there was no room in the Burbank plant for another new project.

An official letter covering this meeting was written on June 19, and on June 24 a Letter Contract for Lockheed's Model L-140 was given. This provided for Lockheed to produce one prototype aircraft at a cost to the government of $495, 210.00, exclusive of a 4% fixed fee for Lockheed.

Between July 20-22 a mock-up inspection of the prototype, now designated as the XP-80, was made at Burbank. Only a few minor changes were seen to be necessary at this point. So far 689 pages of engineering drawings had been required.

By mid August the airframe was actually starting to take shape with the fuselage bulkheads installed and the wings were being skinned with aluminum. The empennage sections had been built and were ready for attachment. But there was no engine, so a wooden mockup had to be fitted. The engine, a Halford HB-1 turbojet, was scheduled for delivery on September 1, but unfortunately it would not arrive until November 2.

Still, the AAF was pleased with the XP-80s progress, and a cost plus fixed fee contract, W535 ac-40680, was approved on October 16 that replaced Lockheed's out of pocket expenses. A total of $515,018.40 was now allocated, which included their 4% fixed fee of $19,808.40.

On November 2 the HB-1 finally arrived. After this engine was installed the XP-80 was moved to Muroc Field on November 13 and ground tests began. The first flight was scheduled for November 17, but as the engine was being run in preparation, the intake ducts inside of the fuselage imploded. It was initially thought that the HB-1 had been destroyed by aluminum being sucked into its compressor section, but a teardown inspection showed that this was not the case. Yet the incident did have a good outcome, as flaws in the compressor vanes that had not previously been noticed were now brought to their attention. If "Lulu-Belle," as the XP-80 was to be fondly named, had actually been flown, the engine might have suffered a catastrophic failure in flight and resulted in the loss of the aircraft.

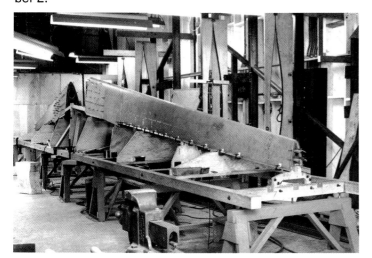

The skinning of the XP-80s wing. Production versions of the P-80 would have fuel tanks in this area. (Lockheed)

On the same date, the aft section of the XP-80 with a dummy H-1B engine installed. (Lockheed)

A month later, on September 18, the XP-80 now has been skinned and its empennage attached. (Lockheed)

On the following day the wing filets were attached. (Lockheed)

A replacement engine finally arrived on December 27 and the first flight was scheduled for January 7, 1944. After a day's delay in waiting for Muroc's lakebed runways to dry sufficiently from recent rains, Lockheed's Chief Test Pilot Milo Burcham took off at 9:10 am.

The first flight lasted for a bare five minutes, as Burcham had neglected to override the landing gear's safety switch that prevented ground retraction of the gear and could not retract the landing gear. He also complained of aileron oversensitivity, due to the hydraulic boost.

After being reassured that the ailerons were as they should be, and being reappraised of the landing gear's safety switch, Burcham was off again at 10:00 for a functional flight check of the XP-80. High out over the desert, he took "Lulu-Belle" to the previously unattainable speed of 490 mph in level flight, and then returned to Muroc to thrill all those that had worked so hard in developing what would become America's first operational jet fighter with a series of high speed passes and aileron rolls.

During the next calendar week Burcham flew the XP-80 three more times to ascertain Lulu-Belle's flight characteristics. While these flights were "seat of the pants" types, they were backed up by a slave instrument panel in the nose gun bay that was being photographed by a 35mm double-frame camera so that Lockheed's engineers could correlate Burcham's written reports with filmed instrument readings.

Burcham's complaints of the way the aircraft handled as it approached a stall, and then fell into one, were of the most consideration. To begin with, there was little warning of an impending stall, and then Lulu-Belle would sharply roll to the right when it went into the full stall with the flaps down. This obviously could be a dangerous situation for a pilot as he prepared to land. Lockheed engineers went to the wind tunnel to develop a new leading edge wing fillet to solve this problem. There were also complaints of "snakeiness," at high speeds, which were resolved through the modification of the rudder fin tip and wing tips from the prototype squared-off version to rounded tips. The leading edge of the horizontal

By September 24 the forward section is partially skinned and the air intakes attached. (Lockheed)

Two weeks later the XP-80 is really starting to look like an airplane. "Comet" was the code name given to the project under wartime secrecy. (Lockheed)

October 13, 1943 and the XP-80 is armed with Browning .50 caliber M-2 machine guns. (Lockheed)

On November 6, 1943 the engine finally arrived and was installed. (Lockheed)

stabilizer was also raised 1 1/2 degrees to improve elevator control.

As the HB-1, "Goblin" (Following the British propensity to name things.), had been derated from 3,000 pounds of thrust to only 2,240 pounds, to extend its service life, following flight tests were conducted through April 13 at reduced power settings. In spite of the derating, the Goblin still produced enough power to push the XP-80 beyond 500 mph, and up to 40,000 feet.

Coinciding with the scheduled first flight of the XP-80 on January 6, Lockheed had submitted their proposal to the Air Force for their next version. Identified as the L-181, this aircraft would be the XP-80A that would be built around the I-40 engine. The XP-80A was eighteen inches longer than the XP-80, spanned twenty-two inches wider, was six hundred pounds heavier, due to the weight of the new engine, and incorporated many internal changes: as shortened but larger and improved air intake ducts, night flying instrumentation, and increased fuel capacity.

The new I-40 engine would be a major improvement and also a source of anal pain. Originally, a contract had been offered to Allis-Chalmers at Milwaukee, WI to mass produce the HB-1 for use in the P-80 program. Due to many factors, several of which were beyond Allis-Chalmers control, these engines all proved to be inadequate. The Air Force finally received three of them via a sub-contract from the U.S. Navy, and these all suffered from manufacturing flaws and were returned to the USN in January 1947 after little use.

The original contract for the improved I-40 engine went to General Electric's plant at Schennectady, NY. But it soon became apparent that they would fail to fulfill the demand for production. Thus, a second choice gave the contract to General Motors Allison Division at Indianapolis. Lockheed would have "considerable difficulty with the I-40 and Allison engines. (A) lack of engines, (B) lack of spare parts, (C) poor design features and poor maintenance. To the end of 1945 this was the major delay in delivery of new airplanes."

Ten days later the armament was removed and replaced by instrumentation that would be photographed during flight trials, which reduced the pilot's note taking and workload. (Lockheed)

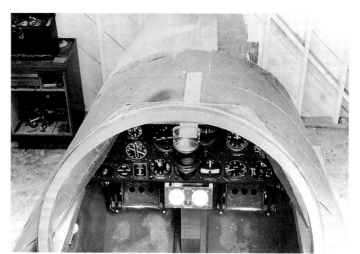

The instrument panel of "Lulu-Belle" prior to the windshield's installation. Quite simple, with only basic engine and flight instruments. Compare with the later panels in the production versions. (Lockheed)

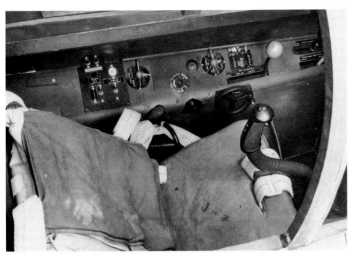

The left side of the XP-80's cockpit with throttle and trim controls, radio and fuel selectors. (Lockheed)

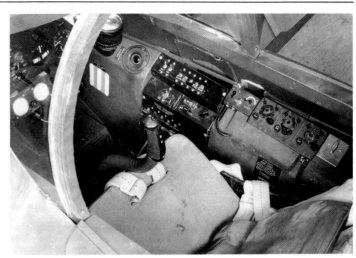

The XP-80's armament selector panel was located on the cockpits right side. Later it was relocated to the forward instrument panel. (Lockheed)

On February 16 a contract supplement letter was received by Lockheed for two XP-80As at a cost of $889,564.00 (not including the fixed 4% fee.) The first example was to be available in 150 days, and the second within 180 days.

The first of these, 44-83021, "The Grey Ghost," was completed in 132 days and was sent to Muroc on June 3. On June 10 Lockheed test pilot Anthony "Tony" LeVier made the first flight with it, and came close to disaster. After 35 minutes into the test flight, LeVier encountered a "split flap" situation where the left flap failed to extend. With the right flap fully lowered, LeVier was faced with an asymmetrical lift situation and corresponding desire for the aircraft to roll violently to the left. He managed to keep his airspeed up to land hot and long on Muroc's dry lakebed without damage to the aircraft.

The Grey Ghost would be further used to determine the XP-80A's flight characteristics, including stability and control tests.

The next example was the "Silver Ghost," 44-83022. It was completed on July 27, three days ahead of the official due date, but two weeks behind Lockheed's own schedule for it. The slippage in delivery being due to Lockheed installation of a second seat in it behind the pilot for an engineering observer. The first flight with this airplane was made on August 1 and lasted for 37.5 minutes. "As a two-place airplane, this XP-80A was considered primarily the engine research article." It would also be flown against the P-51D in maneuverability experiments by Wright Field personnel.

The prototype XP-80, 44-83020, was painted a dark spinach green. After completing service trials, it was placed in storage in 1946, and was later restored by the National Air and Space Museum. It is now on display in Washington, D.C. (Lockheed)

The beginning of the static engine test at Muroc Air Base on November 18, 1943 with the H-1B powerplant. (Lockheed)

As General Hap Arnold, Chief of Staff, Army Air Force, was following the XP-80 developments quite closely, he started to push for an immediate expansion of the program right after he got word of the successful first flights. On March 10 a Letter Contract had been verbally issued for thirteen more examples, to be designated as YP-80As. Accordingly, Contract W-33038 ac-2393 was approved on July 1 by Arnold for the 13 examples, plus one static test model, at a cost of $4,190,424.00 plus the 4% additional for Lockheed. The last of these were scheduled for delivery by March 1945, but as usual, Johnson ramrodded the program into an expedited rate that delivered the last of the YP-80As in December 1944.

Lockheed hoped that eventual wartime delivery production would run at 450 aircraft per month, with a corresponding comparative reduction of their P-38 construction program. But engine production could not attain this rate, nor could the involved subcontractors.

The YP-80A series ran in a block between 44-83023 and -83035, with the second example, -83024, being pulled for modification to a photo reconnaissance aircraft which was designated as the YF-14. All of these examples were to be used for accelerated tests. The first flight of the YP-80A was on September 13 and lasted for 45 minutes. The following day it was transferred to Moffett Field for instrumentation and future use by NACA, the National Advisory Committee for Aeronautics, the forerunner of NASA.

The third YP-80A attempted to make its first flight on October 20 but crashed fifty seconds after starting its takeoff roll. Milo Burcham was taking off from the Lockheed Air Terminal at Burbank on a standard test flight with the intention of climbing to 25,000 feet to conduct controllability tests. Observers noted that the takeoff was normal, but that the landing gear and flaps appeared to retract slower than normal, which indicated a possible engine failure. After attaining an altitude of 300 feet, the Shooting Star turned ninety degrees

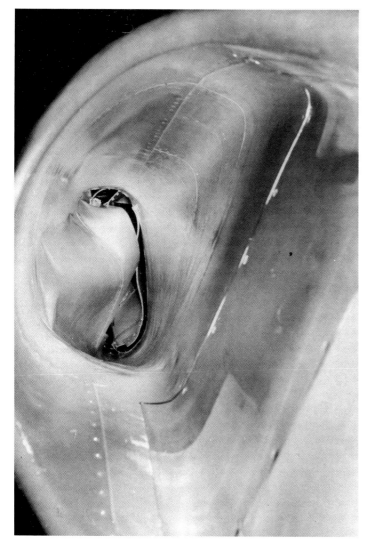
And the result. The implosion of the air intake ducts inside of "Lulubelle's" fuselage. (Lockheed)

The business end of "Lulu-Belle." The nose placement of the machine guns simplified boresighting and negated the problems of establishing a convergence firing pattern, as in wing mounted guns. (Lockheed)

Nicknamed "Lulu-Belle," the prototype XP-80 at Muroc Air Base on December 4, 1943. (Lockheed)

On the hard-pack surface at Muroc, "Lulu-Belle" shows her exceptionally clean lines. (Lockheed)

The XP-80 spanned 37', was 32' 10" long, and stood 10' 3." Her empty weight was 6,287 pounds, with a design gross weight of 8,620 pounds. Note the squared off wing tips and vertical fin. (Lockheed)

The second example of the now named "Shooting Star" was the XP-80A, 44-83021, and this particular aircraft was nicknamed "The Grey Ghost." Lockheed test pilot Tony LeVier had to bail out of it on March 20, 1945 after its engine disintegrated. (via Leo Kohn)

44-85004, the thirteenth example from the first production run of P-80A-1s. This aircraft served in the accelerated testing program at Muroc Field, and then went to Tyndall Field for armament trials. This aircraft finished its service with the 188th Fighter Interceptor Squadron as a maintenance trainer. (Lockheed)

The business end of a new P-80. The two small doors just in front of the nose gear strut are the shell ejection ports for spent .50 caliber rounds. The gun camera is located in the small bulge in the starboard air intake. (Air Force Museum)

to the right, leveled off, and then went into a glide to crash into the side of a gravel pit.

As this was Burcham's first flight in the YP-80A, it was believed that he had not made himself aware of the modification to the aircraft that provided for a emergency fuel system backup in the event of a main fuel pump failure, which was apparently what had occurred. (He should have held the starter button down, which would have cut in the starter fuel pump.) Atypical of accident board findings, the primary cause of the accident was that the pilot failed to complete an emergency landing. The contributing cause was that the engine failed.

44-83026 through -83029 were handled as a group and were dedicated to Project EXTRAVERSION, which sent two of them to England, and two more to Italy. To expedite this program, cannibalization of the other YP-80As had to take place, which meant that although Kelly Johnson had them all available in December, some were now lacking parts and the Air Force would not be able to take delivery of the last YP-80A until February 21, 1945.

Back in April 1944 the Air Force conducted their official inspection of the XP-80 and decided that the aircraft was equal to their expectations in all respects. Thus even though the first of the XP-80A was still under construction at this time a tentative Letter Contract was drafted on April 4, 1944 for 1,000 P-80A-1s. Although this contract was not formalized until December 9, 1944 as Contract W33-038 ac-2527, it was sufficient to encourage Lockheed to gear-up for the mass production of the Shooting Star.

This contract called for a unit cost of $75,913.00 for the first 500 P-80As, $55,709.00 for the second 500. (The second batch would then only be $3,000.00 more per example than the cost of a P-51D.) The first of the first group of P-80As was scheduled for the end of 1945, and the second group by the end of 1946. (This contract would be terminated, in part,

Static testing to determine the strength of the P-80 was accomplished at Wright Field. A combination of lead shot filled bags and hydraulic presses were used to stress the airframe to destruction, to determine just how much physical stress the aircraft could take. Note the fatigue wrinkles. (Air Force Museum)

Lead shot bags are placed upon a P-80s empennage at Wright Field. The standard for the period was a requirement to sustain 7.3 times the weight of gravity without material failure. In practice, the P-80 could withstand 9 G's with a full load of fuel, or 12 G's when nearly empty. (Air Force Museum)

by the end of World War II, for on September 5, 1945 83 contracted for P-80As were deleted, and 123 additional ones were deleted on December 17. But, this later group were reinstated by contract addendum on January 24, 1946.)

Subsequent contract revisions muddled the cost of the aircraft and their numbers. Supplement 6 to ac-2527 on June 30, 1945 changed the unit cost down to $64,096.00, but then it was revised upwards on April 2, 1946 to $83,322.00, for a total contract cost to the taxpayer of $17,639,412.00. This was brought about by the reduction of the numbers of P-80As to be built, readjustment of the delivery schedule, and revisions suggested to enhance the capability of the aircraft.

Several other contracts were issued and then modified or canceled altogether. W33-038 ac-8388 was issued on

February 5, 1945 and called for 3,000 P-80A-1s at a cost of $37,000,000.00. It was terminated in part on May 26 with the end of the war in Europe by canceling 452 aircraft. This contract then had 1,863 more P-80s deleted on August 13 after the dropping of the A-Bomb, and was canceled altogether on September 5.

Another major contract for P-80As, W33-038 ac-7717 had been signed with North American Aviation to build 1,000 P-80As at their Kansas City, KS B-25 plant. North American Aviation having beat out the Glenn L. Martin Company in their bid of $56,775,000.00. Their version would have been identified as the P-80N, and it would have had a 100% percent commonality with the P-80A. Lockheed was to have furnished enough material and design information to get North Ameri-

Accelerated service trials were conducted at Muroc Field with representatives from Lockheed and various departments of the Air Force on hand to conduct testing in their own particular areas of expertise. Tony LeVier, on the far right, and his crew from Lockheed. (Lockheed)

Lockheed's test pilot Tony LeVier. (Lockheed)

First flown on March 27, 1948 by Tony LeVier, the prototype TF-80C was the protégé of the longest serving jet trainer in the world. The USAF still had one in their active inventory in 1994, forty-six years later. (Lockheed)

can started with the new contract. On May 26, 1945 this contract was canceled.

The Army Air Force accepted the first production P-80A-1 in February 1945 and in March the production line was in full swing. Yet there were numerous problems. A large number of production delays were encountered through the lack of parts to be furnished by subcontractors, or parts that were found to be defective to begin with. Engines and other government supplied items, as machine guns, were also behind delivery schedules.

Nevertheless, Lockheed managed to meet their own production schedule until December 1945 when a strike hit General Motors and effected their Allison Division, which then delayed aircraft production beyond Lockheed's control. Then, just as this matter was cleared up, all P-80s with Allison J-33-9 engines, as the I-40 was now designated, had to be grounded because of problems encountered with ancillary equipment.

The first P-80As were sent to Muroc for Accelerated Service Tests and "debugging." These tests were conducted by pilots from Wright Field, Lockheed, and by selectees from the 412th Fighter Group, all to work in concert to get the P-80

Representing Wright Field were Captain Wallace Lein, pilot, and Captain Nathan Rosengarten, Flight Test Engineer. (Lockheed)

48-356, a F-80C-1, was modified by Lockheed at their own expense to become the prototype TF-80C/T-33. It was later further modified to become the first XF-94, and is now on display as such at Lackland AFB, TX. (Lockheed)

The pilot's office of P-80A-5 44-85337. (Air Force Museum)

operational as quickly as possible. All of these pilots were highly experienced fighter pilots, and most were aces, Notable names assigned to the program were the likes of Don Gentile and Steve Pisanos, who had scored 21 and 10 aerial victories with the 4th Fighter Group, respectively. Others were Jim Little and Jim Fitzgerald, Russel Schleeh, and Colonel George Price, who would head-up Wright Field's portion of

the program. The 412th Fighter Group sent Captain's Charles Tucker, John Babel, Jerry Stidham and John Russell. Probably the most recognizable name of them all was Medal of Honor recipient Major Richard Bong, the Air Force's highest soaring fighter pilot with forty kills.

The Service Tests were originally to involve three YP-80As and one P-80A and a total of 200 hours of flying time. But they were extended to cover 500 hours, and these flights resulted in the reporting of over 300 discrepancies.

One of the major discrepancies noted was the inability to jettison the canopy in flight in an emergency. In an incident where Captain Tucker had a partial flameout and thought that the P-80 was on fire because he could see a trail of unburned fuel behind him, which he thought was smoke, he attempted to bailout, only to find that he could not open the canopy. To solve this, Lockheed developed the T-2 canopy remover, which was an explosive charge to blow the canopy off. Subcontracted to Bell for testing, the device was either added to new aircraft, or retrofitted to those that were already built.

Another encountered problem was the loss of the hydraulically boosted flight controls during an engine failure, which

The more complex "office" of a F-80C with rearranged instrumentation and ordnance panels. (Air Force Museum)

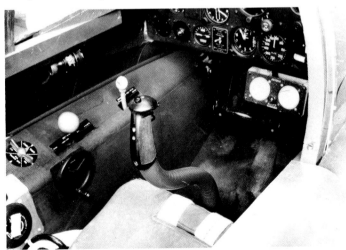

The austere left console of the XP-80. (Lockheed)

By the time the F-80C came along, the left console became more cluttered. This particular example was even more so, as it was modified for evaluation of the F-86s A1C gunsight. (Air Force Museum)

The differences between the P-80A-1 and A-5 versions was the boundary layer control splitter plates inside of the air intakes and relocation of the landing light from the aircraft's nose to the nose wheel landing gear strut (Not installed on this aircraft.), which was replaced by the ADF compass loop antenna. (Air Force Museum)

meant that the boost pumps lost their power source. This could be overcome by manhandling the controls. But the engine driven fuel pumps also lost their power source, so an electrically driven fuel pump was installed as a back-up.

One source of frustration, and some unfounded fear, was that of the phenomenon of "duct rumble." As the air was sucked into the engine ducts, there were areas of both high and low pressure within the ducts, themselves. These two air masses created their own little war within the ducts, which often sounded as a rumble, or sometimes as an organ. With an intake on either side of the pilot, the compressed air within the two ducts fought for superiority, too, and the high and low pressure areas caused the aircraft to "search."

It took some time to ascertain the cause of this rumble, and the correction resulted in the installation of a boundary air control baffle plate inside the entrance of each duct, along with bleed-air ducts to relieve the pressure. Although credit has never been given to the P-80 for its part in discovering this problem, an off-shoot of future experiments with boundary air control discovered that it could be used to good effect and resulted in the usage of some of this wasted compressed air to power ancillary equipment and provide additional lift to an aircraft's control surfaces in later aircraft. The Accelerated Service Tests continued until November 6, 1945 and encompassed a total of 379 flights.

Commencing on July 26, 1944 a combination of flight tests began to determine both what kind of a fighter the P-80 was going to be, and primarily, how to defend bombers against jet fighters, as this was even more of a concern to the AAF at the moment than getting the P-80 into combat. The situation at this time was that Allied bombers were encountering German jet fighters over Europe, and were virtually defenseless against them. Hand held machine guns were worthless, and defensive machine gun turrets could not track at the speed required to follow a jet's path. The first simulated interception trials were run against five B-24s that were escorted by six

P-38s, with Lulu-Belle being the attacking aircraft. Armed with gun cameras, the defenders film showed that no hits were scored on Lulu-Belle while the XP-80 pilot's film showed that he had scored twice on the B-24s in ten simulated gunnery passes. The following day the bombers escort was flown by P-47s, and they managed to "hit" the P-80 twice. On July 29 six brand new P-51Ds were used as escorts, and they were all flown by highly experienced flight commanders. Here, the P-80 pilot was unable to make a successful attack on the bombers, as the Mustang pilots coordinated their defense against him. (Still, he was out numbered six to one.)

In tests against a P-51B, the Mustang was rated as superior in initial acceleration in both dives and level flight. In zoom climbs, the P-51B was superior when the climb was continued to the point of reaching a stall. The Mustang could out turn the P-80 any time below 175 mph. In all other respects the underpowered XP-80 was superior, particularly in the rate of roll, a highly critical factor in combat.

Future development programs eventually resulted in the P-80B-1 and B-5. This version was originally identified as the P-80Z, which was the envisioned ultimate P-80. But, as many of the envisioned revisions to the P-80 design were unfeasible on this aircraft, they were carried through to the future XP-90 project.

The prototype XP-80B, 44-85200, a P-80A-1, originally was constructed with only four .50 caliber machine guns and an Allison J-33-21 engine with water-alcohol injection. It was later modified for the attempt on the World Speed Record by clipping its wingtips and the installation of a smaller canopy, and was redesignated as a P-80R, and named "Racey."

Thus the items that could be incorporated were added to the last 240 P-80A examples under the existing ac-2527 contract, which became the P-80B under Change Order 81. The P-80B-1 had some sixty-five design improvements over the P-80A-5. Paramount in this was to be the installation of an

Lockheed's production line. Note on the nearest example that the plenum chamber doors are off the aircraft, but the empennage control push rods are in place. (Air Force Museum)

ejection seat that was designed, built and installed by Lockheed. Unfortunately this particular seat would not be debugged, installed and become operational for five years. A water-alcohol injection system was added to the improved Allison J-33-21 engine that provided 600 pounds more thrust. The pitot tube was relocated to the leading edge of the vertical fin (But it would be returned to the nose section on the later C model). Browning M-3 .50 caliber machine guns were intended for the B-1 version, but deliveries of them were slow, and they were not installed until the B-5 version, thus the B-1 still carried the earlier M-2 Brownings. Yet as the nose bulkheads were strengthened, they could at least all be fired now, as it had been found that only two machine guns could be fired at a time on the P-80A without causing damage to the aircraft's nose. Note here that a major foreign publication stated in 1948 that the P-80B's wing was thinner than that of the P-80A, and was constructed of thicker aluminum. This is not true! The wings of all P-80s, including the later T-33 and F-94A were all built with the NACA 65 (1) 213 airfoil, and these wings were interchangeable between all models. Historians writing of the P-80 have all picked up upon this error as gospel, unfortunately.

Effective with serial number 45-8478, but not running inclusively, through 45-8717, 209 P-80B-1s were built. From this number, 45-8481 and 45-8566/8595, were further modified to become the P-80B-5. This was the "winterized" version that came as a result of cold weather testing at Ladd Field during the winters of 1945-46 and 1946-47. The P-80B-5 also carried the Browning M-3 machine guns as standard equipment, as they finally became available. These P-80B-5s were all delivered to the 94th Fighter Squadron, which took them to Alaska for cold weather operations, and then turned them over to the 57th Fighter Group.

The final version of the P-80 resulted in the P-80C, which was powered by either the J-33A-23 or J-33A-35 engines that produced 5,400 pounds thrust with water-alcohol injection. The initial contract for these came through Fiscal Year

1947 funds that provided 91 examples of the P-80C-1 and 75 P-80C-5s. These were either allocated to the Air National Guard or to the U.S. Navy. In Fiscal Year 1948, which began in those days on July 1, 98 more F-80C-1s were contracted for, (As the P-80 had become redesignated as the F-80 the previous month.), and the final contract, issued for Fiscal year 1949, called for 692 F-80C-10s.

From the Fiscal Year 1948 contract, the first twenty examples, beginning with 48-356, and the last seven, beginning with 48-913 were modified to become the TF-80C, a two-place trainer conversion. This trainer version was developed and built with Lockheed funds, as Lockheed believed that the aircraft was a necessity, yet the Air Force had to be convinced, first, that it would be a viable program. To accomplish this, the fuselage was extended 29" in front of the wing's leading edge and 12" inches at the wing's trailing edge. A second fully equipped cockpit was installed. The prototype TF-80C, 48-356, and 48-373 from the first batch of 27 were later modified into an all-weather fighter version, identified as the YF-94. The Fiscal Year 1949 contract was similarly modified and resulted in the production of 561 P-80C-10s and 127 TF-80Cs. With the termination of the P-80 contracts in 1949, the TF-80C was redesignated as the T-33A on May 5.

The XF-14 photo reconnaissance version, which was later redesignated as the FP-80A, and then the RF-80A on June 11, 1948, stemmed from the second YP-80A, 44-83024. In general appearance, it was identical to the other YP-80As, with the exception of not having any gun ports. Instead, a window for the camera was built into the lower nose section in front of the nose wheel.

One of the requirements for the training of night fighter crews was the ability to recognize an aircraft by its exhaust pattern in the dark. In most cases each specific aircraft has a recognizable exhaust signature in the dark, due to the placement of its exhaust stacks and emitted flames. Yet, in the P-80 an exhaust flame was only visible at night from directly behind the aircraft. On December 6, 1944 Lockheed test pilot Claypool was up in the XF-14 to work in conjunction with a Lockheed crewed B-25 to attempt to locate the XF-14 in the dark by this obscured exhaust pattern. The XF-14 was operating without its navigation lights on for this test, and for an unknown reason, so was the B-25. The two aircraft collided head-on in flight, and all were lost.

P-80A 44-85260 was then modified with a hinged-forward nose section as a replacement for the lost XF-14 and was redesignated as a F-14A. Painted in a gloss-grey scheme this aircraft's modifications included the installation of oblique cameras, along with the downward camera port.

Thirty-eight P-80As were pulled from the 44-85XXX series for modification to F-14s by Lockheed, and then the block 45-8364/8477 were obtained by contract from the Air Force for additional F-14s. With Korean War demands for even more photo reconnaissance aircraft, many of the P-80As and Cs were later modified by contractors to RF-80 configuration. These being recognizable by their having a slightly bulged

The roll-out of a fighter. (Lockheed)

appearance to their nose section, in contrast to the smooth lines of Lockheed's factory production.

In all, the Air Force accepted a total of 1,731 F-80s and 128 TF-80Cs that stemmed from the initial Shooting Star contracts. The final fly-away costs were $93,456.00 per airplane: $62,050.00 for the aircraft itself, $21,192.00 per engine (installed), $5,536.00 for electronic's, and $4,678.00 for the armament system. Considering the workload placed upon it during the Korean War, the taxpayers certainly got their money's worth.

Early Attrition

As might be expected with the newly developed concept of jet aircraft, the attrition rate was high. Unfortunately, the loss rate was atrociously high for the new Shooting Star, far exceeding all expectations.

A part of this, of course, was due to the newness of the aircraft itself; jet propulsion being spectacularly new. Yet the high accident rate and its causes demanded investigation for several reasons beyond the obvious loss of life and aircraft. A fortune was involved in present and future jet development. Adverse publicity generated by the accidents created a general public roar and Congress was loath to provide funding for development of such new and seemingly farfetched projects in Post War budget cutbacks for something that just might not prove as viable as conventional aircraft, particularly as there was a massive stockpile of surplus aircraft and no present or future plans for their use.

In addition, many "prop jocks," believed that conventionally powered aircraft were supreme to those "blow jets," and all they had to do was to quote the accident statistics to prove it. What good was a jet fighter if all it could do is create a smoking hole?

Brand new F-80C-10s on Lockheed's ramp being prepared for delivery to the 57th Fighter Group at Anchorage, AK. When the 57th FG switched to the F-94, these F-80s went to Korea, and 49-1895 was lost on June 22, 1952. (Lockheed)

Between October 20, 1944 and August 8, 1945 there had been fifteen P-80 accidents. To cite examples: On October 20 Lockheed test pilot Milo Burcham was killed in the second YP-80, 44-83025. On December 6 while conducting aircraft lighting tests the XF-14, 44-83024, and a B-25 were lost in a mid-air collision at night.

The next example, 44-83026, one of the EXTRAVERSION aircraft, was lost in England with Major Frederick Borsodi being killed on January 28, 1945. The preliminary finding indicated the failure of the tailpipe flange which was followed by a fire and explosion. Smoke, or vapor, had been seen emitting from the tailpipe prior to Borsodi turning back towards Burtonwood for an attempt at an emergency landing. (Fitted with a Rolls-Royce B-41 engine, -83027 was damaged beyond repair on November 14, 1945 during an attempted emergency landing in England. It had been retained there for further testing with a new powerplant as the RAF had expressed interest in the design as a back-up to their Meteor).

XP-80 44-83021 crashed on March 20 with Lockheed test pilot Tony LeVier bailing out. He had climbed "The Grey Ghost" to between 10,000 and 11,000 feet to conduct air intake rumble tests. (The aircraft was in standard configuration except that the intake ducts had been reduced 20%). At an indicated airspeed of 450 mph, LeVier heard a "terrific clatter in the aft end of the fuselage, which was followed by a nosing down of the airplane . . . the airplane preformed a number of gyrations, reported consisting of both tumbling and rolling." The tail section of the aircraft was found a half mile east of the remainder of the aircraft, and LeVier either fell out or was sucked out after jettisoning the canopy. He suffered a fractured vertebrae. The cause of this lost was found to be due to a failure of the engine's turbine wheel, as it had been constructed from an improperly cast ingot.

On July 1, 1st Lt. Joseph Mandl, 6th Ferrying Group, was killed in P-80A-1 44-85017 at Long Beach. He had made two previous attempts to get airborne, and on the third attempt the Shooting Star stalled-off on its right wing, skidded through a fence and hit a parked A-26. Observers stated that in all takeoff attempts the aircraft's acceleration had appeared unusually slow. Investigation showed that Mandl had set the flaps to 45 degrees, which was improper for the short runway in use and the aircraft's gross weight of 13,803 pounds.

On August 2 Major Ira Jones was on a ferry mission from Wright Field, Ohio when his 44-83029 crashed thirty minutes after takeoff near Ft. Knox, KY. The aircraft disintegrated in flight. The cause could not be ascertained in this incident.

As mentioned, the United States most noted fighter pilot, Major Richard Bong, was killed on August 6 while making an acceptance flight of 44-85048. Bong took off in weather conditions reported CAVU, Ceiling and Visibility Unlimited, with only a five mile an hour wind. The takeoff appeared normal and Bong climbed out to a point a mile from the field when the P-80A went into a gentle right bank, the canopy was seen to come off, and then the aircraft's angle of bank increased and its nose lowered rapidly. Bong's body, with opened parachute was found fifty feet from the wreckage. Observers in the control tower stated that he had taken off in a shorter than usual distance and made his climb out at a higher rate than usual. A modification to this particular aircraft was a restricter plate attached to the end of the tailpipe to increase engine thrust. The main fuel pump had failed, and Bong had not selected the emergency fuel system that this aircraft was equipped with. In this short this period of time, only 522 hours of flying time had been accomplished in the P-80. (Not counting the mission to Europe).

Between August 9, 1945 and August 31, 1946 there were forty-six further Shooting Star accidents. During this same period, from April 1, 1946 until the end of August, thirty-six of these accidents had occurred and they brought about the deaths of four pilots, major injuries to three, and twenty-seven were uninjured. (The remaining were ground incidents not involving pilots). Thirteen of these P-80s were wrecked, and nineteen had major damage.

Between the period August 9, 1945 and the end of March 1946 the accident rate stood at 1272 accidents per 100,000 flying hours, the base line. The actual flying time for this period having been just 629 hours. From the period April 1 through August 31, 1946 the average changed through an increase in flying time, 8623 hours, which resulted in a figure of 417 accidents per 100,000 hours.

During this later period the statistics showed that nineteen of these accidents were attributed to pilot error; ten to mechanical error, either during construction or maintenance; four more to a combination of the two preceding factors. Four accidents were weather related, and three to undetermined causes.

"The airplane had a high (accident) rate not only because it was a new airplane with mechanical 'bugs' but because the pilots themselves were guilty of the same performance which were exhibited daily by inexperienced pilots."

It is recognized that most aircraft accidents occur during either the takeoff or landing phases of flight. Also, it was recognized that the P-80 differed greatly from conventional fighters in two respects during these phases. It was slow to accelerate on takeoff, and it was more difficult to slow down in the landing phase. Although the P-80 had aerodynamic speed brakes, or "boards," they were not as effective in slowing the aircraft as the braking action of a propeller in flat pitch.

Also, engine response was far slower if a pilot got behind the "power curve" in landing and needed a touch more power to regain needed airspeed. With a conventional engine, all the pilot needed to do was to shove the throttle forward and kick in some rudder to counteract the torque and he could recover the lost airspeed immediately. With the early J-33 engine, the throttle had to be advanced far more slowly to avoid flooding the engine and suffer a total loss of power. With the later engines, the improved fuel control pump overcame this difficulty, but response time still lagged. Although there was no torque or "P Factor" to contend with, anticipation of needed thrust was a prerequisite.

Still, a major factor in early P-80 accidents rested with the pilot and his attitude. The majority of the early P-80 pilots were experienced combat pilots: Young and brash. Often their ego, poor preflight planning or a lack of foresight placed them in a position beyond their ability to save a bad situation in an unfamiliar aircraft. But, experienced pilots could get in trouble over their heads, too. Brigadier General Mervin Gross, commander of the AAF Institute of Technology at Wright Field, OH was killed on a test flight near Brooksville, KY on February 12, 1946 when he took on a test flight and crashed thirty minutes later.

Witnesses stated that they had seen the aircraft flying level, then start to climb. The aircraft stalled and crashed. The canopy was found a half mile from the crash site, but the pilot did not get out of the aircraft.

Further examples:

March 7: The pilot "horsed" the P-80 off the ground on a maximum ammunition load test flight. The aircraft settled back down onto the runway, but suffered major damage when it ran off the end of the runway.

May 24: While approaching for landing the pilot made a sharp "peel-up" for landing, stalled and crashed.

June 13: At Biggs Field, TX a pilot attempted to takeoff, but the field elevation was too high and so was the temperature. The P-80 crashed and was a total wreck. In defense of the pilot, little was known of density altitude and its effect on aircraft operations at this time.

June 27: While conducting an engineering test flight at Scott Field, IL on a P-80A of the 412th FG that was involved in an incident on May 24, the pilot got lost, ran out of fuel and had to bailout.

August 26: On a photo publicity flight the P-80 suffered an engine failure and its pilot attempted a landing on a civilian airstrip. The aircraft bounced, did a half roll and crashed inverted, killing the pilot.

As seen, there appears to be very little in common involved in all of the P-80 incidents except for several where the pilot got in over his head in either exceeding his ability or experience. During the course of other incidents during this same time period, mechanical problems were involved, but the pilot managed to save the aircraft and himself. However, with the exception of problems associated with the fuel control systems in several incidents, there was no single common thread to be found in any of the accidents other than the involved pilot over extending his ability.

As training, with emphasis upon flight discipline, improved, along with experience and familiarity with the P-80, a marked improvement in the accident rate was indicated.

Chapter II: Stateside Fighter Units

The 412th Fighter Group was headquartered at Palmdale Army Air Field, California when they were first introduced to the Shooting Star. At this time the 412th FG was commanded by Colonel Homer Boushey. The Group was composed of the 29th Fighter Squadron which was based at Oxnard; the 31st FS at Palmdale and 445th FS at Bakersfield Municipal Airport.

On October 2, 1944 the 412th FG was notified that they were intended to become the first operational jet fighter group, and ground school classes were started in anticipation of the arrival of the P-80 and an overseas deployment. Less than two weeks later, on October 11, the 412th FG Headquarters relocated to Bakersfield to join with the 445th FS.

The initial complement of aircraft showed the 412th FG was equipped with eighteen P-38s, ten P-59s and eleven P-63s. But on November 14 Major Julis Jacobson, commanding officer of the 31st FS, flew in the first XP-80, 44-83020, to be used for checking out pilots and 1st and 2nd level ground maintenance instruction. The Group was also notified that they would tasked with assisting in the P-80s Accelerated Service Tests at Muroc Army Air Field, California.

Assigned to these service tests were Captain's Charles Tucker, John Babel, Jerry Stidham and John Russell, along with several lieutenants. Tucker was the first of them to get himself into trouble in a P-80, in April, when his cockpit filled with smoke and his engine suffered a partial flameout when several of the burner cans ceased igniting. With unburned fuel trailing behind the aircraft, he at first thought that he was on fire, although there were no fire warning lights. He wanted to bailout, but he could not release the canopy. Tucker set it up to make an emergency landing at Muroc and as the P-80 slowed down, he finally got the canopy open, but by then the initial smoke problems had cleared and he emerged unscathed from the emergency landing.

A Lt. Craig, on loan from Wright Field, had a similar problem, also in April. After a partial flameout at 3,000 feet, Craig set up for an emergency landing at Muroc. Then his engine quit entirely at 800 feet and he was forced to make a belly landing on the desert floor. As an example of just how rugged the P-80 was, although it suffered damage to its flaps and skin, it was repaired and was back flying the next day.

The anticipated delivery date of the P-80s now was lagging so far behind that it was decided to upgrade the 412th FG with Mustangs as an interim fighter, in case they might be called upon for service in the Pacific Theater before they could become operational with the P-80. Coinciding with the end of the war in Europe, the 412th FG received the first of their

The prototype XP-80, "Lulu Belle," was assigned to the 412th Fighter Group in October 1944, and went back to Lockheed in March 1945 after being flown against the best of America's conventional aircraft in evaluation tests, and whipping every one of them. Not too bad for an aircraft known to be underpowered. (Air Force Museum)

new P-51Ds on May 8, 1945 and by the end of the month they had twenty-nine. Major Black, 31st FS was killed in one of these new Mustangs on May 16. By the end of June the 412th FG was completely equipped with sixty Mustangs, and disappointingly enough, transferred out their last P-80 for modifications that had been requested by the detachment at Muroc.

On July 10, 1945 the 412th FG Headquarters relocated to Santa Maria AAF, California, and on September 29 Colonel David Hill replaced Colonel Boushey as their commanding officer. "Tex" Hill had been one of the original American

The P-80A in which "Pappy" Hurbst, commanding officer of the 1st Fighter Group's 27th Fighter Squadron was killed on July 4, 1945 at Del Mar, CA. (via Esposito)

Opposite: A factory-fresh P-80A that has just been delivered to the 412th Fighter Group. The Shooting Star's clean lines made it one of the most photogenic aircraft. (Lockheed)
2.4

One of the first P-80A's assigned to the 412th Fighter Group at March Field in late 1945 is over California's foothills. In later versions of the P-80 the nose mounted landing light was replaced by a compass-loop antenna. Note, too, the location of then SCR-695 radio antenna in front of the speed "boards." (via Esposito)

Volunteer Group Flying Tigers and had 12 3/4 kills with them before they were disbanded and he joined the AAF as first the squadron commander of the 75th Fighter Squadron. And then later, as commander of the 23rd Fighter Group, he destroyed another half dozen Japanese aircraft. All of the P-38s were now gone, being replaced by an additional allocation of Mustangs, a dozen of the new P-51Hs. On November 9, 1945 the 39th Photo Reconnaissance Squadron was assigned to the 412th FG with eleven more P-51Ds and one F-6D. On November 29 the 412th FG was redesignated as the 412th Fighter Group (P-80 Jet) and made another move, this time to March Field, which would finally become their permanent home.

After once again starting ground school classes on the P-80, in October 1945, the 412th FG started sending pilots to Muroc in late November for P-80 training. On December 3 they received the first of their intended operational P-80As. On January 11, 1946 the 412th FG lost its first P-80 in an accident when Lt. Colonel John Herbat had to make a forced landing with it after encountering a severe engine vibration and then a flameout. The aircraft suffered major damage in the gear-up landing.

On January 26 the 412th FG sent Captain John Babel as their representative on Colonel Council's record establishing trans-continental speed run. Babel was the last to depart Long

44-85256 was assigned to the 412th/1st Fighter Group until October 1947, upon which time it went to the Air Training Command at Williams Field, Chandler, AZ. It was destroyed in a crash in February 1949. (USAF)

Captain Martin Smith taxi's-in at Topeka Air Force Base (Later Forbes AFB), KS for refueling during his record breaking trans-continental flight. Total turn-around time was six minutes, including 2:14 spent in the actual refueling portion. (Air Force Museum)

Assigned to the 94th Fighter Squadron (Jet Propelled), Lt. William Reilly won the Weatherhead Trophy Race in 44-85019. This P-80 was later modified into a RF-80 and finished its service life with the 154th TRS. (Olmsted)

Beach, California, at 0958 local time. Two hours and twenty-five minutes later he landed at Topeka, Kansas to take on 627 gallons of fuel in just 1 minute, 54 seconds, spending a bare four minutes total time during the pit stop. Babel made a high-speed penetration over La Guardia Field, New York two hours later and after dark for an elapsed time of 4:23.54. This was just ten minutes longer than Colonel Councill's time, who had not made a refueling stop, and ten minutes less than Captain Martin Smith's time, who had a minor maintenance problem while making his refueling stop at Topeka.

On January 30, 1946 Colonel Bruce Holloway became the commanding officer of the 412th FG (P-80 Jet). Holloway had been the second commanding officer of the 23rd FG in China, relieving Colonel Robert Scott (of "God is My Co-Pilot" fame), and the predecessor of "Tex" Hill in that position. Holloway had racked-up a total of thirteen air-to-air kills and had five more ground kills.

A series of accidents occurred during the next two months that resulted in the death of one pilot and the destruction of several aircraft. On February 8 Lt. Glen Vogan was climbing to 30,000 feet over California when a fire warning light came on. Vogan shut down his engine and returned to March Field to shoot a dead-stick landing. He touched down approximately half way down the runway and ran off the end which caused major damage to the P-80. Four day's later Captain Homer Worley was killed after he took off on a test fight. Witnesses stated that Worley had been flying level and then started a climb. The P-80 entered a stall and then crashed. Although the aircraft's canopy was located a half mile from the crash site, Worley did not escape the cockpit. On March 11 Lt. Clyde Voss had a flameout at 17,000 feet and attempted to dead-stick his P-80 back to March Field. He touched down short of the runway and the aircraft was wrecked, although Voss escaped with minor injuries.

On May 15 the 412th FG dispatched the record establishing Project Comet, the first large-scale movement of a jet

Colonel Bruce Holloway, commanding officer of the 412th and 1st Fighter Group. Holloway was eventually the commander of Strategic Air Command between July 1968 and April 1972. (via Esposito)

To increase maintenance proficiency and esprit de corps, maintenance crews competed to see just how fast a P-80s engine could be changed. This 412th FG crew established the base-line record of just fourteen minutes. Led by Captain Vince Gorden, with M/Sgt Wayne Bond and the rest of the team. (Gordon)

formation across the United States. Project Comet was supported by six C-82s loaded with maintenance people and spare parts, and it came close to becoming a public relations disaster, although fortunately the results were unknown outside of the Air Force.

Twenty-five P-80s were sent on this mission, while all of the remaining aircraft within the Group were cannibalized to prove the required spares: Wheels, batteries, brake pads, etc.

The first leg of the mission was to Davis-Monthan Field at Tuscon, AZ, which was reached in just fifty-five minutes of flying time, where the aircraft remained over night. Succeeding overnight stops were to Ft. Worth, Texas, Memphis, Tennessee, Smyrna, Tennessee, and on to Washington, D.C. on May 19. While enroute aerial demonstrations were flown at most of these locations.

On May 23 Project Comet headed back to March Field, and on May 24 troubles began after they left Chanute Field, Illinois enroute to Tinker Field, Oklahoma. Three of the mission aircraft pilots became lost in weather southwest of St. Louis, Missouri. One pressed on and eventually landed at Muskogee, Oklahoma, while two tried to get into Marris Field at Cape Girareau, Missouri. One got down with minor damage, while the other pilot landed short of the runway and tore the landing gear off of his P-80. This aircraft was taken by truck to Scott Field, Illinois for repair, and would figure in one of the previously mentioned accidents under Early Attrition.

The 412th FG (P-80 Jet) was inactivated on July 3, 1946 and replaced in designation by the 1st Fighter Group. The 1st FG had been previously been inactivated in Italy on July 16, 1945. The assigned 412th FG squadrons were also inactivated, and then reactivated with new designations. The 27th Fighter Squadron replaced the 31st FS; the 29th FS was replaced by the famous Rickenbacker "Hat in the Ring" 94th FS. The 39th PRS was inactivated, with its heritage being allocated to the 101st FS, Massachusetts ANG. (The personnel of the 39th PRS would become the nucleus of the 12th Tactical Reconnaissance Squadron, 363rd Reconnaissance Group that would be activated at March Field on July 29 under Lt. Colonel Leon Grey). The 445th FS was replaced by the 71st FS. Colonel Holloway remained their commanding officer until August 20 when he was replaced by Colonel Gilbert Meyers.

One of the first changes with the activation of the new Group was the movement across March Field from "Dusty Acres," the old World War II temporary site, to permanent quarters and hangers that had been previously occupied by a bomber group.

The new 1st Fighter Group suffered its first loss the following day at an air show at San Diego when Lt. Colonel John "Pappy" Hurbst, commanding officer of the 71st Fighter

Engine maintenance on a 1st Fighter Group P-80A. The aft fuselage was attached with three bolts, and the engine with three more, which made an engine change a "quick-snap" operation. (USAF)

"Maximum" and "Minimum Goose," a pair of "Squadron X's" mission aircraft. "Maximum Goose" belonged to Don Gordon, who had used the same name on his 56th FG P-47 during World War II. (USAF)

On May 15, 1946 Colonel Bruce Holloway led elements of the 412th FG on the first large trans-continental jet formation across the United States. Known as "Squadron X," the mission demonstrated jet airpower to the public for the first time. PN-069 was Holloway's personal P-80. (USAF)

"Yardbird" of the 412th FG's "Squadron X." Each pilot placed his personal World War II score on the vertical fin of his P-80. (USAF)

Preparing for departure from March Field. "Squadron X" was supported by six C-82s with ground crews and logistical supplies. (USAF)

The 412th FG at Andrew's Field, Washington, D.C. The trip east was virtually flawless, but all sorts of problems were encountered on the way home. (USAF)

Squadron, and Major Robin Olds were in the process of making an Immelmann turn followed by a split-ess prior to landing. The maneuver was started at to low of an altitude, and Hurbst did not have sufficient vertical room left to pull out and he crashed in full view of everyone, while Olds barely had enough altitude to avoid crashing, himself. Hurbst had been considered to be one of the most experienced 1st FG P-80 pilots. He had flown Spitfires with the Eagle Squadrons prior to the United States entering World War II, and then had gone to China to fly with the Chinese Air Force before he became the commanding officer of the 74th Fighter Squadron. He had flown 144 missions against the Japanese. (Olds, who had a dozen accredited kills in World War II, would miss the Korean War, but during the Vietnam War he scored four more kills). Hurbst was replaced by Lt. Colonel Phillip Loofborrow, one of the ex-23rd Fighter Group commanders. One of the missions of the 1st Fighter Group was to ferry new P-80s from the Lockheed plant to Newark, New Jersey, where they would be then shipped across the Atlantic Ocean and to be assigned to the 31st Fighter Group. 1st Lt. Bennie Stone was killed on one of these ferry flights on July 11 near Switzer, South Carolina.

On August 1 misfortune again struck the 1st Fighter Group during a flight between Mitchell Field, Long Island, New York and Langley Field, Virginia. Eight P-80s of the 71st Fighter Squadron had been to Mitchell for an airshow, and enroute to Langley afterwards they got into heavy thunderstorm weather and became disorientated. The pilots called for Direction Finding, (DF), steers to get themselves back on course, but apparently the DF controllers became confused by the speed of the aircraft and gave constant changes in compass bearings to fly to the pilots and everyone became further disorientated and lost. One P-80 did get to Langley, while two landed on a road without damage to their aircraft. Three landed gear up in pea patches near Swansquarter, North Carolina. One touched down on a road but swerved off and suffered major damage, while the last one landed gear up in a cornfield and demolished the aircraft. Fortunately, none of the pilots were injured.

In September the pre-World War II air races were started up once again, this time with the new wrinkle of jet propelled events. The first of these, the trans-continental 2000 mile Bendix Trophy from California to Cleveland, Ohio featured Major George Ruddell from the 94th FS, Major Rex Barber

45-8496 of the 71st Fighter Squadron and 45-8501 of the 27th FS, along with other 1st FG P-80s. PN-501 exists today at the ex Chanute AFB, IL. (USAF)

The 71st Fighter Squadron replaced the 445th FS in designation on July 3, 1946. In December 1948 the squadron was assigned to the Air Defense Command from the Strategic Air Command. (USAF)

from the 27th FS, Lt. Colonel Leon Grey from the 12th PRS and Lt. Colonel Phillip Loofbourrow from the 71st FS. Grey finished first, and Ruddell came in second, while the other two were forced out with navigational and mechanical problems.

For the Weatherhead Race at Cleveland the 1st Fighter Group sent four pilots. Lt. John Hancock from the 27th FS, Captain D. Eberhardt from the 71st, Lt. William Reilly from the 94th FS, and Captain John Mouiter represented the Group. Reilly came in first, Moutier placed second, Eberhardt third and Hancock fourth. Fifth and sixth places went to Lt. Walter McAuley and Captain Jack Sullivan, both flying P-80As from Wright Field.

In the Thompson Trophy Race Lt. Colonel Robert Petit, the commanding officer of the 94th FS represented them,

71st FS P-80As on the ramp at March Field. The tip tanks held 165.5 gallons of fuel, of which all but .5 gallon was useable. (USAF)

Captain Robert Pell was from the 71st FS, Major Robin Olds was from the 12th PRS. Wright Field sent Major Gustav Lundquist, Captain Sullivan and Lt. McAuley. Lundquist placed first, Olds, second, and Pell came in third. Lt. Colonel Petit was disqualified for turning inside a pylon, while Sullivan went out with engine problems. (In the conventional engine division, Tony LeVier, in a P-38, came in second place).

A series of accidents and incidents started to occur in October 1946 that almost defied explanation. In three incidents involving the number four pilot in a formation at twenty thousand feet, when a cross-over maneuver was commenced, his aircraft would go into a series of uncontrollable rolls. The pilot of the first aircraft managed to bailout at 2,000 feet, while the pilot of the second one failed to get out at all and was killed. The pilot of the third aircraft lost five thousand feet before he was able to regain control, and then his P-80 flew as though nothing unusual had occurred. Tony LeVier came up from Lockheed and flew this aircraft, and determined that the wing tips and their tip tank shackles were out of alignment, and when the fuel was half consumed (By climbing to altitude.), a combination of asymmetrical fuel balance and wing aerodynamic loading, as caused by the misalignment of the wingtip, created the problem.

During the winter of 1946/47 the 1st FG finally were able to consider themselves "out of the test tube" and that they were now, finally, a combat unit. Yet this was tempered by a reduction in force that struck them by orders from Washington. For example: the 71st Fighter Squadron was reduced by 74% of their officers by forced discharges. which left them with only six pilots and one non rated officer. The enlisted ranks were similarly effected.

Between January 10-12, 1947 the 1st FG sent twenty-one P-80s to the Masters Naval Air Station at Miami, Florida to participate in the "All American Air Maneuvers." This was the first of the true tactical exercises that they would partici-

A 71st FS P-80A-1 after modification that placed the landing lights on the nose wheel strut and a radio compass antenna in the previous location. (USAF)

pate in, a highlight being the interception of forty-eight B-29s out of McDill Field. The only adverse incident being the collapse of a P-80s nose gear on landing, which was repaired overnight.

A shuffle of commanding officers within the Group took place in the Spring of 1947. While Colonel Gilbert Meyers remained as Group Commander, Lt. Colonel Ralph Watson, Commanding Officer of the 71st FS, left for Ohio State University and was temporally replaced by Lt. Colonel Walter Beckham, who had just returned from Selfridge Field where

he had been qualifying the 56th Fighter Group in P-80s. Then on June 17 Beckham left for the University of Florida and Lt. Colonel Gerald Dix became their commanding officer. Beckham had eighteen kills why flying with the 353rd Fighter Group out of England during World War II, while Dix had flown one tour against the Japanese, and then another against the Luftwaffe. Dix had six air-to-air credits, and one on the ground. One of the other pilots transferred out was Captain George Davis, who would later become the first "double ace" of the Korean War and would receive the Medal of Honor, posthu-

Two Lockheed f-80 "Shooting Stars" taking off during Miami All American Air Maneuvers, Miami, Florida, Jan. 8-9-10, 1947. (USAF)

44-5019 of the 94th FS. It was flown by Lt. William Reilly in the 1946 Weatherhead Trophy Race. It later was modified to a RF-80A and finished its service career with Air National Guard.

mously. (Davis had seven kills in World War II and was credited with fourteen more in Korea before being shot down on February 10, 1952).

On June 24 the 1st FG started to receive the first of their new P-80Bs, obtaining nine. Many of their older P-80As were thus transferred to the 4th and 56th Fighter Groups which were just starting to become operational with the Shooting Star.

The 71st Fighter Squadron lost Captain Floyd Soule on July 18 as he was attempting to takeoff from Carrizozo, New Mexico. It was a hot day, and the P-80 was loaded with fuel and the airfield's elevation was above 5,000 feet. It was unfortunately one of those instances where the knowledge of density altitude, temperature and gross weight, and runway length had not yet been discovered to be a fact or in aircraft operations.

On August 7 the 94th Fighter Squadron was alerted that they would soon be going to Ladd Field, Alaska to conduct operational cold weather tests and operations with the P-80. All of their aircraft would be the new, winterized P-80B-5.

Coinciding with this, the pilots were all notified that they would have to fly fifty Ground Controlled Approaches, (GCA's) and get their instrument cards upgraded: And then the squadron was cut back to a meager fifteen hours per pilot flying time because of fuel shortages! The order for the GCA's was soon rescinded.

The 1st Fighter Group was expanded to Wing size on August 15 under the Hobson Plan and the 1st Fighter Wing activated at March Field under Colonel Carl Crane. The 321st Base Unit, the parent unit for the 1st Fighter Group being absorbed by the new wing and redesignated as the 1st Air Base Group. The new Wing and subservient units were further attached to the 12th Air Force.

Between August and the end of the year the 1st Fighter Wing had seven major accidents, with three pilots killed. As with the earlier series of accidents, again there seemed to be no common factor. A pilot practicing for the 1947 Allison Trophy Race at Cleveland ran himself out of fuel, A F-80 assigned to the 36th Fighter Group under Project Squirt, in which the 1st FG was helping to become operational, caught on fire as it was being started. A pilot participating in Operation Combine at Lawson Field, GA flew into the ground while dive bombing. A pilot in a formation of eighteen P-80s hit a buzzard. While landing at Eglin Field, a pilot's engine started throwing turbine buckets and he landed short, killing three cows. A pilot got into a "porpoise" situation while taking off at Ladd

The 1st Fighter Group's 27th Fighter Squadron took the place of the inactivated 412th FG's 31st FS. When the 27th FS converted to F-86s, 45-8487 went to the Air Training Command, and finally to the Air National Guard, ending its career with the 157th FS. (USAF)

The 94th Fighter Squadron took the place of the 29th FS in designation in 1946. In 1947 the 94th went to Ladd Field, Fairbanks, AK for operational cold weather evaluation of the P-80. Upon completion of this exercise, the P-80s were transferred to the 57th Fighter Group at Elmendorf Field, Anchorage, AK and the personnel of the 94th FS returned to March Field to commence Sabre operations. (USAF)

Another formation shot of 412th/1st Fighter Group P-80s over California's mountains. 45-8305 went to Ladd Field with the 94th Fighter Squadron. (Lockheed)

Field and retracted his landing gear and slid to a stop on his tip tanks. He was awarded 100% of the mishap. A pilot flew into a hillside at Ladd while attempting an emergency landing. In addition to all of this, there were 51 engine failures in 1st FG F-80s, with the engines only averaging thirty-seven hours between breakdowns!

Lt. Colonel Donald Hillman and the 94th Fighter Squadron air echelon had arrived at Ladd Field on November 1 after stopping at Hill Field, Utah enroute to have winterized tires put on their F-80Bs. It was a shock to them after sunny California, as the November temperature averaged +9 degrees, with a high of 34 degrees. December averaged +2 degrees, with a low of -23. They flew their first interceptor

missions against the 7th Troop Carrier Group, C-82s of the 12th Air Force on November 18 while the 7th TCG was transporting the 2nd Infantry Division from Delta to Galena, AK during Exercise Yukon. The following day, with Mustangs of the 57th Fighter Group providing top cover, they simulated strafing troops at Galena that were being boarded into more C-82s.

Similar missions were conducted by the 94th FS through March 1948 on the days it was warm enough to fly, in addition to conducting cold weather testing and evaluation of the F-80B. On March 14 their F-80Bs were turned over to the 57th Fighter Group and the 94th FS returned to March Field where they were, essentially, demobilized.

P-80s of the 94th Pursuit Squadron were "put to bed" after their landing at Ladd Field, Fairbanks, Alaska, from which they will operate in arctic exercises. The aircraft are part of Tactical Air Command's First Fighter Group. (USAF)

Although the 94th Fighter Squadron's strength had been bolstered by additional people prior to their TDY to Alaska, the personnel transfers now took them from thirty-two officers and 346 enlisted men down to nine officers, one Warrant Officer and forty-four enlisted men by the end of March. Many of those transferred went to the 14th Fighter Group in Maine that was being reformed with the new F-84. By the end of June their strength was back up to thirty-two officers and 104 enlisted men, and the squadron was effectively reorganized.

While this action was taking place, the 94th FS received F-80A-10s, which were F-80A-1s that were modified by improved versions of the original engines and now featured actually operational water injection systems, provisions for JATO, and an improved cockpit cooling system. Also during this period the remainder of the older F-80As of the 27th and 71st Fighter Squadrons were replaced by F-80Bs.

The 71st Fighter Squadron went to Spokane, Washington for joint air-ground maneuvers, while the 27th FS went to Texas for similar maneuvers. While the 27th FS was conducting air-to-ground exercises at Ft. Hood, a very strange incident occurred that fortunately did have a good outcome. As Lt. Fallon dropped his bombs on the range, one of them skipped back into the air and was struck by the F-80 flown by Lt. Tuchsen. The bomb embedded itself in the F-80s left air duct without exploding and Lt. Tuchsen was able to return to Austin for a successful landing, even though his engine was half starved for air.

The 27th and 71st Fighter Squadrons then went to Brookley Air Force Base, Texas to participate in Operation Combine III. The general opinion among all concerned was that the F-80 was inadequate as a ground support aircraft, as its range was too limited while carrying ordnance, and that it appeared too vulnerable to ground fire. The future would show that they were partially correct in their estimation.

On December 1, 1948 the 1st FG's role, along with all the other state-side F-80 units was changed to that of air defense. On December 20 the 1st FG was transferred to the 4th Air Force and assigned to ConAC, the Continental Air Command, to fulfill this mission.

Although the 1st Fighter Group had been informed in June 1948 that they were slated to become the first F-86 Sabre group, it was not until February 1949 that they actually received their first of the new swept-winged fighters. By the end of the month they had ten Sabres on board and thirty-six pilots qualified in-type. Then in March, confusion reigned, as they were ordered to transfer their Sabres to Turner Air Force Base, while the F-80Cs that were originally intended for the 31st Fighter Group were now to go to the 1st FG. Fighters were coming in from both Lockheed and North American Aviation for acceptance inspections, and then all of the F-86s were grounded awaiting further transfer inspections, while the F-80Cs were assigned to the 1st FG squadrons.

The switch of mission aircraft was rescinded in April and all of the F-80s were then readied for transfer. By the end of the month the 1st FG retained two F-80As, eight F-80Bs and six F-80Cs, with the C models being held for the Group's participation in the First Annual USAF Gunnery Meet at Las Vegas Air Force Base.

On May 1 the 1st Fighter Group sent four pilots and ten enlisted men to Las Vegas AFB for the gunnery meet. Overall, they placed third out of the seven jet teams, with a first place score in the dive bombing phase. Captain George Davis, now back with the 71st FS, hit the towed target during an aerial gunnery mission, but he got back okay. He did believe in forcing his gun barrels right into his target before firing.

On May 1, also, the 1st FG was transferred from ConAc to the Strategic Air Command with the mission of "destruc-

71st Fighter Squadron P-80s over California with their speed boards open to maintain formation with the camera ship. These aircraft later were assigned to Williams Field for use by the Air Training Command. (Lockheed)

Photographed by Lockheed before delivery, this brand new P-80A-5 went to the 62nd Fighter Squadron as their number 54. (Lockheed)

tion of hostile aircraft in the air, in support of bombardment and other friendly types of aviation." In addition to also ferrying Sabres to the 4th Fighter Group, as the 4th FG did not have enough qualified pilots to accomplish the task, they flew out their last F-80 on May 20 and by the end of the month they had seventy-six Sabres on board and a new mission.

The historic 56th Fighter Group, the "Wolfpack," had been reactivated at Selfridge Field, Michigan on May 1, 1946. They were initially the Strategic Air Command's first Very Long Range, (VLR), fighter escort group, and were equipped with P-51Hs. Their first commanding officer was the illustrious David Schilling.

In February 1947 Colonel Schilling and two other pilots went to Williams Field for P-80 familiarization, and the 1st FG sent five pilots and a dozen enlisted men to Selfridge to assist in P-80 training. Then in March, the 56th FG received their first two dozen P-80As and a reorganization of the Group took place. Originally Composed of the 61st, 62nd and 63rd Fighter Squadrons, the 62nd FS had been TDY to Alaska since December 1946 with their Mustangs. In mid April, when the 62nd FS returned, the personnel of the 62nd FS and com-

The jet era caught the Air Force unprepared, as far as pilot protection in the confines of the P-80's cockpit was concerned. To protect the pilot's head from being beaten against the canopy in turbulent air, the Air Force sent the 56th FG surplus tank helmets, which had already seen better days. (USAF)

Colonel David Schilling commanded the 56th Fighter Group, supervising gound strafing and aerial gunnery by the speedy P-80s. Colonel Schilling shot down 23 German planes.

manding officer, 56th FG World War II ace Lt. Colonel Gerald Johnson, were transferred to Grenier Field, New Hampshire to become the nucleus of the newly activated P-51H equipped 82nd FG, VLR, which also assigned to SAC. Coupled with the 56th FG loosing thirty-four additional people to the newly reactivating 4th Fighter Group, the 62nd FS had to be remanned from scratch. Major William Dunham was named as their new commanding officer.

The 56th FG now became the most publicly visible F-80 (With the designation change from P-80 to F-80 in June.) outfit in their historic record establishing Fox Able (Fighters across the Atlantic) mission to Germany in July 1948. What was to be known as the Cold War had just started in March and the Berlin Airlift was just barely underway to supply the entrapped city when Colonel Schilling and several 56th FG pilots decided that they should do something to demonstrate just what the F-80 could do in their most capable hands. And in light of the political situation, what would be better than to fly the F-80 to Europe to bolster the Air Force's presence there? Needless to say, little arm twisting was required in Washington to get the project underway, as the 36th Fighter Group in the Canal Zone was just receiving their own movement orders to Germany, but their scheduled arrival in Ger-

Lt. Kenneth Millikin flew FT-242 on the Fox Able I mission to Europe. It was later improved to F-80C standards, sent to Korea, and was lost on January 18, 1951 after being flown into a tree on a strafing mission. (USAF)

Photographed at the dedication of the new Capitol Airport at Springfield, IL in 1949, this 62nd FS F-80A later was assigned to Missouri's 110th Fighter Squadron. (Conger)

many was six weeks hence and the Air Force was in of immediate need of reinforcing their own image in Europe.

On July 12 Colonel Schilling led the mission off Selfridge with sixteen F-80As enroute to their first refueling stop at Dow Field. Off Dow after a two hour refueling stop, the Fox Able mission arrived at Goose Bay, Labrador to remain over night and meet a flight of six Royal Air Force Vampires that were flying a similar mission, only on a reciprocal course. Diplomacy dictated that the RAF would receive the credit for flying the first trans-Atlantic jet crossing. But the RAF mission was a theoretical goodwill tour, and was not made in tactical squadron strength.

Weather then intervened and the Fox Able mission was delayed several times between Goose Bay, Narsarssuak, Greenland, Iceland and Scotland, thus it took them a total of

A F-80A of the 62nd Fighter Squadron. 56th Fighter Group tiptank markings varied in paint schemes, with these being in the squadron's color of yellow. (Conger)

nine days to arrive at RAF Odiham, England. Yet the total flying time was only nine hours for the 3,725 mile trip. After diplomatic formalities with the RAF at Odiham were dispensed with, Fox Able flew to Furstenfeldbruck, Germany to spend two weeks in providing jet fighter escort support for B-29s conducting show of force practice missions, and to also "show the flag" by making familiarization flights around Germany to demonstrate the F-80.

The return flight were made across the Atlantic Ocean via an identical route, and happenstance dictated that they again met the returning Vampires, at Narsarssuak this time, as the RAF mission was also on its way home.

On December 1, 1948 the 56th FG was relieved from assignment to SAC and assigned to ConAC as an air defense unit.

On May 28, 1949 the 56th FG was tasked with another opportunity to cross the Atlantic Ocean. This mission, identified as Fox Able II, would be a one-way delivery flight to take eleven F-80Bs and a T-33 to the 36th FG at Furstenfeldbruck. This would be the first of the true Fox Able delivery missions that would be flown via the now established enroute ground refueling stops. Fox Able aircraft delivery missions would continue into the next decade, when they were replaced by non stop air-to-air refueled missions that were also pioneered by David Schilling. (Schilling was killed in an automobile accident on August 14, 1956. The following year Smokey Hill AFB, KS was renamed in his honor, and he became the third Air Force F-80 pilot to have an air base named in his honor.)

Fox Able II was led by Lt. Colonel Irwin Dregne, the 56th FG's present Group commander. For two of the pilots, Captains' Russell Westfall and Frank Klibbe, this would be a repeat trip. 1st Lt. Frederick "Boots" Blesse, who would become one of the better known Korean war F-86 pilots, was one of the rookies on the trip. With the exception of one F-80 being damaged on landing in Greenland, the mission was uneventful and successful.

The Wolfpack arrives at Oldham, England on a leg of their historic Fox Able I mission. The SB-17 and C-54 in the background were a part of the mission, providing for air-rescue and logistic support. (USAF)

On the way home during the Fox Able I mission a refueling stop was made at Dow Field, Bangor, ME. #42 belonged to World War II ace Lt. Ray Dauphin. (USAF)

In spite of the successes of the Fox Able missions, the 56th FG appeared to be snake bit in June. They had six major accidents, one of which was fatal. 2nd Lt. Henry French, 62nd FS, was killed in Texas while on a cross-country navigation flight when he encountered a thunderstorm.

2nd Lt. Richard Glenn, also from the 62nd FS, had an unusual experience while flying over Sandusky, Ohio. His wingtip fuel tanks collapsed over the leading edges of his F-80s wings and rendered the aircraft uncontrollable, and Glenn had to belly land his fighter in a field.

In September 1949 Lt. Colonel Dregne was transferred to Okinawa and was replaced by Lt. Colonel Francis Gabreski. Dregne would later take the 51st Fighter Interceptor Group's F-80s into action over Korea. While Gabreski, America's top scoring living ace, would later become the 51st Fighter Inter-

In a fly-by over Munich, 44-85041 of the 56th Fighter Group completes a high-speed low-pass as a part of the Wolfpack's "showing the flag." (Olmsted)

ceptor Wing's commanding officer, when they flew F-86s in Korea.

In October the 61st FS established a new USAF record for flying time in the F-80 by flying 1311 hours during the month. This broke the record established by the 65th FS, 57th FG in Alaska by 131 hours. Each pilot averaged 62 1/2 hours, each. A far cry from today's austere limit of four hours a month.

During April 1950 the 56th Fighter Group converted to F-86As and two of the three squadrons were transferred from Selfridge, with the 62nd FS moving to O'Hare Air Force Base, Chicago, Illinois and the 63rd FS to Oscoda AFB, Michigan.

World War II's highest scoring fighter group, the 4th Fighter Group was reactivated at Selfridge Field on September 9, 1946 from personnel taken from the 56th FG. This was an action that caused a mixed-bag of emotions, as the 4th FG had barely beat-out the 56th FG in the race to see which of the two Group's would be the top scoring Air Force fighter group in World War II. Both had destroyed over a thousand German aircraft during the war. Now the second place finisher was helping to rebuild the winner of that earlier race. The new 4th Fighter Group, under Colonel Ernest Beverly, was composed of the 334th, 335th and 336th Fighter Squadrons, and they obtained a few P-47s, P-51Ds and Hs as initial equipment while still at Selfridge. In March 1947 the 4th FG was transferred to Langley Field and commenced to receive P-80As that were flown in by pilots of the 1st Fighter Group. At this time they too were assigned to SAC's 15th Air Force.

On August 15, 1947 the 4th Fighter Wing was organized under Brigadier General Yantis Taylor at Langley Field, which replaced the old Base Unit as the tenant organization under the Hobson Plan. On December 1, 1948 the 4th Fighter Wing

Arming a 56th Fighter Group F-80A for the Second Annual Fighter Weapons Meet at Las Vegas Air Force Base, NV during March-April 1950. The 100 pound practice bombs were painted blue and filled with sand. They contained a spotting charge for scoring the bomb drop. (USAF)

and attached units were transferred from SAC to ConAC and assigned to the 14th Air Force. This assignment lasted until February 23, 1949 when the 4th FW was reassigned to the 9th Air Force.

The 4th Fighter Group participated in several high visibility exhibitions during the period they flew the F-80. On July 31, 1948 Colonel Beverly led most of the Group as the lead formation of the fly-over airshow during the dedication ceremony at Idlewild International Airport, New York (later Kennedy IAP). At the same time a three-ship 4th FG F-80 formation escorted President Truman's C-54 from Atlantic City to Idlewild, where he gave the dedication address. From September 4-6 the 4th FG's F-80 aerial demonstration team performed at the Cleveland National Air Races.

During the period November 19-20 Colonel Charles Lindberg became jet qualified in the P-80 by 4th FG pilots and flew a gunnery and strafing mission with them.

The only mentioned loss of a 4th FG F-80 pilot occurred on January 9, 1949. The 4th FG had flown to McDill AFB, Florida to participate in an Aerial Demonstration at Miami and the F-80 of Lt. James Hall disintegrated in flight during a high G rolling pull-out while starting a high-speed low-pass maneuver.

On March 27, 1949 the first F-86A arrived, and a week later the 334th FS returned from Ladd AFB where they had been conducting cold weather tests with their F-80s. The switch over to Sabre's was quickly completed. So fast, in fact, that the 4th FG won First Place in their new Sabres during the first annual Las Vegas Field Gunnery Meet just six weeks later.

The 81st Fighter Group was stationed at Wheeler Field, TH with F-47Ns until May 21, 1949 under Colonel Gladwyn Pinkston. But on this date they surrendered their Thunderbolts to the 199th Fighter Squadron (Which kept the best of

Although the 56th Fighter Group first served with the Strategic Air Command as an fighter escort unit, and later with the Air Defense Command in a fighter interceptor role, the pilots also had to be proficient in air-to-ground tactics. Here the Group's Operations Officer's personal F-80 is armed with practice bombs. (Lionel Paul)

One of the 4th Fighter Group's representatives to the 1947 Cleveland National Air Races in September 1947. (Lucabaugh)

them and scrapped the rest.), and they were transferred to Kirtland AFB to re-equip with F-80As that were passed down to them from the 56th Fighter Group as they received newer models.

Composed of the 91st, 92nd and 93rd Fighter Squadrons, the 81st FG was assigned to the 4th Air Force under ConAC with an air defense commitment. They, along with the 81st FG and 81st Fighter Wing, under Colonel Thomas Blackburn, became established at Kirkland on June 17. The 81st FG flew the F-80 for a bare six months. for in December 1949 the 81st FW and associated units switched to F-86As.

With the F-84s and F-86s entering the United States Air Force inventory in strength in 1949, the F-80s previously assigned to regular USAF tactical fighter units in the United States were now transferred to the Air Training Command. These were units at Luke Field, AZ, Moody AFB, Georgia, Nellis Field, Nevada and additional units were established to supplement those already at Williams AFB. Then, with the activation of Air National Guard squadrons during the Ko-

rean War, the ATC realigned the composition of their squadrons and Moody became a training base for all-weather flying training, while Luke became a F-84 training base. Williams and Nellis continued to train future fighter pilots with F-80s until 1954 when the last of these were phased out in favor of F-86s. The remaining F-80s either went to the ANG or Reserve squadrons.

Two additional F-80 squadrons had been assigned to the regular Air Force during the Korean War period. Both of these belonged to the Air Defense Command, which had become separate from ConAC in 1950.

On November 1, 1952 the 49th Fighter Interceptor Squadron was activated at Dow AFB, Maine to replace the 132nd FIS that had been on active duty there during the Korean Emergency. The 132nd FIS, which called Dow home to begin with, returned to State Control at this time and turned their Shooting Stars over to the 49th FIS and received F-51Hs from the Air National Guard Bureau in exchange. The 49th FIS, under Major Reginald "Pappy" Hays, who had been the commanding officer of the 132nd FIS since July, became the squadron commander of this new squadron. The 49th FIS flew the F-80C only as an interim fighter, as the following

44-84992 was the first of the P-80A-1s and it was assigned to the 4th Fighter Group. As expected, it was in demand for airshow participation. (Leo Kohn)

In November 1947 the 4th Fighter Group commenced rotating their squadrons to Ladd Field, AK for cold weather evaluation of the P-80 and the training of their men. Over the next eighteen months all of their personnel and most of their fighters had seen service up there as a part of this program. Hence the Arctic paint scheme on this 335th FS F-80. (Leo Kohn)

44-85456 was transferred from the 335th Fighter Squadron to Sheppard Air Force Base to finish out its career as an instructional airframe. Here students are shown how to "fire-up" a jet. (USAF)

Spring, the F-80s were replaced by F-86Fs and was one of the few ADC squadrons to fly this version of the Sabre.

The 330th Fighter Interceptor Squadron was activated at Stewart AFB, New York on November 27 1952 with F-80Cs also serving as an interim interceptor. They were assigned to the 4709th Air Defense Wing at this time. During the summer of 1953 the F-80s were replaced by F-86As.

For an unknown reason, the 4th Fighter Group repainted the noses of their F-80s that had been to Alaska from their usual squadron color to that of black after they had returned to Langley Field. This particular F-80 had stopped at Kearney Field, NB for refueling on its way back. (Olmsted)

A 4th Fighter Group P-80 bellied-in near Langley Field. A tiptank has been torn off, and the canopy jettisoned. (Actually, only minor damage, and this type of an incident was rather common during the P-80s early era. (Leo Kohn)

This F-80C-1 of the 4th Fighter Group came to grief on August 21, 1949. It appears that the incident involved one of the more traumatic problems that a F-80/T-33 pilot could encounter, that of the gunbay doors opening in flight. When this occurred, the doors became their own canard control surfaces, which were totally uncontrollable by the pilot, and destroyed the aircraft's inherent aerodynamics. (USAF)

334th and 335th Fighter Squadron P-80As on the ramp at Langley Field, VA. Their rudders still have the Arctic Red scheme, indicating that the aircraft had been winterized, while the aircraft's noses are black. (Geer via Isham)

Assigned to the 335th Fighter Squadron, 45-8335 shows a variation in nose and tail markings. A white nose and tail bands, the squadron color, outlined with black piping. (Phillips)

After the 4th Fighter Group switched to F-86s, several of their F-80s went to Japan and were assigned to the 49th Fighter Group. PN-440 was assigned to the 9th Fighter Squadron at this time, and was known as "Stinky." (Conger)

Chapter III: Test Birds

One of the fortuitous results of the P-80 design was the inherent flexibility of the aircraft's form that permitted it to be modified into a test-bed for innovative ideas. During the post WWII period, more "off the wall" ideas were proposed than at any other time in aviation history. Some of these came to fruition, while far more were discarded as unfeasible, but the P-80 was one of the few aircraft that had the capability to develop or disregard many of these programs.

In the P-80 was for the first time an aircraft with a nose section that permitted the installation of these various test items, unencumbered by a propeller and able to attain speeds in excess of 500 mph.

Not including the F-14/FP-80 photo reconnaissance version, which actually was not that much of an technical improvement over the F-5 Lightning camera installations, the P-80's nose permitted the installation of a hook so that the aircraft could be towed in flight. Armament packages that could be swiveled and trained upon a target regardless of the fighter's attitude. Ram jet propulsion, prone cockpit experiments, etc.

Most of these development programs were developed and carried through to various degrees of completion either at or under the direction of the Air Force's Flight Test Division at Wright Field, OH under Colonel Albert Boyd. Boyd was the father of the Air Force's Air Research and Development Command, ARDC. Additional experimental work was conducted by the National Advisory Committee for Aeronautics. The Bell Aircraft Corporation, with their previous and on-going jet programs of their own also involved themselves with P-80 work. Lockheed, of course was in on the ground floor for the first of these programs.

The first of the new programs was the development of a catapault system. In December 1944 the Air Technical Service Command, the forerunner of ARDC, "considered it advisable for Lockheed" to develop a method of catapulting the P-80. There was no actual requirement for such at the time, but it was envisioned that there might be, someday. Lockheed engineers started discussing this with the U. S. Navy in early 1945 and by April the Navy had decided that they were willing to participate in such experiments. Thus, on May 17 the Army Air Force turned over to the Navy two P-80As, one of which had been modified by Lockheed for catapulting. The story on this program is continued in the chapter on U. S. Navy P-80/TO operations. The Air Force, by the way, also wanted Lockheed to work up a similar program for the P-80B, but Lockheed engineers did not believe that it was necessary, as the P-80Bs engine produced more thrust, so this program was dropped.

Another program was radio control. Something that was not entirely new, as the first radio controlled flight had been on August 23, 1937. Lockheed proposed a radio controlled drone version of the P-80 for dive bombing missions on May 3, 1945. Brigadier General F. O. Carroll, Chief of the Engineering Division at Wright Field approved this project on July 19, with the contract for its development going to Bell Aircraft Corporation at Buffalo, NY. -Bell having gained some experience with a similar experiment with their P-59.

The two surviving EXTRAVERSION YP-80s, returned from Italy, were to be used, one as the "mother," and the other as the actual drone, or "robot." As 44-83029 was lost in an fatal accident on August 2 and -83028 was deemed unsuitable, they were replaced by P-80As 44-85407 and 408. The

Preparing for a catapult launch trial at Munsten Field. BuAer 29668 was USAAF 44-85005. (Aviation Week via Esposito)

A Project "Bad Boy" QF-80 with an unusual "buzz number," along with a T-33 chase plane. The radio control equipment was about as sophisticated as the gear the average modeler can purchase today for about $1,000.00, but it was very complicated for its era. (USAF)

Lockheed P-80's visit to Italy. (USAF)

initial contract costs were $56,107.80 with and additional fixed-fee of $ 2,244.31 for Bell. It was not until October 31, 1946 when Bell received the aircraft and were able to send the P-80s to Muroc for proper instrumentation with one for use as a director-ship and the other as the slaved aircraft.

The initial program was limited in expectations: Control of the "robot" was to be within either ten miles of the "mother" or the ground control station. Bank angle of 40 degrees from horizontal, either to the left or right. Remote control of the "robot" by television.

As experience and improvements in radio control technology were gained in the next decade, many of the Shooting Stars saw their last days in a final F-80 drone program. Identified as Project Bad Boy, the dedicated F-80s were re-identified as QF-80s and equipped with flight control equipment manufactured by the Sperry Gryoscope Company. "Bad Boy" was a continuation of the original drone program from 1947 that had continued through 1950 and included the modification of five T-33s to EDT-33s as director aircraft in 1950.

Destined for an inglorious end, 44-85407 became a QF-80 under the Sperry "Bad Boy" Drone Progam. Note that the pilot's seat has been removed and additional radio antennas have been added to the canopy.

A QF-80 in "the Flare" with plenty of observers. (Esposito)

During the later phases of the program, it was divided into two parts. The first was to develop the program and evaluate the F-80s as drone aircraft, while the second phase would be for quantity production of fighter drones.

In 1951 Sperry fabricated twelve sets of drone stabilization and control equipment (DSC-80E), of which eight sets were to be installed in F-80s, to determine how suitable a drone the aircraft could be. Then, in 1953 an additional eighteen sets were ordered, to be installed in a total of fourteen F-80s, but due to delays incurred in the program, the last one was not completed until July 1954. These were to be the actual fighter drone's, similar to the first phase aircraft, only with improved radio equipment and the addition of telemetering.

Two additional items of some innovative thought were also installed. One was a remotely controlled anti-skid braking system, for aircraft recovery upon landing. The other was the addition of cameras, located fore and aft in the Fletcher centerline tip tanks, for recording an attacking aircraft's gunnery pattern. The preserve these cameras in the event the aircraft was shot down, provisions were made to jettison any

Converted to a QF-80 after serving with the 22nd Fighter Squadron, 45-8599 was used to "sniff" for radioactive particles over Nevada after atomic bomb detonations. (USAF)

Toward the end of the Shooting Star's service life, many were converted to radio controlled drones under Project Bad Boy. These were probably the prettiest of them all, with red fuselages with white lettering, and white wings. Unfortunately, most were destroyed by intention. (USAF)

remaining fuel and then release the tanks and lower them by parachutes, which were located in the rear of the tanks to bring them down without damage.

In November 1954 Bad Boy was increased by calling for fifty-five more QF-80s and ten more DT-33s. The conversion would require 2,000 hours of labor for the T-33s and 4,000 hours for the F-80s, including IRAN, Inspect And Repair as Necessary. The reason for the high number of hours required for the F-80 conversion being that the majority of them had been returned from Japan and then stored in the open at McClellan AFB, which resulted in corroded and damaged parts. The cost per F-80 aircraft being modified approximated $102,000.00.

Although the Air Force was not totally satisfied with Bad Boy QF-80s as target aircraft, as their attainable speeds were far less than the fighters that were to be flown against them, these were all that were available to them at the time, as the Air Force could not spare more capable aircraft for conversion. The QF-80 continued to be flown as a drone into the 1960s, both as a target, and in other test programs, as radioactive cloud sampling after an atomic blast, as these missions would have been hazardous to a manned aircraft's pilot.

As the Air Force was always looking for a good high-speed fighter-bomber, the next project was to determine whether the P-80, designed as a fighter, was robust enough to also become a fighter-bomber. As the standard wing tip fuel tanks, 165 gallon capacity, weighed approximately 1,100 pounds, it was felt that the P-80 was structurally sound enough to carry bombs in lieu of fuel tanks. The aircraft's stability on a bomb run had to be determined, for if it was "snakey," accuracy would suffer. Pilot recovery after dropping the bombs had to be explored, for as an example, the tendency to mush out on recovery from a dive bombing pass had proven to be the single drawback of the P-47 Thunderbolt as a fighter-bomber.

Bomb rack development tests were conducted at Wright-Patterson Field initially, and then moved to Eglin and Muroc Fields' for further evaluation. Note how these early racks are aerodynamically flared to conform to the bombs contour. (Air Force Museum)

Bomb loads ranging from 100 to 1,000 pounds were carried by P-80s flown by pilots from the Air Proving Ground Command at Eglin Field, FL during these tests. One P-80 suffered a structural failure of its wing's main spar during this test, "but pilots felt that the P-80 was the best they had ever flown to this goal." Airframe and engine improvements resulting in the P-80C came from this program.

SPEED RUNS

Holding a World Speed Record was naturally a goal for any country. On November 19, 1945 the Royal Air Forces' Gloster Meteor had attained the magic 600 mph mark and the United Kingdom thus possessed this record. At this time the P-80 was rated to 562 mph (With fully military equipment installed.) However, it was felt that the Meteor was going as fast as it was capable of, while the P-80 could surpass this speed.

44-85200 was a P-80A-1 that was used to create the first P-80B, and then it was modified to become the P-80R "Racey." In an attempt to make it faster than production P-80s, its canopy was cut down and NACA designed air intakes were utilized. It is now on display at the Air Force Museum, Dayton, Ohio. (Leo Kuhn)

Accordingly, two P-80As were to be used in attempting to capture the World's Speed Record. One was to be a standard fighter, with machine guns and all, while the second one would be modified, at a cost not to exceed $35,000.00, to clean it up and challenge the record. Preliminary tests showed that the unmodified P-80A could only come close to beating the Meteor's speed, attaining 595 mph. (Increasing the engine's static thrust from 4,750 to 5,400 pounds only increased its Mach from .75 to .777. A 1 1/2 mph gain, and this was felt to be the standard P-80s critical Mach). Thus, they went to the second P-80A, 44-85200, which had first served as the prototype for the P-80B and then was to be highly modified and became known as the P-80R "Racey."

On September 7, 1946 the Meteor IV established a World Speed Record of 616 mph. Then, the Air Force got serious about attempting to break this record, and between September 30 and October 4, 1946 they did their best with the P-80R and a P-84.

One of the later modifications that finally became standard in 1951 was the installation of underwing bomb racks on the F-80C. Note the reinforcing "pads" on the wing's skin. This type of bombrack was later used on the AT-33, the T-Bird modified for use in combat. (Air Force Museum)

Carrying two 30 inch Marquart ramjets, Lockheed test pilot "Fish" Salmon is flying this first flight of P-80 44-85214 that was powered solely by the ramjets for this event. (Aviation Week via Esposito)

Colonel Albert Boyd flashes through the timing gates while establishing a new absolute World Speed Record of 623.8 mph on June 19, 1947 at Muroc. (Lockheed)

Finally, after Major Kenneth Chilstrom broke in the P-80R and set up the course to be flown at Muroc, "Racey" was up to expectations and Colonel Albert Boyd attained an absolute speed record of 628.8 mph on June 19, 1947. Boyd made four speed runs to establish this; at 617.1, 614.7, 632.5 and 630.5 mph. For the first time in twenty-three years, the United States now held the World Speed Record. It was a short-lived feat for the Air Force and the P-80R, however, as on August 25 the U. S. Navy's experimental D-558-1 took the record by twenty-six more mph. The Air Force would recapture the record on September 15, 1948 with the F-86A at 670.9 mph.

Assigned to Wright Field were a series of P-80A-1s for the conducting of all of the wondrous test programs mentioned in the first paragraph. The first one was 44-84995 that was delivered to Wright on May 1, 1945 and was eventually used in the role of being towed by a B-29.

One of the first problems encountered with the new jet fighters was their prodigious rate of fuel consumption. Although they could get from Point A to Point B faster than any conventional fighter, their fuel usage often dictated that there was insufficient fuel remaining at Point B to do anything, or to return to Point A. This obviously would have great ramifications upon the aircraft's future tactical usage. One envisioned solution would be to tow the fighter from Point A to Point B, release it to fulfill its mission, and then either let it return to Point A on its own, or hook it back up to a "mother ship" in flight and tow it back.

In an attempt to expand a jets range, a towing program was started with the P-59 where the Airacomet was towed behind a C-47. This was terminated with the loss of the test vehicle over Arkansas after the C-47 encountered engine difficulties in instrument conditions and the Gooney Bird crew had to cut the P-59 loose, with it's pilot then having to bail out.

Lt. Colonel Pat Flemming under tow. Major Guy Townsend piloted the B-29. (Air Force Museum)

44-85044 in its original scheme, before being modified for prone cockpit tests, and the later gun platform development programs. (Olmsted)

A series of photographs depicting the installation of the rotatable "SchrageMusik" type .50 caliber gun package installed in 44-85044. Another good idea that worked but lacked practicality. (Air Force Museum)

Modified with a rocket launching nose, 44-85116 carried six 38 pound 4.5" diameter rockets. Note the louvers to vent the rocket exhaust gases. (Olmsted)

The P-80 experiment was conducted behind a B-29 dragging five hundred pounds of steel cable that not only provided the tow but also provided electrical power to the P-80 from the B-29's APU. This was so the P-80s electrical supply from its own battery would not be depleted: Necessary to power the flight instruments and airstart the engine. The tow cable was fitted with an attachment ring, while the P-80's probe had a link-hook that was to be releasable by the pilot.

On September 23, 1947 Lt. Colonel Pat Fleming, Chief of Fighter Flight Test, took off to join-up with the B-29 at 15,000 feet. It took several attempts to make the connection, for as Fleming got in too close under the B-29, the bow wave from the P-80 forced the tail of the B-29 upwards. Then, attempting to attach the ring at the limit of the cable's extension, the cable was dancing around in the B-29s slipstream. Finally the link-up was made, and the P-80s engine was stopcocked for ten minutes while the P-80 was towed around.

When Fleming attempted to release the hook, it would not open. He made several attempts at getting it open to no

avail, and then the P-80 slid under the B-29 and the turbulent airstream over stressed the attachment point on the P-80 and Fleming was free. He was now faced with the hook's sheet metal installation folded back over the nose of his fighter and having to land without any forward visibility. (The B-29 was flailed by the cable until it beat a hole in the fuselage and inbedded itself, where upon Sgt.'s Clayton Burn and Frank Corbi, the scanners, safety wired it in place and the B-29 could make its own landing.) The program was terminated at this time and the P-80 was repaired to later serve at Eglin, Muroc, and with the 196th FIS before becoming a instructional airframe.

44-85042 was one of two P-80As used in the testing and development of ram-jet supplemental power, one at Wright Field, while the other example, 44-85214, went to Muroc. This program at Wright Field had originally been started with a P-51D with captured German ram-jet engines, but this aircraft was destroyed when one of the engines exploded in flight and test pilot Paul Chell had to bailout.

This P-80 utilized conventional fuel for both the ram-jets and for its own engine, with a capacity of only fifteen minutes for the P-80's operation. Due to the weight and drag of the ram-jet engines, themselves, the aircraft's critical altitude was twenty thousand feet. So Chell would takeoff and climb to this altitude, ignite the ram-jets and attempt to reach the P-80's critical Mach, somewhere in the .8 range before being forced to shut them down and return to land.

As Chell had endured bailing out of the Mustang, he desired to know exactly what would happen if one of the ram-jet engines failed while at maximum speed, which would leave him with an asymmetric thrust situation. The structural engineers believed that the P-80 would in all probability disintegrate, due to an abrupt side-load. Thus, only a few more flights were scheduled, and then the program was to be terminated. On the last of these flights, Chell returned to Wright Field, but landed on the downwind runway hot and long because of an

Two views of the prone cockpit installation of 44-85044. Robert Stanley, of Stanley Aviation Corp. is in the standard cockpit, while Richard Frost, engineer, is in the prone position. (Aviation Week via Esposito)

Installing 1,000 pound thrust solid-propellant jet assisted takeoff (JATO) rockets. They only burned for 2.5 seconds, but were dramatic in performance. (Air Force Museum)

Billowing white smoke during a JATO takeoff demonstrates the angle of climb attainable though the rockets boost. The pilot was 1st Lt. Richard Dennen, who was assigned to the Wright Air Development Center. (Department of Defense)

The 412th Fighter Group also got in on JATO evaluations, and they were the first to demonstrate its practical use in fighter operations. (Lockheed)

unobserved wind shift by the control tower and the P-80 was extensively damaged.

The second ram-jet powered P-80, #214, carried two American made Marquardt C30-1 engines in two versions, one being 30" in diameter and ten feet long, while the other was 20" in diameter and seven feet long. First flown on November 21, 1947 the engines again would take the P-80 to its critical Mach, but again the fuel consumption negated their value in boosting the fighter's speed.

Tony LeVier had made the first flight, and then was succeeded by H. R. "Fish" Salmon. These flights were made from Lockheed's test base at Van Nuys, and then from their facility at North Base, Muroc Field. Over one hundred flights were made before this test program was curtailed.

Aircraft 44-85044 was used in two major test programs. The first one being the development of a prone pilot cockpit. During this period the standards were to stress a fighter to a 7.33 G point for operational strength. The average fighter pi-

An armament modification attempt to a P-80 at Wright Field to install a 20mm cannon. (Air Force Museum)

This P-80B, 45-8479, was used to develop and test the underwing rocket launching racks at Muroc Air Force Base. Although the top rockets were not supposed to fire unless the bottom ones had already been fired, sometimes when the bottom rocket failed to fire, the top one would fire, anyhow, resulting in some wild trajectories. (Air Force Museum)

Left and right views of the installation of a 20mm cannon in the nose of a P-80. The cannon's rate of fire was considerably slower than either the M-2 or M-3 .50 caliber machine guns, hence the hitting power was less, and this program was dropped. (Air Force Museum)

Preparation for a rocket launch trial at Muroc. The rocket launching "stubs" retracted rearward into the wing after the rockets were fired, to reduce drag. (Aviation Week via Esposito)

ing as a safety pilot and operating the navigational instruments, making the takeoffs and landings, and accomplishing the basic functions of flaps, speed brakes, etc. on demand from the prone pilot.

The flight controls in the front cockpit were mounted on trays that supported the pilot's arms, with a joy stick on each tray. The right stick controlled the vertical attitude, while the left stick controlled the horizontal. This required some practice in operation, but was not detrimental to controlling the aircraft. Test results showed that the prone pilot was able to comfortably fly the P-80 from this position to 8 G's, but he had to monitor the physical condition of the safety pilot at all times, as the safety pilot would become incapacitated before this point. The major drawbacks were found to be the propensity of the prone pilot to encounter vertigo during abnormal flight maneuvers, as he was placed so far in front of the aircraft's normal center of gravity—which would have been changed if an aircraft had been actually been built around this concept. Visibility to the rear was nil, but could have been overcome by mirrors. The required parachute was a back-

lot was expected to be able to withstand three G's on his own, and when wearing a G suit, two more. But with the development of faster aircraft, the need for the pilot to be able to remain functional in combat was foreseen to be as high as eight G's.

As a pilot in a normal cockpit sitting position was faced with a situation of having all his blood trapped in his abdomen and lower extremities and then suffering a gray-out or full black-out in a high G maneuver, it was believed that if he was able to fly from a prone position, he would have a higher tolerance for these physical stresses.

The program started with a centrifuge and then moved into the nose of a B-17 with various control installations. Various head supports were also installed, as this appeared to be the weak point with the program, as the pilot's head became to heavy for his neck muscles to hold up under G loads. Also, his ability to turn his head and see behind him was impossible, and this was an absolute necessity in combat.

In this P-80A rudimentary flight controls were installed in the nose mounted forward cockpit, with the regular pilot serv-

Rocket firing at Muroc Air Force Base to determine the P-80s feasibility as a fighter-bomber. (Lockheed)

A murky photograph at best, but the launching of a 5 inch rocket was difficult to catch on film. (Air Force Museum)

Participating in the 1946 Thompson Trophy Race at Cleveland, Ohio was 44-85247 wearing a spectacular paint scheme for identification during the race. Note the turn-point pylon in the background. It took 515.9 mph to win the race, and several aircraft suffered structural damage as a result of pulling a high number of G's during the pylon turns. #247 was forced out of the race after its aileron boost pump failed. (Leo Kohn)

breaker during flight, just from its normal weight, and unendurable during high G maneuvers, thus an entirely new system would have to be developed to cover an emergency bailout.

After these tests were concluded, 44-85044 was used to develop and test new armament systems. The first one, based up the German SchrageMusik, was a battery four of upward firing .50 caliber machine guns that were mounted on a swiveling platform. These could be could be locked upon a targeted bomber by the P-80s pilot as he flew below it, presumably out of its defensive range and hopefully without detection. The drawback was that every time the guns were fired, the P-80s nose would tuck under from their recoil and accuracy was lost. Later, these were replaced by a battery of four forward firing 20mm cannons, built by Crutis-Wright under a

separate contract, which provided a good forward firing armament, but exceeded the aircraft's cg., due to their weight.

This program was followed by the installation of a rocket launching tube in the P-80s nose. This barrel permitted the firing of six 4.5" 38-pound folding-fin rockets in succession. While it might have had limited success in attacking bomber formations, six rockets would have been an insufficient number to carry. The P-80C would later be equipped for carrying similar rockets in the fighter-bomber role, but these were mounted under the wings.

The other major test and evaluation program was the Jet Assisted Take Off, JATO. In 1945 Lockheed proposed – the use of JATO to reduce the aircraft's required takeoff run. They pushed this program to the Air Technical Service Command in a letter of intent on January 8, 1946. And, after receiving

In addition to flight testing and development, the test pilots assigned to Wright Field were often placed into the public's eye with their new jet fighters. Three P-80As were initially assigned to Wright Field for flight tests, and these were also flown to the first jet National Air Race at Cleveland, Ohio in September 1946. Hence the flamboyant paint schemes. Major Gus Lundquist won the race. Major Robin Olds (1st Fighter Group) placed second. (Air Force Museum)

Weather and a lack of fuel forced Major Russ Schleeh down in a West Virginia corn field in 44-85123, the same P-80 that Lt. Colonel Reilly won the 1946 Cleveland jet race in. Refueled, Schleeh flew it out the next day. (The farmer displayed umbrage at both events. (Air Force Museum)

And the pilot appears to be wearing a fedora! One of the first critical problems discovered with the early P-80s was inadvertent canopy removal: and the proximity of the canopy bow to the pilot's forehead is readily apparent. If the canopy came off in flight, the pilot was going to be incapacitated in some degree, usually with fatal results. This P-80 was assigned to the Bell Aircraft Corporation as a contractor to attempt to solve the problem. (Lockheed)

the go-ahead, completed their portion of the tests by March 14. These JATO units were built by the Aerojet Engineering Corporation, and provided 2,000 pounds thrust for approximately thirteen seconds. The minimum takeoff run was reduced from 4,000 feet to 2,500, and the distance to clear the standard fifty foot obstacle was reduced from 5,150 to 3,450 feet.

Further tests of the JATO program reduced the size of the units to 1,000 pounds of thrust, with two being carried. These units were evaluated by the 412th Fighter Group and became the standard. Although they were used for training and were demonstrated publicly at airshows in the 1940s, they did not become standard equipment until 1951 when they were used regularly by the fighter-bomber squadrons in Korea.

Chuck Yeager prepares to depart Charleston, WV for California. This was the Shooting Star that he flew under the Kanawa River bridge, which upset the CAA (FAA), but Yeager had sufficient status with those in power that he got away with it. (Taylor via J. Smith)

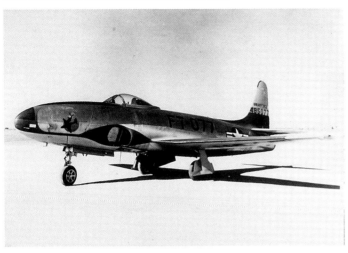

Assigned to Muroc Field/Edwards Air Force Base was 44-85077, which bore their insignia and a nice paint scheme. (Isham)

Also painted in an all-yellow scheme was NASA's (nee NACA) 45-8683. Assigned their identification number of NACA 152, it was based at Langley Field between December 1953 and October 1958. Then retired, it was placed on display at the base's picnic ground. (Olmsted)

Major Charles Yeager "suits-up" at Charleston, WV. 45-8481 was the first of the P-80B-5's and was originally used in cold-weather tests at Ladd Field, AK during the winter of 1947-1948. (Taylor via J. Smith)

The first Shooting Star assigned to NACA was 44-83023, which was assigned to them directly from Lockheed for high-speed tests. On January 13, 1945 it was extensively damaged in a landing accident with Larry Clousing at the controls. Repaired, it remained in NACA's service until January 1947. (NASA va Burns)

44-85299 was assigned to NACA as their number 131. It came to them in December 1946 as a replacement for 44-85029, which had been damaged in an accident and was undergoing repairs. It was scraped in June 1955. (NASA via Burns)

44-85352 in standard Air Force paint, and later in NACA's scheme as their number NACA 112. It served with them longer than any other F-80, between November 1946 and January 1959. (NASA via Burns)

Ex-U.S. Navy BuAer 33868 (48-379) was assigned to NACA in October 1958 to be utilized in developing the guidance system for the Bullpup missile. It was the last F-80 to remain in NACA's service, being retired in February 1960. (NASA via Burns)

The Air Force conducted experiments with caterpillar type landing gear for operations on rough terrain with several types of aircraft. What distinguishes 47-171 from all of the others is that it had also been re-skinned with magnesium in a weight saving experiment. When it had been declared surplus to Air Force needs, it was donated to the city of Canton, OH, and when their fire department discovered what a hazard they had on their hands it was immediately scrapped. (Air Force Museum)

Chapter IV: To Europe

In mid 1946 thirty-two P-80As were sent to the 55th Fighter Group, which had moved from their last WWII base at Kaufbeuren, Germany to Gibelstadt on April 29, 1946. At this time the Group was commanded by Lt. Colonel Horace Hanes, and it was composed of the 38th, 338th and 343rd Fighter Squadrons. The 38th Fighter Squadron would operate the P-80s while the other two squadrons continued with P-51Ds.

The 55th Fighter Group with its three squadrons was inactivated in Germany on August 20, 1956 and was replaced "in designation" by the 31st Fighter Group, which was reactivated this same day, with Hanes in command. The 31st Fighter Group had the 307th. 308th and 309th Fighter Squadrons assigned, and they replaced the three 55th FG squadrons in respective sequence.

In January 1947 Lt. Colonel Frederick LeFebre became the 31st FG commanding officer, and he was succeeded by Major Allen Stanton the following month. One month later Colonel Dale Fisher became CO, and then Lt. Colonel Donald Blakeslee was named commanding officer in May. Blakeslee was noted as having been the dogmatic commander of the highest scoring Air Force WWII Fighter group, the 4th.

On June 25, 1947 the 31st Fighter Group was transferred to Langley Field, VA "Less Personnel and Equipment" in the continuing shuffle of unit designations and assignments. The men of the 31st FG in Germany were then transferred to other units in Europe, their P-51s scrapped, and the P-80s returned to the United States with little being recorded of their operations with them.

In March 1948 the Berlin blockade, with all of its repercussions, began. At this time there was only one viable USAF Fighter Group remaining in Europe, the 86th Fighter Group, flying P-47s. Immediately plans were made to reinforce the 86th FG with a fighter group of P-80s. In the meantime, to "show the flag," Colonel Schilling led an element of the 56th Fighter Group with a dozen F-80As from Selfridge Field MI, as related elsewhere in this book, that July via the North Atlantic route to show resolve in the matter. This, of course, was backed up by sending B-29s to England, and hundreds of men and transports to fly what became the Berlin Airlift.

The 36th Fighter Group, with the 22nd, 23rd and 53rd Fighter Squadrons was based at Howard Field, Panama Canal Zone at the time the selection for their transfer to Europe was made. They were equipped with P-80Bs that they had picked up in October 1947 at March Field under Project Squirt, after flying P-47s since their reactivation at Bolling Field, DC. Their first commanding officer was Lt. Colonel Henry Spicer, and it was Spicer, a dynamic firebrand of an officer, who led a portion of the Group to Howard Field in October in the longest overwater flight accomplished to date with jet aircraft, a mission of 1,700 miles.

Exactly why the 36th FG had been sent to the Canal Zone in the first place has been lost to time. It would seem that there would be little military use for a high performance tactical fighter in that area at that time. Certainly there was little threat from any of the Pan American nations against American interests that would call for the United States most modern fighter. Nonetheless, the 6th Fighter Wing's all-weather squadron that was also based in the Canal Zone also received more modern aircraft at the same time, upgrading from P-61s to P-82s.

On July 12, 1948 the 36th Fighter Group was alerted for their transfer, and all of their F-80s were readied for shipment via aircraft carrier to Scotland. Upon arrival at Glasgow , Scot-

With Post-War operational "buzz letters," this 55th Fighter Group P-80A was returned to the United States, and was then assigned to the 56th Fighter Group. (Sanders via Esposito)

A 55th Fighter Group P-80A with all of its joints sealed for transport back to the United States after service in Germany in 1946. The 55th FG being inactivated in August. (Sanders via Esposito)

A "plane Jane" all-grey P-80A of the 55th Fighter Group at Gibelstadt, Germany in 1946. (Sanders via Esposito)

land, the aircraft were offloaded, inspected, and then flown to Furstenfeldbruck, near Munich, Germany, arriving there in August.

In January 1949 Lt. Colonel Spicer was transferred, and he was replaced by one of the best known Colonels in the Air Force, Hub Zemke. Zemke ramrodded the 36th FG until December, when he was transferred to the Group's parent 2nd Air Division, and Colonel William Daniel took over the 36th Fighter Group.

During this period the 36th Fighter Group found themselves in the midst of a highly visible and both USAF and world-wide political situation that was sometimes unfortunate for those involved. At this time every movement of their aircraft was open to political and public scrutiny. This was an era where the 36th FG represented the sole USAF jet force in Europe, while the United Kingdom also had some jet fighter strength, they were considered the "prototype air force," for while they had a lot of aircraft types in development, they had little actual airpower. The other Allied European nations were all flying antiquated reciprocating engined fighters, and all of these were in limited numbers, as those countries were trying to rebuild after WWII devastation and resultant economic depravations.

As noted, the 36th FG had three commanding officers during their F-80 era. The squadron's had the same situation, as it seemed to those involved that the door to the commander's office was a revolving one. The 22nd Fighter Squadron had three CO's also during their F-80 time in Europe, the 23rd FS two, and the 53rd FS three. Some of these men rotated home at the end of their overseas tour, while some incurred the displeasure of others and were transferred to less meaningful positions, and others moved up through promotions. The general feeling was that one was to neither make a mistake nor bring attention to one's self or else one was going to be in deep trouble with someone else and find themselves railroaded.

One of the side effects of this was a lack of stable leadership within the effected units. And this, along with the Group's tactical mission, may have contributed to the Group's high accident rate.

The primary mission of the 36th Fighter Group was that of tactical air support, and air defense was their secondary role. (The 36th FG was redesignated as the 36th Fighter Bomber Group in January 1950). In comparative numbers to other F-80 units, the 36th FG had a terrible attrition rate. This was brought on by several factors, as there is never a single cause for such things.

The weather over Europe was a major factor in many accidents, particularly in those involving younger pilots that had little experience with instrument flying. The tactical training mission required a lot of low altitude airwork in less that desired visibility, European fog and rain or snow. Inadequate fuel and POL storage, and facilities for proper maintenance was a contributing factor, as most of the installations remained in damaged condition from the war years. A high workload was also placed on the 36th FG to participate in both air-to-ground and air-to-air missions to keep the Group in a combat ready status, and also to fly cooperation missions with the ground forces for their own training. This placed a massive amount of job related stress upon all involved, as no one wanted to let the unit down in the performance of its mission.

To cite an example of the flying and mission conditions faced by the 36th Fighter Group in Europe:

In January 1949, one F-80 of the 22nd Fighter Squadron had to make a wheels-up landing, while four others were damaged when they went off the end of the runway at Furstenfeldbruck. Contaminated hydraulic fluid was determined to be the culprit. Contributing were inadequate storage facilities, and the lack of adequate monitoring of its condition, through inexperience and workloads impressed on supervisory personnel.

In April 1949 the squadrons went TDY to Malta for training, returning in May. While in Malta, Captain Vince Gordon, 22nd FS, started working up a solo aerobatic routine, which was later expanded upon to include four aircraft, to demonstrate the USAF's and the F-80s prowess. In June they again went TDY, this time to England to participate in Operation Foil, a test of the air defenses of the United Kingdom.

Operation Foil was the first joint USAF-RAF exercise since the end of WWII and involved the USAF's 36th FG and B-29s, along with Vampires, Meteors, Wellingtons and sundry other RAF aircraft. As far as the 36th FG's role was concerned, the exercise was a complete success, with the exception of the F-80s inability to intercept the RAF photo-reconnaissance Spitfires that were operating above 40,000 feet.

Also, in June, the 36th FG received their first replacement aircraft since they had left Panama, eleven F-80Bs and a TF-80C that had been ferried across the Atlantic Ocean by pilots of the 56th Fighter Group.

On July 25, 1949 the 36th FG flew to Gibelstadt, Germany for two weeks of air-to-ground gunnery and dive bombing training. The F-80s tip tanks were removed and the shackles used for carrying bombs. (Their range office on the Schweinfurt Range was Lt. Ben Fithain, who would later score the first F-94 kill in the Korean War). This exercise was soon followed by another trip to England to work with the RAF at Odiham, participating with the RAF in their gunnery training.

The 22nd Fighter Squadron suffered a major loss on August 24 during a navigational training flight from Rome. Italy to "Fursty." The flight of four F-80s got split-up on their way home and then encountered a severe thunderstorm. Lightening blinded all of the pilots, and the formation was split with all of the pilots attempting to go "lost wingman" and assume their own navigation after loosing sight of their flight leader, Captain George Gleason. The Number Two man, Lt. Wallace, then had to bailout after encountering extreme turbulence. The Number Three man, Major Earnest Harris, the 36th FG's Operations Officer, crashed fatally near Augsberg. Gleason managed to land safely after ordering the Number Four man, Lt. Durlin, back to Rome.

On September 6 it was back to Giebelstadt for three days, and then back to "Fursty," for a week, and then to Kitzingen,

Germany on September 15 to participate in Operation Harvest, which was a combined operation of almost all of the Allied military forces in Europe. This was followed by a TDY to Wiesbaden on September 27 to participate in Operation Hooelle in support of a French Army exercise. In October the 36th FG went back to England to demonstrate the F-80s firepower to the RAF at Tangmere.

With the air-to-ground exercises over for the fall season, the 36th FG then practiced their air-to-air work during the winter. Primarily, their targets were B-29s flying out of England, under the control of "Racecard," the 501st Aircraft Control and Warning Squadron at Freising.

The winter weather also brought about the necessary modification to the F-80 to burn 100 octane fuel, as the usual JP-1 made for hard starting in the lower temperature ranges. In addition, work was done to improve the F-80s anti-icing systems.

On January 15, 1950 the three squadrons started sending detachments to Wheelus Air Base, Tripoli for gunnery training in better weather conditions, for preparation for the May USAF Gunnery Meet at Las Vegas AFB, NV. Of the six pilots selected from the Group, 1st Lt.'s Cuthbert and Charles Pattillo, twin brothers, represented the 22nd FBS. The 36th

Thunderbolts and Stars over the Alps. The 86th Fighter Group F-47s were the last of the type in operational Air Force service. The F-80s are from the 23rd Fighter Squadron. (USAF)

A 36th Fighter Group formation led by a 23rd Fighter Squadron P-80B. #10 was from the 22nd FS, which used red as their squadron color. #70 was from the 53rd FS, which sported a green lightning bolt. (USAF)

(now) FBG would place eleventh overall in the meet. The 36th FBG's commanding officer, Colonel William Daniel, placed third in competition with all of the other participating fighter group commanding officers in their own special event. As an historical sidelight, this was the last fighter meet for the USAF F-47 Thunderbolt, and the 86th FBG came in third in the Conventional Class.

Air-to-air interception work continued through the Spring of 1950, with the squadrons undergoing Operational Readiness Tests, ORT's, in March, and the Group in April. All evaluations were deemed satisfactory.

The 36th FBG's aerobatic team became official in May 1950 and were named the "Skyblazers." To clear up several misconceptions about the history of the Skyblazers: The team originated from the 22nd FBS, and not the 23rd FBS that later took over the name when they were flying F-84Es. The original pilots were Captain Vince Gordon, the Pattillo twins, and Lt. Lawrence Damewood. The first official shows were flown at West Raynhum, England; Paris, France: Gutersloh, Germany and Brussels, Belgium: All in May 1950.

The rotation of the three squadrons back to Wheelus Air Base began again in June. But, when they got down there they started having numerous engine failures because of

contaminated fuel, and all of their aircraft had to be grounded for engine and fuel system purging.

Upon the Group's return to Germany in July, they found themselves placed on a Red Alert status, as the Korean Conflict had just started, and no one was sure if things were going to escalate in Europe, or not. Their role then shifted to that of primarily air defense, and they started flying "Sniper Missions." These consisted of two or more F-80s being scrambled against "bogies" at the direction of "Racecard."

Air defense missions continued until August 26 when the Group was dedicated to participate in Operation Champaign, a field maneuver being conducted by the French Army. For participation, they squadrons staged from Kaiserslautern, Germany. These were the first missions conducted by flying from the Autobaun since WWII. On the last mission of this exercise the 22nd FBS lost 2nd Lt. Charles McAbee at Verdun. The Group's mission had got into some bad weather just ten miles from Kaiserslautern, and McAbee apparently became disorientated and crashed.

Operation Rainbow began on September 11 and bad weather continued through its duration. This time the 23rd FBS suffered a loss, 2nd Lt. Richard Gregory being killed on September 17. The 23rd FBS was flying from Rhine Main,

A mass lineup of 36th Fighter Group P-80Bs at "Fursty." Their movement from Panama to Germany was the largest deployment of jet aircraft during the decade. (Esposito)

Berlin at the time, as "Willie Air Force," the "friendly force." The 22nd FBS also lost a F-80 this day, due to a shimmy damper failure that caused the aircraft to go off the end of the runway. The pilot, Captain John Pedigo, was uninjured.

On September 18 the first of the replacement F-84Es arrived via a Thunderjet "Fox Able" mission. Transition training began immediately, and on October 21 the 36th FBG's F-80s were ferried to Burtonwood, England for refurbishing, storage or shipment back to the United States.

For almost two years there were no operational F-80s in Europe, but then the escalation of the Korean Conflict via the intervention of the Chinese Communists and the threats of a further escalation of the Cold War in Europe forced the creation of the North Atlantic Treaty Organization, NATO, and the reinforcement of the Allied nations by the United States. Several new USAF units were formed, mostly fighter, that initially came from the earlier activation of most of the Air National Guard and Reserve squadrons, and many of these units were then sent to Europe to bolster those few USAF that were already there.

The 10th Reconnaissance Group's last mission aircraft before inactivation in 1949 had been the RF-51D at Pope

Field, NC. The 10th RG was reactivated at Furstenfeldbruck, Germany on July 10, 1952 under Lt. Colonel Barney McEntire when the Air National Guard's 117th RG was redesignated as the 10th RG and the 117th RG's designation was returned to State Control. At this time, also, the 10th Tactical Reconnaissance Wing was activated, only they were headquartered at Toul-Rosieres Air Base, France with Colonel Dixon Allison as their commanding officer.

It was a situation of slightly placing the cart before the horse, as the Wing and Group were not activated until after its first operational squadron, the 38th Tactical Reconnaissance Squadron had been. The 38th TRS had been activated on June 25 to replace the 160th TRS, Alabama ANG, who term of active duty was up.

Also activated on July 10 and assigned to the 10th TRG was the 32nd TRS with RF-80As and the 42nd TRS with RB-26s. As the 38th TRS replaced the ANG's 160th TRS, they were stationed at Neubiberg, Germany while the 32nd TRS commenced operations from Furstenfeldbruck. On May 14, 1953 the 38th TRS relocated to Spangdahlem Air Base, Germany, and two weeks later they were joined there by the 32nd TRS. The 32nd and 38th TRS's started supplementing

Another "plane Jane" P-80A of the 55th Fighter Group. Its plenum chamber doors are off for maintenance. (Sanders via Esposito)

45-8598 was the personal F-80 of Colonel William Daniel when he commanded the 36th Fighter Group at Furstenfeldbruck, Germany in 1949. Decals for this particular F-80B came with the reissued Monogram 1/48" scale model kit. (Olmsted)

The 23rd Fighter Squadron commanders P-80B-1 over California prior to departure for Panama. The 23rd FS used a medium blue as their squadron color. (USAF)

their RF-80s with RF-84Fs in 1955, but it would not be until the following year before they were entirely phased out in favor of the Thunderstreak.

The 66th Reconnaissance Group was one of those USAF Reserve units that was activated as a result of the Korean Conflict. They were activated on May 1, 1951 to replace an Air National Guard unit that was being returned to State Control. But two weeks later their designation was inactivated, as the action proved to be unnecessary at the time. The 66th RG was reactivated again as the 66th Tactical Reconnaissance Group on January 1, 1953 at Shaw AFB, SC under Lt. Colonel Stanley Irons. (The administrative 66th Tactical Reconnaissance Wing was also activated at this time, under Colonel Jacob Dixon). The new 66th TRG was composed of the 30th, 302nd and 303rd Tactical Reconnaissance Squadrons, of which the 30th TRS would be equipped with RB-26s, while the 302nd and 303rd TRS's would receive RF-80As. The 19th TRS would be activated later and assigned to the Wing, flying RB-45Cs.

On march 27, 1953 Colonel G. H. Fulcher became the new Wing Commander. On July 7, 1953 the Wing, Group and squadrons were moved to Sembach Air base, germany and were assigned to the 12th Air Force, Colonel Harvey Henderson became the Group commander with this movement. Operations with the RF-80A were short lived, as the 66th TRW was one of the first overseas units to receive the new RF-84F, in 1954.

"Brown's Dog" belonged to the 22nd Fighter Squadron, 36th Fighter Group. (Olmsted)

OPPOSITE: Early-on evaluation of the P-80 indicated that the airframe's size and shape, and current engines, did have their limitations. To improve on these limits, an entirely new aircraft was developed, the XP-90, which bore a distinct family resemblance to the P-80. Powered by two J-34 engines, the two examples built (46-687 and -688) suffered from a lack of thrust, and both wound up as ground targets for A-Bomb tests after their design was rejected by the Air Force. (Lockheed)

P-80s of the 1st Tow Target Squadron at March Field. The P-80 in the rear eventually wound up with the Planes of Fame Museum at Chino, CA. (Beggs)

44-85480 of the 56th Fighter Group's 62nd Fighter Squadron taxi's out for takeoff at Selfridge Field, MI. (via Menard)

44-85161 of the 62nd Fighter Squadron during the period when the Air Force could not decide exactly what "buzz numbers" to assign the F-80. Originally "PN" was assigned, for "Pursuit P-80," the "FN" for "Fighter F-80," and the settling for "FT." (via Menard)

44-85043 of the 334th Fighter Squadron. It had just emerged from the repair shop after being heavily damaged in September 1948 as a result of a forced landing. (Larkins via Isham)

45-8339 of the 336th Fighter Squadron at Langley Field. The 4th Fighter Group only flew the F-80 for two years, 1947-49. (via Menard)

45-8355 on the runway at Langley Field. Note that the plenum chamber doors on the top of the fuselage are open, drawing more air into the engine. They would automatically snap closed as flying speed was attained. (via Menard)

Captain Vermont Garrison's F-80 when he flew with the 334th Fighter Squadron. Garrison became the oldest jet ace of the Korean War while flying F-86s with the 4th Fighter Group. He passed away in the Spring of 1994. (Picciani)

4th Fighter Group P-80As in July 1948. During this period the 4th had just been assigned from ConAc to SAC, to serve as a fighter-escort group. Due to the P-80s short range, this was soon proven not to be feasible, and in December they returned to the air defense role. (via Menard)

Assigned to the 336th Fighter Squadron, this P-80 sports the Arctic Red tail and black nose, which indicates that it had been one of the 4th FG's aircraft that had been to Alaska. (via Menard)

Designated as a TQF-80F, this Shooting Star was setup for either piloted flight or NOLO (No Live Operator) drone flight. (via Isham)

Designated as a JQF-80F, 45-8519 was based at Holloman AFB, NM in 1963, being one of the last operational Shooting Stars. (Swisher via Isham)

Assigned to Edwards AFB was 44-85288, in which among its many roles it was used to develop high visibility paint schemes. Note the orange example in the background. (Picanni)

A pristine F-80C of the 44th FBS at Clark Field. When the 18th FBG sent the 12th and 67th FBS's to Korea they were left with seventy F-80Cs, and few pilots to fly them. (Cantwell)

Taxiing-out at Clark for a gunnery mission at "Happy Valley." (Cantwell)

Placed on permanent display at NAS Willow Grove, BuAer 33824 was 47-221. (Conger)

The Acrojets started with P-80As and finished with F-80Cs. 49-481 had been one of the few F-80Cs that had previously been assigned to the 1st Fighter Group. The remainder were among the handful of F-80C-10s that did not see service in Korea. (Lockheed)

45-8354 was assigned to Vermont Garrison when he led the 4th Fighter Group's F-80 aerobatic team and the 334th Fighter Squadron. In Korea, Garrison would destroy ten MiG-15s with the 4th Fighter Group's 335th Fighter Interceptor Squadron. (Picanni)

Colonel John W. Mitchell's F-80 at the 1950 USAF Gunnery Meet. His aircraft bears the colors of all three of his Group's squadrons. (William Larkins)

48-891 was definitely one of the most photographed F-80s, but the jets were something new and impressive. (via Mullet/Isham)

The 132nd Fighter Squadron had more experience with the F-80 than any other Air National Guard squadron, being the only ANG squadron to continue to fly the F-80 during their Korean War activation. (Paulson via Menard)

Assigned to the 127th FIS and delegated the role of a target tug. This was a somewhat hazardous role, particularly of the attacking pilot pressed his run on the towed sleeve too closely. (via Geer/Isham)

Serving as a target-tug with the 182nd Fighter Squadron at the end of its service life, 45-8576 had earlier served with the 94th Fighter Squadron, the 57th Fighter Group, and the 3525th Combat Crew Training Wing. (Paulson via Menard)

Texas was the largest, state-wide, ANG user of the F-80, with all three of their fighter squadrons flying the type for various lengths of time. The correct serial number of this Star is 45-8607, which wound up as a display aircraft at NAS Hensley, Dallas, TX. (J. Keer via Isham)

45-8490 originally served with the 1st Fighter Group. It finished its active duty with the 188th FIS, and then went to Cannon AFB, NM as a display aircraft. (via Kaston/Isham)

45-8549 of New Mexico's 188th FIS high over the desert. It is fitted with 35mm cameras on the leading edges of its wings for ordnance delivery photographs. (via Kaston/Isham)

This 185th Fighter Squadron F-80 shows evidence of having fired its upper machine guns on a gunnery range. The early F-80 examples had problems with the nose bay bulkheads cracking when all six guns were fired, and since the ANG only fired for practice, there was little point in firing them all, to begin with. (J. Geer via Isham)

After originally having served with the 4th Fighter Group, 45-8344 finished its career with Oklahoma's 185th Fighter Squadron. (Picanni)

One of the "Minutemen" F-80s of the 120th Fighter Squadron that was based at Denver's Buckley Field. The aerobatic team flew under the radio call-sign of "Redeye," while their support ship used "Blackeye." (Menard)

Alaska's 144th FBS at Gowen Field, Boise, ID during the 1954 All ANG Gunnery Meet. (Paulson)

Seen at the 1954 Gunnery Meet. The 144th FBS F-80 bears the standard Arctic Red paint scheme, while the 120th FIS F-80 is pained for use as a target towship. (Paulson)

49-663 was the personal F-80 of Captain Richard Penrose, 36th Fighter Bomber Squadron. The photograph was taken in July 1950. just before the squadron switched to Mustangs. (Penrose)

49-691 was assigned to the 36th FBS, and then to the 49th FBG. It was lost over North Korea on October 26, 1950, but the cause and the involved pilot could not be identified. (Esposito)

At Johnson Air Base, Japan just before the Korean War began: FT-475 was "Hall's Hearse," belonging to 1st Lt. Ralph "Smiley" Hall. It was destroyed in an accident on July 10, 1950. The second F-80 is 49-696, which now belongs to the Air Force Museum. 49-703 and -759 were both lost through combat related incidents. (McLaren collection)

"The World's largest fighter pilot." Lt. Colonel C.H. Williams, and his crew chief. 49-1882 crashed on a gunnery range on March 5, 1952. (O'Donnell)

Leaving Japan enroute to Korea in July 1950. A pair of 36th F-80Cs without underwing ordnance, but with the extended-range Misawa tip tanks. 49-696 ended up with the Air Force Museum. (Fletcher Meadows via L.B. Sides)

49-849 came to the 8th Fighter Bomber Squadron from the 25th Fighter Interceptor Squadron in January 1951. It was destroyed during an emergency landing at Tague on February 24, 1951. (Butcher)

Headed for a target in North Korea at 25,000 feet. 49-829 is carrying 5" HVAR's on "trees." It crashed on takeoff on a combat mission on April 3, 1951 and was a total loss. (Butcher)

Preparing a 35th FBS F-80C for a mission over Korea in July 1950. Note that the rockets have yet to have their warheads attached. This particular F-80 later went to the 25th FIS and was heavily damaged by AA fire on January 25, 1951. Repaired, it was transferred to the 16th FIS, and it was lost on April 28 with 1st Lt. Lee Schlegal. (Fletcher Meadows via L.B. Sides)

A flight of four 8th Fighter Bomber Squadron F-80s headed home after a mission over North Korea in early May 1951. Atypical of the Korean War F-80 attrition, 49-522 was lost on May 11 and 49-1826 was written-off as a result of battle damage in June. 49-555 was transferred to the 35th FBS when the 49th FBG switched to F-84Es. (Butcher)

49-534 of the 8th FBS. It was reassigned to the 51st FIW and became a ground instructional training aid as a result of battle damage. (Butcher

Up on jacks for landing gear maintenance at Tague. 49-1820 was lost on June 2, 1951. (Butcher)

An engine change at Tague. Note that the flight control push rod are folded up over the canopy to get them out of the way. This F-80 was shot down on June 13, 1951. (Butcher)

36th FBS F-80Cs being refueled prior to a mission. 49-662 was destroyed in a landing accident on June 26, 1951. (Esposito)

Chapter V: In The South Pacific

The decision to send the P-80A to the Pacific Theater of Operations during Word War II was viewed "very strongly, both ways" within the Air Force hierarchy. One element wanted the P-80 in combat as soon as possible, to counter the Japanese threat of their own jet propelled aircraft. (The United States was aware that the Japanese were experimenting with jet propelled aircraft, but the degree of their expertise and the number of these aircraft was an unknown factor). And also, to show further Allied air superiority to friend and foe alike.

The other element had no desire to push the P-80 into a combat role that they felt that it was not ready to undertake. There were just too many inherent "bugs" and technical problems that had not yet been surmounted. This element got its way, indirectly, as a result of the Atom Bomb.

Initially, it had been planned to send six P-80As to the Pacific Theater for testing, in a program identical to the Extraversion portion to Italy. This was rejected by the Air Force, as there was an inadequate number of trained personnel to support the second program at the time, and if it failed "The future of jet aviation would have been set back many years." However, if the war had continued, plans were formulated to send 150 P-80As to Europe, and 150 more to the Pacific Theater.

Although the 412th Fighter Group had been declared to be the first operational jet fighter group and they had been told that they would be the first jet combat unit to deploy overseas, their involvement with the P-80's operational testing, individual proficiency and public relations programs prevented this from happening. Instead, the 18th Fighter Group at Florida Blanca, Luzon (Approximately thirty miles south of Clark Field), was selected to be the first Pacific Theater based Air Force combat operational jet fighter unit.

The ramp of the 18th Fighter Group's P-80As at Nichols Field after delivery via aircraft carrier in 1946. The anti-corrosion sealing tape remained on all the aircraft for months until qualified people could get them airworthy. (Lucabaugh via Olson)

One of the first P-80As assigned to the 18th Fighter Group at Nichols Field. The aircraft all bore the standard all gloss-grey paint. (Lucabaugh via Olson)

Exactly how and why the 18th FG was selected for this role has been lost to time. At the time the decision was rendered the Philippines were already in the back-waters of the war and the aerial assault against the Japanese home islands from closer islands was well underway. Then, with the dropping of the A Bomb in August 1945 and the official surrender of Japan in September, the point became moot.

Nevertheless, the decision had been made and the pipeline opened to transfer a minimum of a squadron's worth of P-80As to the Pacific Theater. (Twenty-four aircraft, plus spares, for a total of thirty-two). The first of these arrived via aircraft carrier shipment to the Philippines Islands in March 1946 and were assigned to the 67th Fighter Squadron at Florida Blanca. At this time, the parent 18th Fighter Group was under the command of Colonel Victor Hagen. These early P-80s were all gloss-gray in color, with red noses, the squadron color of the 67th FS. During this period, the 12th and 44th FS's continued to fly P-38s, and then switched to P-51Ds in late 1946, as there were to be no more P-80As forthcoming. In fact, most of the P-80As that had arrived remained parked in storage until August when the Group gained sixteen jet pilots from the 412th Fighter Group and the Air Proving Ground Command at Pinecastle Field, FL and actual flying and training was able to commence.

The first loss of one of these P-80As occurred on September 9 when Major Henry Trollope, commanding officer of the 67th Fighter Squadron was killed immediately after attempting to takeoff. At this time all of the Group's Shooting Stars were grounded pending an investigation into the cause of the accident.

On August 7, 1946 Colonel Hagen rotated home and he was replaced by Colonel Homer Boushay. Five months later, on January 14, 1947, Boushey and three other pilots flew a record over water mission. Departing from their new base at

The 44th Fighter Bomber Squadron served as an Operational Training Unit with F-80s, in addition to its other duties, for the 18th Fighter Bomber Group while the Group was stationed in Korea and was flying Mustangs and Sabres. Here crew chief Dave Crooks is preparing his charge for a practice strafing sortie at the "Happy Valley" gunnery range. (Crooks)

"Where's our pilot?" 47-563 of the 44th FBS and its ground crew. The "2311" on the F-80s nose was Lockheed's construction number. (Cantwell)

Laoag, they took off at 0400 and climbed to 30,000 feet enroute to Bataan, Tarama, on to the Sakishima Islands, and to their destination of Yontan, Okinawa. They covered a course of 752 miles in just two hours, averaging 380 mph. Upon arrival, each aircraft still had approximately 180 gallons of fuel remaining, which proved that effective cruise control fuel management was possible in jet fighters.

For this particular mission, navigational assistance over the ocean was provided by B-29s, and it was proved that such an escort was unfeasible for jet fighters. The Superforts were just too slow. Colonel Boushay suggested to the Air Force that for future missions of this sort several P-80s should be modified to provide for a navigator position in its nose, similar to the P-38 "Droop Snoot." The suggestion was deemed "timely," but unfeasible because of cost effectiveness. In addition, the P-80Bs now in production would be delivered with the AN/ARA-8 Airborne Homing Adapter, and those after the 385th example would also be fitted with the AN/ARN-6 Radio Compass for long range navigation. In addition, if any further long-range flights were to be made, the P-80s would, in all probability, be escorted by the new B-45, as it was the only suitable and comparable aircraft envisioned at the time.

By November 14, 1946 the Group had forty-five pilots qualified in the P-80A and ninety-four in the P-51. (Many of these being qualified in both types, which was authorized at that time).

In March 1947 the 18th Fighter Group's P-80As were again loaded upon an aircraft carrier at Manila Bay and returned to the United States, as it had proved to be unfeasible to have them operating so far out on the logistical pipeline. Also at this time, the 18th Fighter Group was all but officially inactivated, being stripped of all aircraft and personnel, and existing only "on paper."

On October 1, 1947 Lt. Colonel Joseph Kruzel was named as the new 18th FG commander and the reconstituted Group was relocated to Clark Field, turning Laoag over to the fledgling Philippine Air Force. At this time the 18th FG received P-47Ns, which they flew for a year before turning them over to the Chinese Nationalist Air Force, and they received P-51Ds in exchange.

Under the Hobson Plan, the 18th Fighter Bomber Wing was activated at Clark Field on August 18, 1948 under Brig. General Robert Oliver. Colonel Marion Malcom became the 18th FG's commander on September 3, 1948, and he was replaced by Lt. Colonel Harry Norman on July 24, 1949.

In September 1949 five pilots with previous jet experience were sent TDY to the 49th Fighter Group for requalification in F-80s. These pilots were then tasked with training the remainder of the Group's pilots in the new jets.

Commencing on November 9, the 18th FG started to replace their Mustangs with brand new Shooting Stars, with the 67th FS, under Major Lewis Sebille, being the first to receive them. Maintenance training was conducted by a Mobile Training Unit that had been sent TDY from Chanute Air Force Base, IL. As expected, everyone involved was trained on the hydraulic, fuel and engine systems, which were all radically different than those on the Mustang. There was no one left in the 18th FG that had previous experience with the P-80As.

On December 20 Lt. Donald Upshaw had a flameout on takeoff and was forced to belly-in his F-80C in a rice paddy ten miles north of Clark. Although he was uninjured, the Star was the Group's first jet write-off during this era.

Personnel changes within the Group saw the arrival of nineteen new pilots during the Fall of 1949, almost all of them being brand new 2nd Lieutenants. Major James Bothwell, commanding officer of the 12th Fighter Squadron, also rotated home, being replaced by Major James McKown.

A few problems in making the switch from conventional fighters into jets did crop up. "The JP-1 fuel was so heavy that it wouldn't ignite from the igniter plugs so we were forced to carry 100 octane in the leading edge tanks for start-up and shut-down. This meant running the engine on gasoline to 'purge' of JP-1 before shut-down. Another problem we had was chipped and thrown turbine wheel buckets. Any time a bucket was thrown or chipped, it meant an engine change," related Lt. Colonel Ed Hodges. An engine change was required every 10 - 12 flying hours.

Hodges also related another incident of some interest: Two pilots ferrying F-80s to the 18th FG from Japan had to make emergency landings at Laoag while enroute. One aircraft had ten chipped buckets, and one had been thrown. The other had six chipped buckets. Hodges and Major Sebille went to Laoag to refuel these aircraft from 55 gallon fuel drums and then continued the ferry flight to Clark Field. (Lou) "Sebille flew the one in worst shape. He was like that."

Both Hodges and Colonel "Bud" Biteman agreed that there was little problem in flying a "good ship" out of Clark Field, even though the field elevation was high, and so was the usual ambient air temperature, humidity, and density altitude. Clark did have dual eight thousand foot runways.

One crash at Clark Field involved the 18th FG's TF-80C (T-33) and a young Lieutenant who would become rather well known in the future. As he was taking off, the engine started throwing buckets and Daniel "Chappie" James stop-cocked the throttle and aborted the takeoff, but the trainer went off the end of the runway with a jolt, and the canopy jammed closed. James, unbuckled his parachute and harness and stood up in the cockpit, breaking the canopy free with his back. He then extricated the unconscious "Spud" Taylor from the rear seat. "Chappie" was a big guy in more ways than one, and he later became the Air Force's first black four star general.

A new speed record was established on April 20, 1950 when Captain Robert Meyers and Lt. Phillip Conserva aver-aged 445.77 mph during a 1500 mile ferry trip from Itazuki, Japan to Clark Air Base. They reduced the previous record time by thirty-three minutes, with an elapsed time of three hours twenty-two minutes.

On June 16, 1950 Lt. Colonel Ira "Ike" Wintermute assumed command of the 18th Fighter Bomber Group (So redesignated on January 20, 1950). Nine days later, the North Koreans crossed the 38th Parallel and immediately thereafter, on July 4, Headquarters Far East Air Force ordered the 18th FBG's parent 13th Air Force to form a provisional squadron of their most experienced Mustang pilots remaining within the Group for service in Korea. Volunteers were drawn from the 18th's three squadrons and Group Headquarters and they were transferred to Japan, sans aircraft, to form the "Dallas Project."

The contingent arrived in Japan on July 11, and were commanded by Captain Harry Moreland from the 12th Fighter Bomber Squadron. This unit, now identified as the "Dallas Squadron," was immediately sent to Tague, South Korea to combine with "Bout One," the shipment of ten Mustangs to the South Korean Air Force with American advisors commanded by Major Dean Hess. (The author of Battle Hymn.) The two units were combined as the 51st Fighter Bomber Squadron (Provisional).

Although the pilots had been told that there were to receive a minimum of four hours in the Mustang to requalify, they got one hour, the ferry flight from Johnson Air Base where they picked up the aircraft, to Ashiya where they stopped to refuel and had their aircraft armed. And then they set off for Korea and a new war.

On July 28 Headquarters 18th FBG was moved to Tague and the 51st FBS (P) became redesignated as the 12th FBS. At this time, the 67th FBS, under Louis Sebille also became operational in Korea.

Installing an ejection seat into 44th FBS 49-615. Although Lockheed had developed an ejection seat for their F-80s early on in its career, they did not become a standard item until late in the aircraft's life and most were added "in the field" by maintenance crews. (Cantwell)

Assigned to the 12th Fighter Bomber Squadron in the Philippines prior to the Korean War, 49-876 later went to Korea to fight with the 36th Fighter Bomber Squadron, while the 12th FBS had to revert to Mustangs. Post Korea it was sent to Ecuador as their TF-867, and then returned to China Lake, CA to serve as a target at the Weapons Center. (USAF)

On August 4 Major Robert Dow, commanding officer of the 12th FBS in the Philippines, rejoined his squadron as commander. Captain Moreland reassumed his position as their Operations Officer. On the following day Major Sebille dove his Mustang into his target at H'amchang and became the first United States Air Force recipient of the Medal of Honor, posthumously. Indicative of the rest of the Korean War for Mustang pilots, the 18th FBG lost a total of eighteen Mustangs by the end of August.

With the dispatch of the 18th FBG and the 12th and 67th FBS's to Korea, the 18th Fighter Bomber Wing at Clark Field was now left with just the 44th FBS as their tactical unit, and they continued with F-80C's. On December 1, 1950 the 18th FBW designation was transferred to Korea "Less Personnel and Equipment," and they absorbed the 6002nd Air Base Wing at Pusan. Thus, at this time, the 44th FBS was assigned to the newly designated 6200nd Air Base Wing at Clark Field. It would not be until 1957 before the three squadrons were reunited under the 18th FBW banner at Clark when the Wing returned from Korea.

Although the 44th FBS was autonomous from the 18th FBG, in Korea, the relationship with the 18th FBW placed

Colonel Richard Montgomery, commanding officer of the 51st Fighter Wing on Okinawa in 1949, poses with his personal F-80B "Angel Ende II." In September 1950 the 51st FW's "B" models were returned to the United States and replaced with the "C" version that the Wing took into combat. (Air Force Museum)

them in the position of serving as the Operational Training Unit, OTU, for the other two squadrons. (As the 26th FIS would be for the 51st FIW, and the 41st FIS was for the 35th FIW). This action created hardship and confusion for all involved, particularly since the original Mustang pilots had all been in a position of being overseas for a long time and many were about ready to return to the United States. Now, the replacement pilots were to become combat ready under the 44th FBS in F-80s in the Philippines, and then were transferred to the 18th FBG in Korea to learn how to fly the F-51, which was a new experience for most, and then fly combat in an unfamiliar aircraft. A morale busting effort.

Those pilots that had originally volunteered for combat with the 18th FBG were placed in an even more unhappy situation. Most of them went to Korea and flew between 50 to 55 missions and then were rotated back to Clark Field when replacements for them arrived from the United States. Yet due to the lack of a viable replacement rotation policy and foresight, and clear thinking as to the ramifications of their action, Headquarters FEAF really "stuck it to these pilots." These men were told that since they had flown combat missions in Korea, they had to adhere to the policy of flying 100 combat missions before they could return home, regardless of the time served overseas. Thus they had to return to Korea to complete a 100 mission tour. Those pilots in the Far East that had managed to duck flying combat missions altogether were not effected, and even though they were rated pilots, if their three years overseas were up, they could return to the States without having to fly combat.

For some of these it meant flying F-80s at Clark Field, going to Korea in Mustangs, returning to Clark and F-80s, back to Korea and Mustangs. Others managed to return from Clark and get themselves assigned to F-80 units, but no matter how it was handled, it was a morale breaking situation that was received bitterly by those that survived, and many did not.

With the dispatch of the two 18th FBG squadrons to Korea in July, and two from the 51st Fighter Interceptor Wing from Okinawa in September, this left only two USAF tactical squadrons to protect the expanse of the Pacific Ocean outside of Japan. This created an interesting political and military quandary for the USAF, which was handled with a flair.

In 1949 the Chinese Nationalists had been forced from mainland China to Taiwan, nee Formosa, and this is were the 18th FBG's P-47Ns had gone, to bolster the Nationalists forces. And, although the US Navy was patrolling the strait between Formosa and the mainland with their own limited resources, there was little actual military equipment and personnel available to provide any sort of United Nations support to the Nationalists if the Communists were to escalate from the present stand-off.

Chiang Kai-shek and his Nationalist army, as weak as it was, constantly agitated the Chinese Communists into thinking that he would return to China. He even offered troops to the UN for service in Korea, even though he had none to spare beyond his own defensive operations, in a political effort to gain more UN support. The threat of an invasion of Formosa by the Communist Chinese was believed to be real.

In either case, the United States, either militarily or politically, did not want and could not afford an escalation of military action in this area by either side. The US was forced to show military resolve in their desire to keep these two political groups apart.

The Air Force's F-80 participation in this effort involved flying "faker" missions to Formosa by pilots of the 44th FBS out of Clark Field and the 26th FIS of the 51st FIW from Okinawa. It was believed, apparently correctly, that these missions would enforce the image of strength and resolve of the United States to both the Nationalist and Communist Chinese people.

On alternate days, a flight of four F-80s of the 44th FBS would be dispatched from Clark Field to Taipeh, Formosa where they would conduct low-level maneuvers where the maximum number of Nationalist Chinese could see them. They would then land, dine and refuel; takeoff and conduct more low-level airwork, and then head for Naha Air Base, Okinawa to spend the night. At the same time, four more F-80s of Claude "Tex" Hanley's 26th FIS would be conducting the same type of operations in the opposite direction, spending the night at Clark Field. And then the two flights would repeat the process in reverse the following day.

The low altitude airwork over Formosa showed the US presence there to the Nationalists, and then the climb-away to 30,000 feet from Formosa in both directions by the jets was sure to show on the communist radar screens and indicate that the island was not being ignored by the United States.

Another situation also involved communist forces, albeit guerrillas, in the Philippines. The Hukbalahap's, communists better known as the "Huks," kept a constant political and a quasi military pressure on the US forces and Philippine government in their attempts to gain political control of the Philippine Islands.

Again. the 44th FBS F-80s were kept in a state of readiness, with armed guns, to thwart any attacks that the Huks might attempt against the friendly Philippine government or the US presence. Their main mission was to protect the Clark Field military reservation. The airbase, itself, only encompassed a small portion of the southeast corner of the reservation. The entire area involved some 99 square miles, which could only be loosely guarded by ground patrols.

To protect the field from the air, dawn patrols were flown by the 44th FBS at 500 feet, with the pilots pulling a constant 3 G's to stay within Clark's confines. As this appeared to have little deterrent to the Huk movement, it was decided to turn the remainder of the installation into a gunnery and bombing range. After giving two weeks notice to the civilian population to abandon the area, the 44th FBS was turned loose on any and all non military structures on the reservation. Armed with their machine guns and 2.5" rockets, the pilots leveled everything. Several secondary explosions were observed from many of the abandoned huts, indicating that they had indeed been used by the Huks as supply buildings.

Eventually, as the Korean War progressed, all of the low flying time 44th FBS F-80Cs were rotated to Japan and Korea for combat. They were replaced by the war weary examples that had gone through FEAMCOM for major overhaul. When the Shooting Stars were replaced by F-86s in late 1953, those F-80s in better condition were returned to the United States for use by the reserve forces, while the war weary ones were scrapped overseas.

Japan and the Far East Air Force

In 1948 the three tactical fighter groups based in Japan were all flying Mustangs, but this changed during July when the 49th Fighter Group received their first F-80As. At this time the 49th FG was stationed at Misawa Air Base, Japan and was commanded by Colonel Lewis Hughes. The 49th FG was composed of the 7th, 8th and 9th Fighter Squadrons. Also at this time, the 49th Fighter Group fell under the command of the 314th Air Division.

The first F-80 arrived on July 6, being flown in from the depot at Tachikawa AB, Japan by Lt. Laurin Schmidt, the engineering officer of the 9th Fighter Squadron, and it was assigned to the 9th FS. On July 20 the 9th FS flew its first airshow to demonstrate the F-80, with three of the four F-80s then available, and thirteen Mustangs. On August 18, Lt. Colonel Robert Kirtley became the new Group commander. By the end of August the 9th FS had ten pilots rated as combat qualified in the F-80, and had twenty-five F-80s and nine Mustangs in their inventory. The 7th FS lost their first pilot and Shooting Star during the month when 1st Lt. Wages, their engineering officer, was killed in a takeoff crash. It was believed that the fuel was contaminated.

26th Fighter Interceptor Squadron F-80s over Okinawa. Although the 51st FIW switched to F-86s in November 1951, the 26th FIS continued to fly F-80s through the Korean War period. (USAF)

Originally assigned to the 49th Fighter Group's 9th Fighter Bomber Squadron, this F-80C missed the Korean War by being reassigned to the 26th Fighter Interceptor Squadron on Okinawa, the OTU for the 51st FIW. It was destroyed in an accident on January 16, 1952 at Naha Air Base. (via Esposito)

The transition training into the Shooting Star at this time might be considered as spastic, as there were only enough aircraft available for two squadrons, and everyone wanted to become jet qualified. In November, the 9th FS sent six pilots to the 8th Fighter Squadron to fly Mustangs again, as all of their own were gone at this time, and received eight pilots from the 8th FS to learn to fly the F-80. One of the new pilots came close to killing himself and wrote off a F-80 in this process. He "lost it" while on an instrument flight and the aircraft went into a high speed dive. During the pull-out recovery, the skin was pulled from the fuselage over the engine and the wings were bent. The "G Meter" was peged-out, so there was no way of knowing exactly how much stress had been placed on the aircraft, but he had come pretty close to having it come apart on him.

Throughout the winter months of 1948-49 the flying was reduced because of the notorious bad weather at Misawa and environs of northern Japan. In January 1949 the F-80As were fitted with the new K-15 gunsight, which was immediately termed as "Wandering Willie," as the pip could not be kept on the target. These would soon be replaced with the more reliable K-14 sight of WWII fame.

As the 49th FG became proficient with the F-80 and when the weather permitted, they started participating in exercises. One was a fighter escort mission for 3rd Bomb wing B-26s, but the big mission was to Okinawa. On February 22 they left Misawa, with Yokota as a refueling stop. However, the weather got in the way, and it was not until February 24 that they could take off on the next leg, to Itazuke. Again the weather did not cooperate, and they were delayed at Itazuke until February 26, and they finally got to Naha that day. They flew back to Itazuke on February 28 and encountered more bad weather, and did not get back to Misawa until March 2. All of the weather delays were taken in stride by the more experienced pilots,

and it did provide excellent instrument training for the younger ones, who would have to call upon this knowledge in another eighteen months.

Training continued through the spring and into the summer months with the squadrons and pilots commencing training in air-to-ground work with the F-80 on the Mito gunnery Range. On March 18 the 7th FS lost another pilot when 1st Lt. John Brown crashed near Hanawa, Japan on a return flight from Yokota. Weather was believed to have been a factor. Brown had flown 19 combat missions over Europe before being shot down and had to spend eight months as a resident of a Luftwaffe POW camp.

On June 13 the 49th Fighter Group suffered one of the highest losses of the peacetime Air Force. A pair of Mustangs from the 8th Fighter Squadron had been scrambled on a practice interception mission, and when they returned to Misawa they found a flight of Mustangs from the 35th Fighter Group overhead. They "bounced" them, and Lt. Young had a fatal mid-air collision with the lead 35th FG flight, fatally injuring himself and Lt. Hurley from the 35th FG. Compounding this tragedy was that the destroyed Mustangs crashed directly on the 9th Fighter Squadron's ramp. Two crew chiefs were killed, and one seriously burned. Twelve F-80s were totally destroyed, and three more extensively damaged.

As the 9th FS was to participate in their first Operational Readiness Test with the F-80 the following day, they had to borrow aircraft from other units in order to meet the challenge.

The F-80 supply line finally started to catch up with the rest of the 49th FG's needs in June, with brand new F-80Cs arriving to re-equip the 7th and 9th FS and to be assigned to the 8th Fighter Squadron. By the end of June the 8th FS had three F-80Cs, along with twenty-three of their weary Mustangs remaining. Finally, by November, there were a sufficient number of F-80s on hand and air and ground crews trained that the 49th FG was considered as combat operational with the Shooting Star.

In January 1950 the last of the aged F-80As were transferred to Naha and the 51st Fighter Wing. The 49th Fighter Group was also elated in that they had just won the Far East Air Forces (FEAF) Aerial Gunnery Meet, and were thus qualified to represent FEAF at the Las Vegas Gunnery Meet in March. -They placed 4th at Las Vegas, while Lt. Colonel Stanton Smith, the 49th FG's commanding officer since January 20, 1950 won the Group Commander's competition.

The usual training programs continued through the winter and until the end of spring. The first two weeks in June were spent in preparation for maneuvers at Komaki Air Base by the 9th FS, while the 8th FS went to Tachikawa on June 15 to participate in an airshow at Tokyo. As this show was canceled, the 8th FS stayed at Tachikawa until June 22 when they flew to Yokota to participate in an amphibious maneuver. Thus, when the Korean War started the 49th Fighter Group's squadrons were scattered far and wide.

The 35th Fighter Interceptor Group

The second FEAF Mustang Group to convert to Shooting Stars was the 35th Fighter Intercepter Group, which had been designated as such in January 1950 while still flying F-51Ds. During this period the 35th FIG was commanded by Lt. Colonel Jack Dale, and they were based at Johnson Air Base, Irumagawa, Japan, near Tokyo.

The first F-80s arrived on February 14, 1950 and in the midst of transition training, the 35th FIG was ordered to relocate to Yokota Air Base, which was accomplished on April 1. During June 5-8 the 35th FIG had their first Operational Readiness Test with the F-80s, and at this time they had 74 F-80s on hand. On June 25 they were in place at Yokota and their life would become one of turmoil.

The 8th Fighter Bomber Wing

During the Korean war the 8th Fighter Bomber wing would find itself as the parent unit for all of the FEAF tactical forces. However, prior to the Korean War, the 8th FBW was the last of the Mustang fighter groups to switch to jet fighters. This was accomplished in May 1950.

The 8th FBW had been stationed at Ashiya until March 25, 1949 when they were transferred to Itazuke Air Base. Colonel John Price being their commanding officer. The subordinate 8th Fighter Bomber Group was led by Lt. Colonel Charles Chitty at this time. On May 1, 1950 Colonel William Samways would become the Group Commander.

Okinawa

The 51st Fighter Group had been reactivated at Yontan, Okinawa on October 15, 1946 as a redesignation of the 413th Fighter Group. Hence, the old 1st, 21st, and 34th Fighter Squadrons became the 16th, 25th and 26th Fighter Squadrons, respectively.

On January 14, 1947 while under the command of Colonel Loring Stetson the 51st FG received their first four F-80s, a combination of As and Bs, with their being flown from Luzon to Yontan by pilots of the 16th Fighter Squadron. This was the same date that the 18th Fighter Group made an identical flight.

On May 26, 1947 with the 51st FG now under Colonel Homer Boushey, they moved to Naha Air Base, on the other end of Okinawa. Their mission at this time was the defense of the Ryukyus Islands with a combination of Thunderbolts and F-80s.

By the end of February 1948 the 51st FG was completely re-equipped with F-80s and working under radar control of the 529th Aircraft Control & Warning Group. They were under twenty-four hour alert status with the war in China between the Nationalist and communist forces going on. The F-80s stood daytime alert during this period, being known as "Hopkins Flights", with either two F-80s being airborne at the time on airborne patrol or standing five minute runway alert. Two additional F-80s were on fifteen minute alert. The attached 4th Fighter (All-Weather) Squadron took the night hours with their P-61s. Additional missions and exercises were conducted with, or against, US Navy forces and/or USAF B-29s in and around Okinawa.

On August 18, 1948 the Hobson Plan went into effect and brought about the activation of the 51st Fighter Wing as the parent unit for the 51st FG. Their original parent unit, the 301st Fighter Wing became the 301st Fighter Division at this time, but their commander, B/General Hugh Rush was transferred to be the commander of the 51st Fighter Wing.

To strengthen the image of US airpower on Okinawa, the 1st Air Division at Naha was inactivated on December 1, 1948. Its replacement was the relocation of the 13th Air Force Headquarters, which was relocated "Less Personnel and Equipment" from Clark Field to Kadena, and the movement of the ex 1st Air Division personnel to Kadena from Naha. The new Commanding Officer of the 13th Air Force was Major General Charles Meyers, the ex Commanding Officer of the 1st Air Division.

One of the more interesting exercises the 51st Fighter Group took part in during May 1949 was the hypothetical situation of when "Nation X spilled armed forces over the South Korean border and overran that country in a matter of hours." The 51st FG received a score of 87.9% for their part of the exercise, defending Okinawa and the Ryukyus, the highest score by a FEAF unit. After this exercise was concluded the last of the USAF forces in South Korea were withdrawn from the peninsula.

On May 15, 1949 the 13th Air Force returned to Clark Field "Less Personnel and Equipment," and they were then replaced by the 20th Air Force, which came to Kadena under the same circumstances from Harmon Field, Guam.

On June 29, 1949 between typhoons "Delta" and "Gloria," the 51st FG flew forty-one F-80s from Naha to Yokota Air Base to escape further storm damage. This was believed to now establish a record for the longest over-water mass formation of jet aircraft. ("Gloria" destroyed five aircraft, and caused major damage to 53 more, with minor damage to 35).

Administrative changes in June 1950 brought Lt. Colonel Irwin Dregne to command the 51st Fighter Interceptor Group (So redesignated on February 1, 1950.) Dregne had previously commanded the 56th Fighter Group. The following month Dregne was relieved by Colonel Oliver Cellini, the previous commanding officer of the 52nd Fighter (All-Weather) Group.

On June 26, 1950 the 51st Fighter Interceptor Wing was placed on a "Red Flash Alert" with eight F-80s to be fully combat loaded and committed to a five minute alert status. This action was followed by having the attached 4th Fighter (All-Weather) Squadron, now flying F-82Gs, being sent to Japan for combat duty. The 4th F(AW)S had just been attached to the 51st FIW two days previously, after being assigned to the inactivated 347th Fighter (All-Weather) Group and attached to Headquarters 20th Air Force prior to this action.

During the early summer months the Wing was in the process of converting from the older F-80As and Bs to F-80Cs. On July 1 they had eighteen of the improved models, and gained a dozen more during the month, but one was destroyed in a taxi accident. Also, during this period, the squadrons were pulling rotational duty to Yontan, an airstrip that was considered as "primitive," and was utilized by the Wing as field training site.

On September 6, 1950 the 51st Fighter Interceptor Wing was alerted for movement to Itazuke Air Base, Japan. This movement would involve the 51st Fighter Interceptor Wing and Group along with the 16th and 25th Fighter Interceptor Squadrons. The 4th F(AW)S, which had returned from Japan in July would remain on Okinawa for night and inclement weather defense, while the 26th FIS would also remain behind for daylight hours defense. The 26th FIS would also serve as a replacement training unit for the squadrons in combat, and would rotate pilots and ground personnel to Japan and Korea.

The main body of the 51st FIW was transported to Itazuke on the Sergeant Antolak and they departed Okinawa on September 20. Two days later sixty-one F-80s of the 16th and 25th FIS's flew to Itazuze, landing at 1330 hours. The Antolak docked at Moji, Japan on September 25, and this contingent completed the trip via rail. Upon their arrival at Itazuke, the 51st FIW was assigned to the 5th Air Force, with attachment to the 8th Fighter Bomber Wing for logistical and administrative support.

Chapter VI: Recce Stars

The initial role of the F-14/FP-80 was to train personnel in new high-speed photo reconnaissance techniques, as this version of the Shooting Star they were now receiving was considerably faster than any of the reconnaissance (commonly called recce) aircraft then in the Air Force's inventory. By a good 100 mph, which meant far more emphasis had to be placed upon fuel management, because of the jet's fuel consumption at low altitudes, and pin-point navigation to and from the targeted areas.

To accomplish this, many of the initial missions were of a "swords into plowshares" nature. Training missions were flown for the Department of Agriculture, the Army Corps of Engineers, municipalities requiring photo mapping, and for sundry other reasons in addition to those desired by the military for their own purposes. Then, with the Cold War beginning in 1948, recce targets became those of a tactical nature. Yet, strangely enough, the 1949 Post War budget cuts then forced a reduction of Air Force units, and the recce units were the first to be cut back or inactivated. A year or so later the Air Force was forced to reactivate many of these units and create additional ones to help counter the communist threats that were cropping up around the world.

The first of the F-14/FP-80 tactical reconnaissance groups to be activated was the 363rd Reconnaissance Group. It was activated at Brooks Field, San Antonio, TX on July 29, 1946 and at that time it was commanded by Colonel Russell Berg.

Assigned reconnaissance squadrons were the 12th, 161st and 162nd. Note here that the block of squadron designations assigned to the Air National Guard, 101-199 encompassed these later numbers, although these particular squadrons bore no relationship to the similarly identified ANG squadrons, particularly Alabama's 160th that later became a RF-80 recce squadron.

The 12th Reconnaissance Squadron was activated at March Field on July 29 and absorbed the personnel and equipment of the recently inactivated 39th Reconnaissance Squadron, 412th Fighter Group. The 161st RS was activated August 31 and was assigned to Brooks Field with F-6Ds and FP-80s, and they moved to Langley Field, VA on November 1. The 162nd RS was also based at Brooks Field, and they were equipped with B-26s. They followed the 161st to Langley on December 20. The 363rd RG, now under Colonel James Smelley, also moved to Langley in December.

On June 24, 1947 the 160th RS was relieved from assignment to the 10th RG in Germany and assigned to the 363rd RG at Langley, to be equipped with FP-80s. Coinciding with this move, the 12th RS was relieved from assignment to the 363rd RG and was assigned to the 67th RG. The 160th RS was temporally deactivated on April 26, 1949 and when they were reactivated on September 1, 1950 they be-

44-83024 was the prototype YF-14. It only has a camera window below its nose in front of the nose wheel. It was lost in a mid-air collision with a B-25. (Air Force Museum)

44-84998 was modified by Lockheed to become the second F-14A. Note the hand crafted boundary air control ducts, which were slightly larger than those found on the mass production versions. (Department of Defense)

The third prototype of the F-14 was 44-85201 and it had three camera viewing ports in front of the nose wheel, along with one on each side. (Air Force Museum)

Discussing the placement of the internal camera equipment in a F-14s nose, and the general arrangement of its internal camera bay. The recce version's nose section rotated upwards for easy access, but crews had to be careful with it in windy conditions, lest the hinges were damaged. (Air Force Museum)

came B-26 equipped. On September 23, 1949 the 161st RS relocated to Shaw Field, SC and gave up their Mustangs, but they would continue to fly RF-80s until 1955 when they were replaced by RF-84Fs. The 162nd RS was relieved of assignment to the 363rd RG on July 28, 1950 and transferred to the 5th Air Force in Japan.

On April 2, 1951 the 17th Tactical Reconnaissance Squadron (Photographic) was activated at Shaw and assigned to the 363rd RG (Now Tactical Reconnaissance Group.) with RF-80s. They too would continue with the RF-80s until 1955 when they were replaced with RF-84Fs.

The 67th Reconnaissance Group was reactivated at Langley Field on May 19, 1947. As an "on paper" group, they were transferred to March Field on July 25 "Less Personnel and Equipment." Major Edwin Larson served as an interim commanding officer, and two weeks later he was replaced by Lt. Colonel Arvis Hilport. On August 16 the noted Colonel Leon Grey became the commander of the 67th RG. On November 25 the 67th Tactical Reconnaissance Wing was organized at March Field under Colonel Arthur DeBolt and this Wing was in turn attached to the 1st Fighter Group for control purposes.

Initially assigned to the 67th RG were the 11th and 15th RS's. The 11th RS remained at Langley "on paper" until September 1, 1947 when it too was moved to March Field, to fly B-26s. The 15th RS had been assigned to the 67th RG with F-6Ds on May 17, but on July 24 the relationship was terminated and they were reassigned to Lawson Field, GA and the 10th RG that had returned from Europe.

On July 29, 1947 the 12th RS joined the 67th RG from the 363rd RG with RF-80s and on June 14, 1948 they were redesignated as the 12th Tactical Reconnaissance Squadron (Photographic). The 67th RG was similarly redesignated at this time, as the 67th Tactical Reconnaissance Group. The 67th TRG, by now under Colonel Loren McCollom, and its squadrons was inactivated on March 28, 1949, but they would be reactivated in Korea on February 25, 1951. The remain-

der of their F-80/RF-80 history will be found in the Korean War chapter.

The 8th Tactical Reconnaissance Squadron (Night Photographic) was all by itself at Yokota, Japan when they converted from F-15s, (later redesignated as the RF-61C.) the Northrop "Reporter" modification of the P-61 Black Widow, in 1949. The 8th TRS (Photographic), so designated on August 1, 1949 reported directly to Headquarters 5th Air Force. On June 29, 1950 the 8th TRS established a detachment at Itazuke, Japan for Korean War operations, and on July 9 the entire squadron moved there to become attached to the 8th Fighter Bomber Wing for logistical and administrative purposes. On September 26, 1950 the 8th TRS was assigned to the newly constituted 543rd Tactical Support Group and then moved to Tague, South Korea on October 2, 1950. The remainder of their history appearing in the Korean War chapter.

The 10th Tactical Reconnaissance Wing was activated at Furstenfeldbruck, Germany on July 10, 1952 as a

Assigned to the 363rd Tactical Reconnaissance Group, this RF-80A visited Kerney Field, NB in the Spring of 1948. It seemed that the Air Force could never quite make up their mind as to where to place the "buzz codes" on these aircraft. (Olmsted)

45-8435 was a Lockheed built FP-80A-5 that was assigned to the 66th Tactical Reconnaissance Wing. Observe the smooth blend of the nose section into the fuselage, in contrast to the later "in the field" conversions. The 302nd TRS used red chevrons, the 303rd TRS used blue. (Leo Kohn)

redesignation of the 117th Tactical Reconnaissance Wing, which was scheduled to return to the Air National Guard. The Wing commander was Colonel Allen Dixon, while the 10th TRG commander was Lt. Colonel Barney McEntire. McEntire would later become the commander of the South Carolina ANG and he was killed in a F-104 crash on May 25, 1961. Congraree Air Base, South Carolina would be renamed in his honor on Novermber 10, 1961. Assigned to the 10th TRW were the 1st and 42nd Tactical Reconnaissance Squadrons with RB-26s. The two RF-80 squadrons assigned were the 32nd TRS at Furstenfeldbruck, which replaced South

Carolina's 157th TRS, and the 38th TRS at Neubiberg, Germany which replaced Alabama's 160th TRS. (So, here one can see that there had been two 160th TRS squadrons operating at the same time that were not in any way connected. One assigned to the 363rd TRG at Shaw AFB, SC with B-26s, and the other to the 117th TRG at Furstenfeldbruck with RF-80s). In November 1952 the Wing/Group moved to Toul-Rosieres, France for a short period, and then moved to Spangdahlem, Germany in May 1953.

The role of the 10th TRW was to provide both day and night tactical reconnaissance, along with weather recce, over West Germany and along the Warsaw Pact boarders. On May 4, 1953 the 38th TRS relocated to Spangdahlem and On May

The first assignment of the F-14/FP-80 was to the 39th/12th Reconnaissance Squadron of the 412th/1st Fighter Group. The squadron was commanded by Colonel Leon Grey during its early months, and Grey won the 1946 and 1947 Bendix Trophy Races in this aircraft. (Lockheed)

The 363rd TRG, under Colonel John Dyas, was based at Shaw AFB, SC after being reactivated during the Korean War emergency. Here one of the RF-80As is visiting Baltimore, MD's Friendship Airport. (Lucabaugh)

A 8th Tactical Reconnaissance Squadron RF-80A near Yokota Air Base, Japan. Their pre Korean War markings were quite nondescript. (Wilson via Esposito)

17 the 32nd joined them there. In 1955 the Wing re-equipped with RF-84Fs and some RB-57As.

The 66th TRW activated at Shaw AFB on January 1, 1953 with the wing commanded by Colonel Jacob Dixon and the 66th TRG commanded by Lt. Colonel Stanley Irons. The intention of this activation was to replace the 118th TRW, an Air National Guard Group composed of the 106th, 155th and 185th Tactical Reconnaissance Squadrons that had been based at Shaw with RF-51Ds and then RF-80s during their Korean War mobilizations.

The 66th TRW was composed of the 19th TRS with B-45s and the 30th TRS with RB-26s. RF-80As equipped the 302nd and 303rd TRS's. By the end of 1955 the 30th TRS has switched to RB-57s and the 302nd and 303rd TRS's to RF-84Fs.

The 432nd Tactical Reconnaissance Group was activated at Shaw AFB, SC on May 18, 1954. It first commanding officer was Colonel Frank Sharp, and he was replaced by Colonel John Foster in 1955. (The 432nd Wing was established on May 23, but it was not activated until 1958).

Assigned to the 432nd TRG were the 20th, 41st and 43rd TRS's. The 41st TRS was initially equipped with RB-26s and the 43rd TRS with RB-57As, while the 20th TRS received RF-80As. The 20th TRS flew the RF-80s from Shaw for just a year in a training role, and in 1955 they were replaced by RF-84Fs.

The 23rd Fighter Group had a rather unusual history as far as the Shooting Star was concerned. This Group, The "Flying Tigers," had replaced the original American Volunteer Group in China and fought with the 14th Air Force during the remainder of WWII, to be inactivated on January 5, 1946 "on paper" at Ft. Lewis. WA. The Group was then reactivated on Guam on October 10, 1946 with P-47s and assigned to FEAF. But on April 25, 1949 they relocated to Howard Air Force Base, Panama Canal Zone to fly RF-80s.

Although the three assigned squadrons, the 74th, 75th and 76th were all identified as "fighter" squadrons, their role, apparently, was that of photo-recce over the Canal Zone. On

Another 363rd TRG RF-80A in pre Korean war markings. They sometimes got carried away with their checkerboard markings. (Esposito)

45-8374 of the 8th TRS. When the 8th TRS was redesignated as the 15th TRS, this RF-80A was named "Mary Lou." (Esposito)

Down in the rough at Yokota Air Base after a landing gear folding incident. (Wilson via Esposito)

September 24, 1949 the Group and the three squadrons were inactivated.

Little of the 4th Tactical Reconnaissance Squadron is known. They were assigned directly to the Caribbean Air Command at Rio Hato, CZ on August 26, 1946, and then further attached to a Provisional, unnumbered, Composite Reconnaissance Group between February 1 and July 28, 1948, and then to the 5620th Composite Group: with actual assignment transferring them to the 6th Fighter Wing on June 1, 1948. Between 1947-48 they flew F-6D Mustangs, and RF-80s from 1947-49. On June 17, 1948 they were redesignated as the 4th Tactical Reconnaissance Squadron (Photographic), and they were inactivated on March 14, 1949. Apparently their major claim was that their RF-80As were faster than the F-80Bs of the 36th FBG!

During the Korean War the 160th Fighter Squadron was redesignated as the 160th Tactical Reconnaissance Squadron and switched from F-51Ds to RF-80As before deploying to Europe. 44-85473 was one that Lockheed selected at random for conversion to a RF-80 while 45-8399 was intentionally built as one of the RF-80 series, as were the other two examples. (Esposito)

Modified to a RF-80 by a sub contractor from a regular F-80, this example had previously served with the 56th Fighter Group. Note the bulge in the radio compass housing and the more bulky appearance of the aircraft's nose in general. (Leo Kohn)

44-85160 had previously served with the Kansas Air National Guard's 127th Fighter Interceptor Squadron as a F-80A-11 before it was modified to a recce version and assigned to the Alabama ANG. (Leo Kohn)

45-8466 as built by Lockheed as a RF-80A-5. Again note the smooth blend of nose to fuselage over those later modified by contractors. (Leo Kohn)

The pilot's instrument panel of a RF-80 with camera switches, film counters, and blinker lights to show when the camera's were in operation replacing the K-14 gunsight. (Air Force Museum)

Chapter VII: The United States Navy

Assignment of the P-80 to the United States Navy came from two separate evaluation programs. The US Navy, early on, had expressed interest in the P-80, as it was well in advance of their own FD Phantom (Redesignated as FH-1 on July 27, 1947.), and FJ Fury programs. Strangely enough, the first evaluation program came from a desire of the Air Force to determine the suitability of catapulting the P-80 in December 1944 when they "Considered it advisable for Lockheed" to develop a method of catapulting the P-80 off of an aircraft carrier deck, as it was envisioned that this would be a good way of delivering the aircraft to operational units in a combat theater. In reality, similar fly-away deck-launch programs had been utilized operationally to deliver P-40s to Africa during Operation Torch in 1942, and the Navy continued to deliver P-39s and P-47s to islands in the Pacific theater in this fashion during the war. Almost all of the Air Force fighters, including the comparatively huge P-61 Black Widow had been evaluated for feasibility in this sort of delivery program.

Although the U.S. Navy was initially reluctant to involve itself in this particular P-80 program, as they could not see any immediate need for aircraft carrier delivery of the P-80 during the later stages of World War II, they did agree on April 4, 1945 to participate in a ground based catapult development test program.

On May 17 the Army Air Force turned over to the Navy two P-80As, one of which had been modified by Lockheed for catapulting. (The AAF also desired to furnish the Navy with two P-80Bs for this program, but Lockheed engineers balked at the idea, as the P-80B had a more powerful engine, and they did not want to devote the time or resources to install catapult equipment on these aircraft).

The first P-80A delivered to the U.S. Navy was 44-85000, and it was re-serialed as BuAer 29667 under the Navy's aircraft serial number system. It was flown to Patuxent River Naval Air Station, "Pax River," by a relatively unknown Lockheed engineer that was also a Naval Reservist, by the name of Najeeb Halaby. (Halaby became the first administrator of the Federal Aviation Agency when it was created from an "Administration.")

Between July and December 1945 the USN conducted simulated aircraft carrier operations with this P-80 on the runways at Patuxent River. Assisting Halaby was Ed Owen, the Navy's Project Officer. Although the pilots were in agreement over the general flight handling characteristics of the P-80, it proved to be definitely unsuitable for carrier operations. The reasons were numerous, with almost all being related to the characteristics of the early jet engines: low thrust, slow throttle response, and a lack of deceleration when the throttle was "cut" at a point 10-15 feet above the simulated carrier's deck. The P-80 would "float" between 600-800 feet at this time, instead of settling to the deck, which would have placed the aircraft well beyond the actual aircraft carrier's deck before it was ready to touchdown.

The second P-80A furnished to the Navy did not become available to them until December 18, 1945. This aircraft, 44-85005, became BuAer 29668. The delay in delivery was due to Lockheed's aircraft carrier catapult modifications. Lockheed had installed three catapult hooks, one behind the nose wheel doors, and one under each wing near the fuselage. They also installed a catapult hold back ring and an arrestor hook under the fuselage and between the flaps. This was the only P-80 to be fitted with an arrestor hook.

Marine ace Major Marion Carl was checked-out in this aircraft on December 18 at Muroc, and two days later he started to fly it to Patuxent River. It took him ten days to get

Lt. Colonel Marion Carl, USMC, Launches off the USS Franklin D. Roosevelt on November 1, 1946 while conducting carrier trials of the P-80/TO. (USN)

One of the NAS Miramar based TO-1s. The markings were atypical for the period, nondescript. BuAer 33867 has 265 gallon tip tanks. (Esposito)

Assigned to VCN-1 at Miami, FL was this TO/TV-1, a P-80C-1, in 1950. This unit was to provide jet qualification for future Navy all-weather pilots. (USN)

there, due to weather and other factors. Ed Owens continued to be the Project Officer as the program continued.

Two different catapult systems were utilized at Pax River to ascertain launching suitability. One was electric, and the other hydraulic. These catapult types were both proven to be satisfactory, with limitations. It was viewed that the P-80s wings lacked sufficient inherent strength to permit continuous aircraft carrier operations in an operational configuration (ie, with tip tanks). There was not enough strength to permit high "G" acceleration on catapult launches without overstressing the tip tank shackles and either loosing the tanks or bending the P-80s wings.

After the catapult trials were completed, it was time to conduct the arrested landing trials. On September 13, 1946, eight months after this P-80 came on board, Major Carl made eleven arrested landings. Carl, after experimenting with many different approach configurations, determined that the best approach method was to approach the carrier deck at 105 mph and to take the "cut" at about fifteen feet above the deck. This insured that the P-80 would touchdown at 101 mph with a six foot per second sink rate. Of course, all of this would change with the actual approach to an aircraft carrier deck, with the inherent wind over the deck.

On November 1, 1946 Major Carl flew four running take-offs, two catapult launches, and made five arrested landings on the aircraft carrier Franklin D. Roosevelt. The normal deck

takeoff's were "hairy" to say the least, as the FDR had a deck length of only 924 feet, and the P-80 required a 900 foot deck-run with a headwind of thirty-five knots. The catapult launches were the first ever made by a jet aircraft.

VMF-311 was the U.S. Marine's only squadron to receive the TO-1 in squadron strength, and they flew them for only a year. (Esposito)

After the 49th FBG converted to F-84s, this F-80C was transferred to the 35th FBS. Surviving the experience, it finished its career with the Alaska ANG. (Butcher)

A 49th FBG F-80 makes a JATO takeoff at Tague Air Base. JATO was an absolute necessity during the summer months in Korea, because of the combat loads, ambient air temperatures and short runways. The failure of a bottle to fire always resulted in the loss of the aircraft and injury, or worse to the pilot. (Butcher)

An 100 hour engine inspection taking place on a RF-80 of the 67th TRW at Kimpo Air Base. Note on the port Fletcher tip tank that the seal plate on the tank has been removed to work on its attachment lugs. (Newman via Menard)

An indicator of just how rough and foreboding North Korea could look from 25,000 feet during the winter months. Wind-swept peaks and snow-filled valleys. Escape and evasion by a downed pilot in this country was almost an impossibility, although some made it. (Butcher)

49-847 enroute to North Korea with 110 gallon napalm tanks. Some of the tanks were painted yellow, some brown, and some were natural metal. She was lost in an accident at Suwon Air base. (Butcher)

49-793 of the 8th FBS undergoing a 100 hour inspection. The tip tanks readily show where the two extra sections have been added to increase their capacity. (Butcher)

Charging the machine guns on a 49th FBG F-80 prior to takeoff. The napalm tanks have yet to have their fuzes installed. Korean winters were noted for their severe cold, hence the bundled-up ground crew. (Butcher)

A J-33-35 engine at K-2, Tague, awaiting installation in a F-80. (Butcher)

500 and 1,000 pound GP's and napalm tanks in the storage dump at K-2. 49-527 in the background belonged to the 7th FBS, and went to the 35th FBS when the 49th FBG switched to Thunderjets. (Butcher)

Ready for action. Armed with 250 pound GP's. 49-734 in the background was lost on May 12, 1952 with 1st Lt. William Slade, 35th FBS, being killed by North Korean AA fire. (Butcher)

The 45th TRS oversprayed the tops of several of their RF-80As in an attempt to camouflage them from MiG-15 pilot's eyes. This particular recce Star was written off in an accident on August 11, 1952 during a period of heavy rain. (Newman via Menard)

49-438 of the 45th TRS. The polka dot markings came as a result of one of their Mustang pilots bringing back a bolt of material from Japan, to be used for scarves, and the motif was carried through to their aircraft. (Picanni)

Tague Air Base, South Korea February 1951. F-80s of the 8th FBS are readied for a mission. 49-847 had previously belonged to the 25th FIS, hence the not as yet applied new squadron markings. FT-860 was lost in March, to flak damage. (Butcher)

Columbia was the second South American nation to receive F-80s under the Reimbursable Assistance Program. In March 1954 they received six T-33s, which were followed by F-86s in 1956, and then F-80s in 1958. (Esposito)

Uruguay was the last Organization of American States country to receive the F-80, in June 1958. Note that the upper .50 caliber machine guns have been fired, by the blast residue. (Boruck via Jack Smith)

The same aircraft after restoration from a captive airframe and bearing the markings of the famed "Acrojets," which also called Williams "home." It was placed on display later at Holloman AFB. (Keer via Isham)

A P-80A assigned to Williams Field, Chandler, AZ. For a period Williams used a full checkerboard on their aircraft's vertical fin for identification, while Las Vegas/Nellis used a partial checkerboard in the same yellow and black. This example was lost in an accident in February 1949. (USAF)

"Chief Blanket Ass," is the insignia of the 169th AS, Illinois ANG. 45-8357 when it was on display at Phillips Park, Aurora, IL. (McLaren)

44-85182 was a F-80A-1 improved to F-80C standards and assigned to the 3595th CCTW. The 3595th used the checkerboard paint scheme, while the attached Fighter Weapons School added the bullseye. (Isham)

Some F-80s did survive to inspire future airmen. 44-85171 went to Lackland AFB, where it was awaiting a new paint scheme. (C. Kaston via Isham)

In 1984 45-8357 was moved from Aurora to Robbins AFB, GA and restored in its original 56th Fighter Group markings by the AFRES. It was one of the original "Fox Able" mission F-80s to Germany. (R. Leader via Isham)

45-8501 was a P-80B that had served with the 27th Fighter Squadron. It later went to Chanute AFB, IL as an instructional airframe. Aviation historian David Menard was instrumental in having it painted in the markings of the F-80C that Major Charles Loring flew when he perished in Korea. (McLaren)

Now on display at Oshkosh, WI and in the hands of the Experimental Aircraft Association, 48-868 had been assigned to the 132nd Fighter Interceptor Squadron at DOW AFB. Rest assured that the EAA will handle her with well deserved TLC. (McLaren)

In 1949 the Smithsonian Institution obtained "Lulu-Belle," and in 1976 they commenced restoration of her. After years of painstaking work and attention to every detail, she was rolled out for the cameras before being placed on permanent display in the National Air and Space Museum. (Lockheed)

"Panther Queen" was the personal F-80 of Colonel Samways, commanding officer of the 8th Fighter Bomber Group. Samways was the highest scoring F-80 pilot, with four air-to-ground kills. Later this F-80 was transferred to the 16th FIS, and was bellied-in on August 20, 1951. (Fletcher Meadows via L.B. Sides)

49-1872 was originally assigned to the 8th FBS, 49th FBG. Now assigned to the 45th TRS, this F-80 was one of those they used for armed-recce and escort for their RF-80s. Post Korea, she went to Ecuador as their TF-872, and then wound up at China Lake, CA as a target for Navy pilots. (Newman via Menard)

49-503 of the 36th FBS. It was later assigned to the 80th FBS and was lost on January 24, 1952 when 1st Lt. Jerry Bingham was attempting an instrument let-down to reach his North Korean target. After entering the clouds he was never seen again. (Esposito)

Replacing .50 caliber machine guns in 49-847. There were major problems with the gun barrels in both the F-51 and F-80, as the barrels tended to rupture, due to their own age, and that of the ammunition, due to poor storage conditions of both prior to the war. (Butcher)

Bombing up! Loading a
1000 GP bomb on 49-844
at Tague Air Base. This
8th FBS F-80 was lost on
May 11, 1951 as a result
of a takeoff accident on a
combat mission.
(Butcher)

Carrying two 260 pound
fragmentation bombs and
extended range tip tanks,
a 8th FBS F-80 trundles
along side of Tague's
single runway. Most of
the runway was PSP,
pierced steel planking,
that rattled and undulated
under the heavy laden
fighter-bombers. It also
had a propensity for
cutting tires and causing
accidents. (Butcher)

49-718 was badly damaged in a mid-air collision over Kimpo Air Base on November 10, 1951 while serving with the 8th FBG. Rebuilt, she went to the 45th TRS. (Newman)

The TO/TV Shooting Star continued in Navy service through the mid to late 1950s, giving them a naval service life of just a decade. (Esposito)

Assigned to NAS Whiting Field, FL BuAer 33822 was the second TO-1 obtained by the USN, ex 47-219. (Esposito)

The arrested landings were flown as computed with a gross weight of 10,000 pounds, which gave the P–80 a stalling speed of 98 mph. Thus Carl targeted 105 mph as his final approach speed with a power setting of 82%. At this setting the I-40 engine required four seconds to "spool-up" to 100% power, which was the very minimum deemed safe in the event he was forced to take a wave-off. The P-80s stalling speed in this configuration was 98 mph, so at all times the aircraft was at a critical point it its flight envelope.

In all, the P-80 was determined to be unsuitable for aircraft carrier operations. The deck-run takeoffs were not at all feasible, as they were too long and too slow. Only one aircraft could be launched at a time. Catapult launches would be a necessity at all times, and it was too slow of an operation. The slow engine response time made all landing attempts hazardous, particularly in the event of a wave-off. The P-80 had a tendency to bounce and rock upon landing, and the arrestor hook often skipped the arresting wires. Fuel consumption at low altitudes and in the landing pattern was so high that the fuel state became critical after only a few minutes of low level air work or practice landing approaches. The wing's inherent lack of physical strength would not permit the carrying of tip tanks to extend its range at all.

On February 13, 1947 BuAer 29667 was lost in a belly landing on Deal Island, near Patuxent River. Lt. John Thomas was flying it at the time. Its engine lost fuel pressure, rpm, and the engine started to vibrate, and he was forced to make an emergency landing on the island with it. Prior to this, it had been used to evaluate the jet versus prop situation, putting it up against other Navy types in simulated air-to-air combat.

On June 4, 1947 BuAer 29668 came apart in the air at Pax River killing Lt. Donald Umphres. While he was doing an aileron roll at 200 feet and 500 mph, the tail came off the aircraft. Apparently because it was overstressed while in the inverted portion of the roll and the pilot inadvertently lowered its nose in an improper attempt to recover the aircraft at too low an altitude and too high an airspeed.

In a left break over NAS Whiting Field. The TO/TV was the primary Navy jet trainer until deliveries of the F9F caught up with the demand for an adequate navalized trainer. (USN)

BuAer 33868 was 48-379 and it was originally assigned to Mustin Field, Philadelphia, PA. It then went to NAS Oakland as their number 108. (Esposito)

As they say: "A gear-up landing occurs in two forms, those who have, and those who will." BuAer 33850 was 47-1397. (Esposito)

In March 1946 the U. S. Navy received 44-85235, BuAer 29689. It was assigned to Marine Corps Air Station Mojave, CA for use as a monitor and chase aircraft for Naval guided missile programs. In October 1946 this program relocated to Point Magu, CA and on August 29, 1947 BuAer 29690, 45-8557, a P-80B, was also assigned to the missile chase pro-

gram. They remained in service until July 1952 and 29689 was scrapped, while 29690 wound up in the collection of Walter Soplata, an aircraft collector in Ohio.

Even though the U.S. Navy and Marine air arms had entered the jet era with their FD's and FJ's, their production was lagging behind the desired rate and these aircraft had already proved to be unsuitable for extended operational fleet use. In the future were the F9F Panther and F2H Banshee, and in the mean time, the FD and FJ were relegated to the jet training role. To increase the capability of the Navy's Training Command to furnish jet pilots, the Air Force agreed to furnish the Navy with fifty examples of the P-80C (now F-80C). The Navy thusly designated them as the TO-1 (Which, in turn, was redesignated as the TV-1 in 1952.), T= Trainer, O= Lockheed, the "O" being changed to "V" on April 1, 1952.

These F-80Cs/TO-1s came from the initial batches of F-80C-1s ordered in Fiscal Year 1947 and 1948: Seven from the first allocation of 1947 Air Force serial numbers, and forty-three from the second series. Assigned BuAer numbers as 33821/33827 for 47-218/224; 33828 for -525; 33829/33832 for -601/604; 33833/33847 for -47-1380/1394; 33848 for 48-382; 33849/33864 for 47-1396/1411 and 33865/33870 for 48-376/381 (48-356, the first of the FY 1948 F-80Cs was modified to the TF-80C two-seat trainer which became the T-33/

Assigned to NAS Kingsville, TX and ATU-200, BuAer 33860 was 47-1407. (Esposito)

Another NAS Kingsville based TO-1 caught just after liftoff and with its landing gear just beginning to retract. (Esposito)

TV-2, and the first twenty aircraft in this new series ran to 48-375).

Upon delivery from Lockheed, these new TO-1s were assigned to the U.S. Navy's VF-52, JTU-1/ATU-3/200 and VCN-1, along with Marine squadron VMF-311. VMF-311 was based at MCAS El Toro, CA. It was commanded by Lt. Colonel John Conden. Their initial training with the TO-1 took place at two separate locations. The squadron's ground personnel initially trained with the Air Force's 1st Fighter Group at March Field, while the first four Marine pilots qualified "in type" at Williams Field, Chandler, AZ in F-80s and then returned to El Toro to fly their own aircraft and to train the remainder of the squadron. With the start of the Korean War, VMF-311, now under Lt. Colonel "Spike" McIntyre, converted to F9Fs and went to Korea in November 1950.

Little is known of the U.S. Navy's TO-1 operations other than VF-52 was commanded by Commander Ed Pawka. VF-52 kept the TO's for just a year, but did manage to become proficient jet pilots in the process. After switching to F9Fs in 1949 they won PacFleet's Battle Efficiency "E" award for FY 1949. Jet Training Unit -1, JTU-1, was redesignated as ATU-3 (Advanced Training Unit) and then ATU-200. They were based at NAS Kingsville, Texas. VCN-1 became identified as "FAWTUPac," one of the strange Navy acronyms that wound up painted on the sides of their TOs as "FALLWEATRAPAC." All of this roughly translated to Fleet All-Weather Training Unit, Pacific. VCN-1 was mostly concerned with evaluating all-weather Grumman fighters and training aircrews, in Corsairs and Skyraiders until the F3D Skynight became available. Apparently they used the TO strictly for night and instrument training in jet fighters. As apparently the Navy had never intended to use the TO in fleet operations to begin with, when they obtained sufficient F9Fs and F2Hs to furnish their training squadrons with the newer jets, the TO-1s were sent to join the FJs and FDs in assignments to the Naval Air Reserve Training Command and they were assigned to Whiting Field, FL; Oakland, CA and Seattle, WA where they continued to be flown until they could be replaced by more suitable naval fighters in the mid- to late 1950s.

Although the TO-1 was never suitable for aircraft carrier operations, the refinement of the design that brought about the T-33/TV-2 eventually brought about a future improvement in the form of the T2V Seastar. First flown on December 15, 1953 the T2V had a considerably larger and raised cockpit, leading edge flaps, boundary layer control, and was equipped for aircraft carrier operations with catapult and arresting gear equipment. It was "Car-qualified" in July 1957 and 149 examples were produced for naval service and they remained in use for decades.

Chapter VIII: Aerobatic Teams

There is a distinction to be made between what is an "aerobatic team" and an "aerial demonstration team," although it is purely an academic one to the layman. But to the "professionals," it is a bone of major contention. Massive umbrage is usually taken by those members of an aerial demonstration team when they are referred to as an aerobatic team, although it basically boils down to which team has the official sanction and funding for their operation. Three F-80 teams were aerial demonstration teams by official definition, while there were others that did not enjoy this prime distinction. In all, it mattered little to the observer, or the taxpayer who was funding the team in one form or another to begin with. The pilots generally flew the same or similar acrobatic routines, and all placed their lives on the line in the process of doing so.

Acrojets

The first P-80 team was known as the Acrojets. Their initial routines in jet precision flying were originally developed to demonstrate to future P-80 pilots just what the Shooting Star could do, and safely.

At the time the Acrojets were formed at Williams Field, AZ, which was the primary jet training base then, the early jet fighters did not enjoy the highest safety record, for several reasons. Among them was the instances of pilots transitioning into them from conventional fighters often utilized their old techniques, which just did not work with the jets. As again, the jet engine response time was not as quick as with a reciprocating engines, both in taking off and in the landing approach. In addition, the fledgling jet pilot was bombarded with horror stories of the short-comings of these aircraft and they were unnecessarily intimated by the thought of flying them.

To inspire confidence in the new jets, the Acrojets were formed in 1948 with the original idea of simply demonstrating to other pilots what the P-80 could do. Their flight routines were simple formation maneuvers that student pilots flew every day, only they were flown with a panache that the students had not yet attained. Eventually "the word" got out that the Acrojets flew an impressive airshow and the parent Air Training Command called upon them to start demonstrating their work at other ATC bases, such as Las Vegas and Luke Fields.

As their own experience as a team and further publicity evolved, the Acrojets were called upon to participate at various airshows around the United states. Cleveland's National Air Races in September 1948, Chicago's Air Force Association Convention in July 1949, and the Miami Air Maneuvers, for examples.

OPPOSITE: The Acrojets were the first bona fide jet aerobatic team. In 1949 they converted from F-80As to Cs, and in 1951 they switched to T-33s. The team broke up in 1952. (USAF via Isham)

An Acrojet diamond formation over the Arizona desert. Aerobatics were far smoother, and the aircraft were able to fly closer together in the P-80 than in conventional fighters, as the Red Devils and the P-51s, since they didn't have torque and propeller clearance problems. (USAF)

In 1948-49 the lead was flown by Major Howard "Swede" Jenson, 1st Lt. Michel "Smoe" Smolen had the right wing position, while Captain Benjamin Yeargen had the left wing. The slot man was Major Walter "Lefty" Selenger. Later that year Yeargen was transferred to Las Vegas Air Force Base, and his position was taken over by Major Jones "Jonsey" E. Bolt. There were two alternate pilots, Captain's Robert Tominson and Eldon Kapal. Contrary to the young and bold image of fighter pilots, all of these men were WWII veterans that averaged the hoary age of thirty.

When the Korean War started the Acrojets efforts were reduced, as there was no little opportunity for them to practice, as the Air Training Command had to then place all of their resources towards training new pilots. A limited number

The Acrojet pilots inspect their Shooting Stars at their home base of Williams Field, "The Fighter School." (USAF)

Vince Gordon and his first Skyblazer P-80. Gordon flew his routines without an oxygen mask, and wearing a throat microphone, as pulling high G's during aerobatics would cause the mask to slip down off his face. His routines were also flow without tiptanks, as loosing one would have caused a disaster. (Gordon)

of performances continued until 1953, with the team now flying T-33s, but when the decree came down that they had to fly their aircraft with tip tanks, which reduced the aircraft's performance, the Acrojets discontinued the unit. Major Selenger was shot down and killed while leading the 36th FBS in Korea. As time progressed, "Smoe" was promoted to Lt. Colonel and led the Skyblazers in Europe in their F-84 era with the 36th FBG. Tominson later took over the Skyblazers when they became a part of the 86th FBG.

The Skyblazers

The Skyblazers officially became an aerial demonstration team in May 1950 with Captain Vincent Gordon as their leader. Twin brothers, Cuthbert and Charles Pattillo as wingmen, and Lt. Lawrence Damewood in the slot position. In July 1950 Captain Harry Evans took over the team from

Now that is a low pass! Vince Gordon makes a solo run between the control tower and a hangar in England while leading one of the first Skyblazer airshows. (Gordon)

Gordon, who returned to the United States to form the F-86 equipped Sabre Knights teams.

The Pattillo brothers, Cuthbert being the 22nd Fighter Bomber Squadron's engineering officer, and Charles a flight leader in the squadron, had been a part of the 36th Fighter Bomber Group's representatives to the 1950 Air Force Gunnery Meet at Las Vegas, NV. As time progressed, they both flew with the Thunderbirds during their F-84F period and eventually both became general officers before they retired from active duty.

The "Silver Sabres"

The actual name of Silver Sabres was not applied to this acrobatic team during the period they flew the F-80, for the obvious reason that it was not a F-86. However, this 4th Fighter Group team was led by the same pilot during both its short lived F-80 and F-86 aerial demonstration periods.

During the team's early Shooting Star era the 4th FG sent this team out to do their acrobatic routines without a name being applied to them at all. But it mattered little, for they flew their airshows with aplomb and were content to do so as such.

Their leader was Captain Vermont Garrison. (Garrison was the oldest of the Korean War aces, being born in 1915. He had eight kills during WWII, and would score ten more in Korea, the last at the hoary age of thirty-seven.) The original slot man was 1st Lt. Lawrence McCarthy, while 1st Lt.'s Beriger Anderson and Erwin Hesse were the left and right wingmen, respectively. Their first public display was the National Air Races at Cleveland, OH in September 1948.

By February 1949 1st Lt. James Roberts became the slot man, and McCarthy took over the role of the solo pilot. And then in June the team's make up changed with 1st Lt. Calvin Ellis taking the right wing position, while Lt. Colonel Benjamin Preston took the slot, while Roberts became the solo pilot.

In March 1949 the 4th Fighter Group started flying F-86As and the Silver Sabres were named as such, with Garrison still in the lead. However, the 4th FG headed for Korea in November 1950 without Garrison, as he was transferred to Nellis AFB for a period. He formed another team there, known as the Mach Riders, also with F-86s, and continued with them until his own transfer to Korea came through.

"Polarjets"

One of the more short lived F-80 precision flying teams was the Polarjets. Formed under a Major Popovich, the squadron commander of the 66th Fighter Squadron, 57th Fighter Group, the team was made up of three aircraft, with the wingmen being a Capt. Brooks and Lt. Olden. Apparently they only were in existence during the summer months of 1949. One of the more interesting items of the team, however, was that they were the first jet team to use colored smoke during their routines, red, yellow and green, the squadron colors of the 57th FG's three squadrons.

A F-80C-1 of the Florida Rockets. This example was the mount of Lt. Colonel Bill Haviland, the team's leader. (Menard)

"Florida Rockets"

The Florida Air National Guard has never been a unit to hide its light under the proverbial basket, as anyone who ever saw their beautifully painted Bicentennial F-106 can attest. After the 159th Fighter Squadron became proficient with their F-51Ds they formed a yellow-nosed Mustang team known as the "Roman Candles," a semi unauthorized team that often found themselves in hot water with the brass after flying an exhibition.

With arrival of F-80As in 1949 a new team was formed with the first four Shooting Stars received, and they took up the name of the Florida Rockets. Led by squadron commander Colonel Bill Haviland, the wingmen were Lt.'s Harvey Howell and Bud Haefel, with Lt. Bill Yokley as the slot man. The Rockets existed until October 1950 when the 159th went off to war.

"The Minutemen"

The Minutemen also had their start while flying Mustangs before the Korean War, but at that time they were not recognized as an aerial precision team by name. After the Korean war the Mustang team was rebuilt in 1953, but an official name for themselves was not adopted until 1956 when they were flying F-80s.

The original F-80 pilots were squadron commander Lt. Colonel Walter Williams, who had also led the Mustang teams. Lt. Richard Hoeholt flew the slot position, while Majors Warren Harvey and Ranger "Arch" Curran were the wingmen. In January 1956 Harvey left the ANG and Hueholt moved to the left wing position, and Captain Robert "Bob" Cherry joined the Minutemen to fly the slot position. In June 1956 Hueholt also left the ANG and Cherry moved to his left wing position, with Captain John T. Ferrier joining the team as the slot man. At this time a solo pilot was added to their routine, Major Wayne Coomer. (Captain Robert Jankovsky was his alternate.) This permitted someone to always be in front of the crowd during airshows. During the summer of 1957 Coomer

Colorado's 120th Fighter Squadron and their Minutemen F-80s at Buckley Field prior to an airshow. (Williams)

Colonel Walt Williams, originator and leader of the Minutemen. There was no doubt in anyone's mind that witnessed this team in action that they were the best aerial demonstration team in existence in the mid to late 1950s. (Not to slight any of the other teams, but the Minutemen had an advantage in equipment, with both their F-80s and F-86s being lighter and more maneuverable than the aircraft flown by the other teams. (Williams)

The "Corkscrew" in action, whereupon the wingmen roll around the flight leader and slotman. (Williams)

The "Bombburst" as performed by the Minutemen and their Shooting Stars. (Williams)

left the unit, and his place was taken on the right wing by Lt. Robert "Bo" Odle.

The Minutemen were noted for not only the usual formation aerobatic maneuvers, but for several of their own creation, too. The "Squirrel Cage Break" announced their arrival. It was a two-hundred seventy degree turning roll that dove into a split-ess maneuver that brought the aircraft underneath the remainder of the formation at a ninety degree angle that was guaranteed to rattle the coolest of the control tower operators. The "Eiffel Tower" took four F-80s up in a vertical climb, while the solo pilot took the elevator up through the middle at high speed. They also flew a routine heretofore never flown by any team, and none since, either. The "Corkscrew," where the wingmen slow rolled around the lead and slot men at high speed.

On June 8, 1958 after the Minutemen had switched to F-86s, Captain Ferrier was killed while flying an airshow at Dayton, Ohio. The Minutemen had taken their F-80s far and wide as the only official Air National Guard Aerial Demonstration Team, being the first official team to visit the territories of Hawaii and Alaska, along with performing in most of the United States. (They had missed only five when the team was terminated in 1959.)

The Minutemen perform during a "severe clear" day over Colorado. (Williams)

Chapter IX: North To Alaska

On August 15, 1946 the 343rd Fighter Group was inactivated at Shemya Army Air Base, Aleutian Islands, as a part of the Army Air Force program to retain only low-numbered Wings, Groups and Squadrons. At this same time under this program, the 57th Fighter Group was activated at Shemya as the replacement unit. The new squadrons were the 64th, 65th and 66th Fighter Squadrons, which replaced, in designation, the 11th, 54th and 344th Fighter squadrons, while the 343rd's 18th FS was totally inactivated.

Initially equipped with P-38s, the 57th Fighter Group immediately started receiving P-51Hs as their mission aircraft. However, due to logistical, manning requirements, weather, and other problems, the 57th Fighter Group was relocated to Fort Richardson Army Air Base, Anchorage, Alaska in March 1947. At this time they were under the command of Colonel Morton Magoffin. Also at this time, the 57th Fighter Group represented the sole tactical Air Force fighter unit in the area, being only assisted by a single all-weather squadron in their air defense endeavor.

A year later the 57th FG commenced transition training into the P-80Bs that were handed down to them from the 94th Fighter Squadron at the end of their TDY period to Ladd Field. The first of these aircraft were assigned on March 14, 1948 to the 65th Fighter Squadron and pilot training began at Ladd Field under the tutelage of the 94th FS, while many of the enlisted men were sent to California for maintenance training. These twenty-seven P-80Bs had been "pickled," with their engines removed, prior to the 57th FG being able to accept them.

This then became a period of extreme turmoil for the men of the 57th FG, as on March 15 the 64th FS had been ordered back to Anchorage from Marks Field, Nome, where they had spent the winter on TDY. On March 20 the 57th FG was ordered to become fully combat operational, due to the Berlin situation. The Group was participating in Operation Yukon at the same time, providing escort to C-82s and tactical support to Army maneuvers. Most of the Mustangs of the 65th FS were out of commission awaiting spare parts. It was noted that it took almost a year to obtain there required parts, and they were short of people to install them when they did arrive.

However, by March 26, the date the 57th FG was ordered to be combat operational, the 65th FS had seven P-80s combat ready, along with all of their Mustangs, and they were placed on combat alert. Fifty of the Group's sixty-five P-51Hs were also ready for action. The 57th FG remained on full alert status through June 10, with all aircraft armed and carrying external fuel tanks.

After June 10, one squadron remained on full alert status, while the other two were placed "on call." All pilots and maintenance people were attending the Mobile Training Unit. During this period the Group lost four pilots in fatal accidents, but all were flying P-51s at the time.

On July 1, 1948 the Hobson Plan went into effect. At this time the 57th Fighter Wing replaced the Base Unit at Anchorage, with Colonel Thomas Mosley as commanding officer.

In August the 57th Fighter Group was fully operational with F-80s, and the 65th was redesignated as a Fighter Squadron (Jet) on August 3, while the 64th and 66th were so designated on August 20. The Mustangs were placed in storage, and the ferrying of new F-80Cs from March Field, California commenced with the first flight of eight arriving on August 27

Off to Alaska. The 94th Fighter Squadron deployed to Ladd Field in the fall of 1948 to conduct operational cold weather tests of the F-80B. At the completion of these tests, the 94th FS returned to March Field to be restructured and then to switch to the F-86A. Their F-80s were turned over to the 57th Fighter Group, so that unit could commence switching from F-51Hs. (USAF)

The 57th Fighter Group over the Knik glacier. Some mighty rough country for a pilot in a single engine jet to be over.

In April 1948 the 57th Fighter Group at Elmendorf Field received the first of their own F-80Bs from Lockheed after winterization modifications. Each of the three squadrons developed their own characteristic paint schemes for the aircraft from this point. (USAF)

under Project 97682. This first flight was led by Major John Winkler, 57th Fighter Group Operations Officer, with refueling stops at Edmonton, Ft. Nelson, White Horse and Ladd Field. The first of these F-80Cs went to the 64th Fighter Squadron, and the remainder to the 66th FS, while the 66th FS would continue with P-80Bs for a period.

On August 23 the 65th FS went TDY to Ladd Field for F-80 gunnery training, and on August 31 the Group suffered its first fatal accident with the Shooting Star. Lt. Jim Lane was returning to Ladd from a gunnery sortie when battery acid

Unbuttoning a 64th Fighter Squadron F-80C-5 prior to flight. The 64th FS used yellow trim on the nose of their aircraft, along with yellow bands on the wings, inboard of the Arctic Red wingtips. (USAF)

leaked and ate through the radio wiring below the cockpit and caused an electrical fire. Lane's bailout attempt was unsuccessful.

With the mission "to provide fighter air defense and fighter support for land, air and naval units," the Group remained on a semi-alert status through September 6, 1948 when they were given a week off for intensive ground training, including both aircraft maintenance and survival training. The Group returned to limited flying status on September 13, but at this time all F-80s were grounded. It had been discovered that their exhaust cones were being distorted when a pilot had a "hot start," and the distortion caused the turbine blades to then rub against the shroud and be ground down or chipped.

(These hot starts could stem from several factors. One was through having the wind blow up the tailpipe when the engine was being started. The back pressure would then cause the unignited fuel to light. It was spectacular, but not particularly dangerous. The other situation came from either a misadjusted fuel pump or improper starting procedures, which allowed fuel to pool-up in the lower engine chambers. The back pressure when this fuel was ignited was tremendous and sometimes catastrophic to the engine).

By the end of September only eleven Mustangs remained in the 57th FG inventory, all of the others either being flown to the United States for service with the ANG or pickled. But, it was not until November 1 that the F-80Cs were again released for flight after inspection for their cone and turbine problems. The engine problems continued,

The first allocation of Fiscal Year 1949 F-80C-1s went to the 57th Fighter Group in Alaska to replace their older F-80As and Bs, which then were assigned to the Air Training Command. Here the snow had to be swept from the aircraft's wings before flight, as a surprising minute amount was enough to destroy the aircraft's aerodynamics. (USAF)

however, as by December 1 sixteen engines had to be replaced because of the turbine problems.

On December 8 the Group suffered another F-80 loss when a flight of two Shooting Stars were scrambled on an air defense mission. Immediately after they took off and explosion was heard, and it was discovered that 1st Lt. Edward Maidhof had crashed into a warehouse at Elmendorf.

The following day another pilot was taxiing out for a flight, and when he checked his fuel deicing system his engine exploded. It was discovered that the Fluid Injection System shut off valve had been safety wired in the partial off position. This permitted alcohol to be injected directly into the engine, and it was believed that this was the factor involved in Lt. Maidhof's crash.

Highlights for January 1949 included a mission flown by Major Taras Popovich, commanding officer 66th FS, and

On the bombing range, a 66th Fighter Squadron F-80 pulls up from a skip-bombing run with one practice bomb remaining for the next pass. The impact of the first one is barely discernable in the snow. (USAF)

wingmen to Barter Island, the northern most point ever reached by jet aircraft at this time. Another was when the Group sent twelve F-80s to Kodiak Island on January 12 to participate in Operation Micomex-49A with the US Army and Navy. Assigned to provide the air defense of the Kodiak Naval Air Station from attacks by the USN, the Group fended off a major assault by Bearcats and Skyraiders on February 6 by shooting them all down. (On gun camera film, of course).

Colonel Magoffin moved to Deputy 57th Fighter Wing Commanding Officer on January 22. He was replaced by Colonel Bingham Kleine as Group Commander.

The last eight of the new F-80Cs arrived in February as a part of the ferry mission that had commenced the previous July. Seventy-seven aircraft had been delivered by the Group pilots, assisted by twenty-five pilots from the Tactical Air Command. One pilot and aircraft had been lost enroute. The old F-80Bs were all returned to the United States, those with low hours being sent to Williams Field and the Air Training Command, while the high-time aircraft were sent to McClellan AFB, CA for overhaul first.

Winter-spring of 1949 was one of adverse weather conditions. In March there had been only eighteen days where the weather was suitable for flight. Still, during the three month, January-March period, the 57th FG managed to fly 2,604 hours. Flying remained reduced by weather through April and May, and then when the weather improved, the Air Force was forced to place a limitation on the amount of flying time in all F-80 flying units. The Bendix Corporation at South Bend, IN was struck by its employees. This plant produced the F-80s main fuel control valves, and the stock level supplies had to be maintained. Accordingly, each pilot was limited to four flights of only 30 minutes duration per the duration.

In spite of this restriction, the "Polarjets" were created, and with the restriction on flying time being expanded to ten hours per aircraft per month in July, operations returned to a more normal condition. Also during the summer months, the Group received their first T-33s, with two being assigned to each squadron for navigation and proficiency training.

By the fall of 1949 the 57th Fighter Group found themselves in the same situation faced by all of the other Air Force units. Budget limitations forced many of their pilots out of the service involuntarily. In October they lost twenty-one officers, and now had more aircraft than they had pilots. The restriction on flying hours now meant nothing.

In December 1949 the 66th Fighter Squadron went TDY to Ladd Field for cold weather training, a mobility exercise, gunnery and tactical exercises, and practice interceptor work against "hostile" F-82s of the 449th Fighter Squadron.

As most of the problems with "hard starts" had been resolved, the 66th FS now encountered problems with "cold soak" in the frigid Fairbanks area winter weather. The extreme sub-zero temperatures were found to cause contraction of the J-33 engines' turbine shroud ring, which reduced the spacing between the ring and the compressor blades. The ensuing friction wore down the tips of the blades, as well

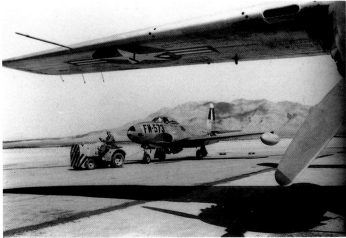

After a forced landing on frozen tundra, members of the 57th Fighter Group built skis to enable the aircraft to be flown back to Anchorage. Note the bits of tundra still hanging from the gun barrels. (AAHS)

A 1950 visit to Las Vegas Air Force Base by the 65th Fighter Squadron for the Second Annual Air Force Gunnery Meet. (Air Force Museum)

as causing cracks in either the blades or the shroud ring, and markedly reduced engine life. The short term answer was to hanger over night any aircraft intending to be flown the following day, while the long term answer was improved metallurgy and accordingly modified engines.

With the Second Annual USAF Gunnery Meet scheduled for March 29, 1950 at Las Vegas NV, preparations for assembling a team to participate took place during the winter. Two pilots from the 64th FS, Captain Douglas Holmes and Lt. James Jarvis, did some impressive scoring to get on the 57th FG's team. Holmes got 100% in ground gunnery, while Jarvis got 96% in aerial gunnery. This was when 10% was enough to be considered as qualified, and 24% was considered as outstanding.

Colonel Kleine took the 57th FG's team south in March, but they only ranked in 10th place at the end of the meet. It should be noted, here, that there was less than a one full point spread between the 10th and 12th place finishers.

In May 1950 two F-80Cs were lost in the wilds of Alaska, but details on these crashes are unknown. The hulks of these aircraft remained visible on the ground for years. Then in the 1970s the USAF hired a contractor to go around Alaska on a dog sled and blow apart with dynamite all such aircraft, as they were a target for scavengers and considered a liability to the government.

The F-80s period with the 57th Fighter Group began to close in April 1951 with the arrival of the F-94A and a reassignment of the Group from a tactical to an air defense unit. Most of the Shooting Stars were ferried to Lockheed for overhaul by subcontractors in flights of four or eight, and after training in California, the same pilots returned to Alaska in the F-94. Several of the F-80s remained in service with the Group into 1952 as target tugs and as pilot proficiency trainers, however.

49-429 was also forced down in the wilds of Alaska, on February 13, 1951. It too was recovered by the use of skis. (USAF)

Chapter X: The Air National Guard

The Air National Guard flew the F-80 in two different and contrasting time periods within their history. Prior to the Korean War, the ANG was largely viewed as a "flying club" for a selected few. This was due to many factors, few of which could be blamed upon the ANG, itself. Until 1954 they had the advantage of being able to fly as often as they desired when ever they wanted, with unlimited flying hours and fuel available to them. After the Korean War the situation within the ANG had drastically changed, due in part to the fact that 80% of the ANG had been mobilized during that war, and many of the units had been more than indoctrinated in combat.

In the beginning, the Post WWII ANG was envisioned to include 84 flying squadrons and 430 supporting units, spread more or less equally among the States and Territories, depending upon each State's population and ability to support these units. Although all supplies and some 96% of the budget would be provided by the federal government.

The allocation of aircraft, twenty-four to each flying squadron, was to be P-47s, P-51s or A-26s. There were to be no medium bombers or transports assigned to the ANG as mission aircraft. All of the fighter squadrons were to initially be committed to the new Air Defense Command, formed March 21, 1946 under Lt. General George Stratemeyer.

This commitment would remain in effect through the early months of the Korean War, although the ADC was replaced as a command by the Continental Air Command, ConAc, on December 1, 1948 which also absorbed the Tactical Air Command.

Basically, P-47Ds or Ns were assigned to eighteen squadrons along the east coast or in the southeast portion of the United States, while P-51Ds were assigned to thirty squadrons west of the Appalachians. A-26s were assigned to twelve squadrons, all located near larger municipalities. By the end of Fiscal Year 1948 sixteen more P-51 and five more P-47s squadrons had been added, which at that point gave a total of seventy-three flying squadrons and 320 other units.

As these squadrons were being formed and grew to a point large enough to be Federally Recognized as a squadron, plans were already underway to equip at least some of these squadrons with jet aircraft. On December 20, 1946 a letter contract was issued to Lockheed to produce 60 examples of the P-80B-1, and an amendment to this contract was issued on January 31, 1947 to provided an additional eighty aircraft, of which sixty were to be assigned to the ANG. On March 5, six of the contracted for aircraft for the ANG were deleted by revision of the contract, because of cost overruns. (At this time the fledgling ANG was already having funding difficulties of its own. Although the original budget request had been for a total of 536 million dollars, by the end of Fiscal Year 1949 only one quarter of the requested funds had been made available).

Three squadrons had been selected for early conversion from conventional fighters into the Shooting Stars, whether by geographical or political design being an unknown factor. The 196th Fighter Squadron at Norton Air Force Base, San Bernadino, CA; the 173rd FS at Lincoln AFB, Lincoln, NB; and the 132nd FS at Dow AFB, Bangor, ME. All were to be so equipped in 1947. A year later the 158th FS at Chatham Field, Savannah, GA and the 159th FS at Imeson Field, Jacksonville, FL followed suit. The 126th FS at Mitchel Field, Milwau-

Nebraska's 173rd Fighter Squadron was known as the "Cornhuskers," and flew for a period with the radio callsign of "Husker." Hence the corn related "Cornpopper" identification to 48-867. In 1950 the Air National Guard separated from the Army National Guard, and the "NG" on their aircraft was revised to "ANG." (via Slowiak)

Maine's 132nd Fighter Squadron at Dow Field, Bangor, was one of the first recipients of the new F-80C-1s in Fiscal Year 1948. Note the State Seal below the canopy. (John Antaloci via L. Paul)

In 1948 the Air Force decided to modernize the Air National Guard from conventional fighters to jets. Yet the ANG was totally unprepared for this action, as they had no qualified pilots, ground crews or facilities to operate these aircraft. Hence, all of these brand new F-80C-1s allocated to the ANG had to be held in storage until the ANG could accept them. (Lockheed)

kee, WI was the last of the pre Korean War F-80 units, not receiving theirs until September 1949. By this time, too, the ANG was truly entering the jet age, as ten other squadrons were in the process of converting into F-84s.

The 196th Fighter Squadron (Single Engine) was the first ANG squadron to replace their P-51Ds with P-80Bs in June 1947 and on August 1 they were redesignated as the 196th Fighter Squadron (Jet Propelled). They flew the Shooting Star until October 10, 1950 when they were activated into Federal Service and converted into F-84Es. When the squadron was released from active duty they relocated to Ontario, CA and equipped first with F-51Hs and then F-86As. Two of the 196th FS pilots, Bob Love and Cliff Jolley having become aces with F-86s in the meantime while flying with the 4th Fighter Group in Korea.

One of the first F-80C-1s to the Air National Guard was 48-884 which went to the 196th Fighter Squadron. It later served with the Ecuadorian Air Force. (via Menard)

The 173rd Fighter Squadron (SE) also replaced F-51Ds with F-80Cs commencing in December 1947 and were likewise reidentified as "Jet Propelled" on August 1, 1948. Atypical of the era, the squadron, under Lt. Colonel John Campbell, conducted the transition pretty much their own way. The pilots, in groups of five, went to Williams AFB for conversion training, usually wearing civilian clothes under their flying suits. ANG people had that option at the time. As originally there was little fuel storage available for the JP-1 at Lincoln, flights were usually limited to a meager fifteen minutes in the local area, or they were made to Kearney AFB, NB where more fuel was available to permit flying a longer period. In October 1950 the 132nd Air Base Group was established at Lincoln and Lt. Col. Campbell was promoted to "bird" colonel and selected as the Group commander. Major Fred Bailey became the new commanding officer of the 173rd.

On April 1, 1951 the 173rd FS was activated into Federal Service and transferred to Dow AFB, Maine to serve with the Tactical Air Command with F-51Ds. In January 1952 the Strategic Air Command took over Dow AFB and the 132nd FBG was relocated to Alexandria AFB, LA. The following January they were released back to the State of Nebraska and returned home to continue flying F-51Ds for a period.

The 132nd Fighter Squadron (SE), (Having only a coincidental numerical relationship to the 132nd FBG.)replaced their P-47Ns with F-80Cs in the summer of 1948 and were officially designated as Jet Propelled on August 1. On February 25, 1951, while under the command of Lt. Colonel Lawrence Smith, they were Federally activated at their home base of Dow AFB, and they would remain there, now with an Air Defense Command commitment. They would be the only ANG squadron to continue to fly the F-80 as their mission aircraft during the Korean Emergency. In June 1952 Smith was transferred overseas and was briefly replaced by Captain Clayton Hobbs, and then in July, Major Reggie "Pappy" Hays became their squadron commander. Upon release from Federal Service, on October 31, 1952, their F-80s were transferred to the 49th FIS, which was activated as their replacement. At this time the 132nd FS received F-51Hs. Two years later they would fly the off-shoot of the F-80, the F-94.

The 158th FS (SE) at Chatham Field, Savannah, GA converted from P-47Ns to F-80Cs during the summer of 1948 and on August 1 were designated as the 158th FS (JP). On March 31, 1949 they moved to Hunter Field, also at Savannah, and remained there until activated during the Korean War call-up, on November 1, 1950. At this time they were redesignated as the 158th Fighter Bomber Squadron. Re-equipped with F-84Es, the 158th FBS joined the 116th FBW and went to Misawa Air Base, Japan to fly both ground support missions in Korea and to provide aerial defense coverage for Japan.

The 159th FS (SE). led by Lt. Col. Bill Haviland, switched from F-51Ds to F-80Cs in July 1948, and were redesignated as the 159th FS (JP) on August 1.

All set for an airshow at Boston, this 132nd FS is teamed up with a 33rd Fighter Wing F-86A for the publics enjoyment. (Harlandwood via Isham)

Georgia's 158th Fighter Bomber Squadron was one of the few squadrons to apply a "sharkmouth" motif to their F-80s. (Esposito)

In March 1950 the 159th, now designated as a Fighter Interceptor Squadron, and its parent 116th Fighter Interceptor Group, represented the Air National Guard at the Second Annual USAF Gunnery Meet at Las Vegas AFB, NV. They came in at eighth position, scoring 175.84 points out of a possible 800.

The 159th FIS was activated during the Korean War, on November 1, 1950. On this date, the 159th also became identified as a Fighter Bomber Squadron, and, along with the 158th and 196th squadrons, they were transferred to George AFB, Victorville, CA to commence transition training into F-84s, with this being completed by April 1951.

These three squadrons made up the flying elements of the 116th Fighter Bomber Wing, commanded by Lt. Col.

Howard Galbreath, were transferred to Misawa, Japan by aircraft carrier commencing July 10, 1951. By August 10 the three squadrons were in place in Japan and flying combat missions. This Wing was the first to participate in Operation High-Tide, aerial refueling of F-84s during actual combat operations.

The 126th FS (SE) was the last of the Mustang squadrons to switch to the Shooting Star before the Korean war. Based at Milwaukee's General Billy Mitchel Airport, the squadron was commanded by Major Paul Dowd. The switch to F-80As took place in September 1949, and in November 1950 the 128th Fighter Interceptor Wing was activated at Milwaukee, which included the sister 176th FIS at Madison, WI. In January 1951 the squadron and wing was activated into Federal Service and relocated to Truax AFB, Madison, WI to fly air defense missions. This move now co-locating them with the 176th Fighter Interceptor Squadron at Truax, where the 176th was split between flying F-51Ds and early F-89s as All-Weather fighters. The F-80s were soon recalled to the Air

48-868 was assigned to the 132nd Fighter Interceptor Squadron prior to the Korean War and was activated into the regular Air Force along with the rest of the squadron. Note the traces of the original ANG markings after the USAF markings were applied. The actual damage in this incident was minor and the F-80 was repaired. It now belongs to the Experimental Aircraft Association at Oshkosh, WI. (Esposito)

A 159th Fighter Squadron F-80 firing on a gunnery range. Note the open shell ejection doors and the empty .50 caliber casings falling away. (Esposito)

While 44-85487 and -85489 were converted to RF-80As by Lockheed, -45488 remained a F-80A and was assigned to the 126th Fighter Squadron, the last of the pre Korean War ANG squadrons to receive the F-80. (Paul Stevens)

45-8612 had previously served with the 36th Fighter Group, and then became known as the "City of Wichita" when it was assigned to the 127th Fighter Interceptor Squadron. It is in pristine condition for participation in a Rick's Trophy Race. (KS-ANG)

Training Command and the 126th, now also designated a FIS, replaced them with F-51Ds for the duration, and then eventually received F-89Ds.

Post Korean War

As mobilized Air National Guard squadrons were returned to State control after their period "not to exceed twenty-one months" expired they were faced with a total rebuilding program in terms of both personnel and aircraft. Many of their original men had either elected to remain on active duty with the regular Air Force as a full time career, had been separated from their original units and assigned to combat units beyond the twenty-one month period (Not always necessarily by choice!), or elected to resign from the ANG upon release from Federal Service.

As most of the ANG squadrons had been Federalized, in one form or another, they lost their original mission aircraft in the process. As these squadrons were returned, they once again received hand-me-down obsolete or obsolescent equipment from the USAF as interim aircraft until more modern

aircraft became available. Almost all of those sixteen jet-equipped pre Korean War era squadrons received F-51Hs as interim aircraft until jets once again became available.

Shooting Stars were brought back from the Far East Air Forces or were transferred to the ANG from Air Training Command billets. All of these were in the atypical "flown hard and put away wet" condition. High airframe hours for some, and down right war weary for others. All required major overhaul, and in the case of the earlier versions, uprating to F-80C standards. All of this took time, and it was not until late 1953 that these F-80s became available to ANG squadrons.

On July 1, 1950 the Continental Air Command had been revised to include several new several sections, with ADC and TAC being discontinued as individual commands. Yet on January 1, 1951 the Air Defense Command and Tactical Air Commands were again reactivated, with ConAc still retaining control of the reserve forces. With the Korean War over,

44-85180 previously served with the 55th Fighter Group in Germany, and now is bearing the markings of the 126th Fighter Interceptor Squadron during their Korean War activation and in service with the Air Defense Command. (Esposito)

A pair of 117th Fighter Interceptor Squadron Shooting Stars begin their takeoff roll. The 117th designation was transferred from Pennsylvania to Kansas in February 1957 and the F-80 was the newly activated squadron's first mission aircraft. (via Geer/Isham)

Based at Ellington Field, Houston, Texas, the 111th Fighter Interceptor Squadron, the "Ace in the Hole" squadron switched from F-51Hs to F-80s in January 1955 and thirty months later switched to F-86Ds. (Menard)

the mission of the ANG was also revised to include roles beyond being ready for mobilization, and most units were now "tasked" with commitments to either the ADC or TAC. This role soon increased to full time commitments, and in 1954 the ANG took on full time assignments to the ADC by starting to stand "runway alert" with several squadrons being so committed. (This program became so successful that now the ANG has virtually all of the air defense assignments within the United States).

The tactical role had also changed after the Korean War and ANG F-80s were assigned to the Tactical Air Command in two roles: Those of fighter bombers, with a secondary role of air defense; and of tactical reconnaissance. Two quite distinctive and separate functions.

Commencing Fiscal Year 1954 the ANG had seventy-three flying squadrons, of which fifty-three either were jet equipped or were in the process of making the switch from conventional fighters.

Twelve of the Post Korean War F-80 squadrons were assigned to the Air Defense Command as their primary role: the 111th, 117th, 124th, 127th, 159th, 166th, 173rd, 174th, 182nd, 187th, and 188th.

The 111th "Ace in the Hole" Fighter Interceptor Squadron was based at Ellington AFB, Houston, Texas when they were activated with the 136th Fighter Group on October 10, 1950. After serving twenty-one months on active duty and distinguishing themselves in Korea, they were released from active duty and redesignated as the 111th Fighter Interceptor Squadron on July 10, 1952. (The designations "Single Engine" and "Jet Propelled" being dropped as superfluous, previously).

The 127th Fighter Bomber Squadron was redesignated as a Fighter Interceptor Squadron on July 1, 1955. 0-5892 was a well traveled Star, as she had previously served with the 94th Fighter Squadron, the 57th Fighter Group, and the Air Training Command before assignment to the 127th. (Isham)

Assigned to the Des Moines based 124th Fighter Squadron, 44-85190 later went to the Texas ANG's 182nd FS. (Leo Kohn)

Under the command of Major Robert Taylor, the 111th FBS initially received F-51Hs, were redesignated as a Fighter Bomber Squadron January 1, 1952, and once again redesignated as a FIS on July 1, 1955 after becoming operational with F-80As that had been modernized to F-80C standards. (The refurbished aircraft being identified as F-80C-11s). On July 1, 1956 the 111th FIS commenced to participate in the active ADC runway alert program, being on active duty from a half hour before sunrise until a half hour after sunset each day with armed Shooting Stars. This program continued until the receipt of F-86Ds in the summer of 1957 when they went on full twenty-four hour alert status.

Kansas had two fighter squadrons during the 1950's, with the 127th Fighter Interceptor Squadron being the first to be equipped with F-80s. The 127th was returned to state Control in July 1952 after flying F-84s in France during the Korean War. Initially re-equipped with F-51Ds and based at Wichita AFB, Wichita, KS (Renamed McConnell AFB in April 1954, the base is named for two brothers, and not the Korean War ace, Joseph McConnell, as generally assumed). The "Jayhawks" received F-80Cs in June 1954 and were redesignated as a FIS on July 1, 1955. In January 1958 they transitioned to F-86D Sabres.

Bearing somewhat confusing serial number depictions that reflected a policy change. The "0" prefix indicated that the aircraft was over ten years old. (And not obsolete, or obsolescent, as often stated). 0-5104 (44-85104) began its career with the 1st Fighter Group, and retired from the 182nd Fighter Squadron. (N. Taylor via Isham)

The other Kansas squadron was the 117th FIS which was activated at Hutchinson on February 23, 1957. The unit's designation having been picked up from Pennsylvania after their squadron of that number had been inactivated. (Pennsylvania's 117th squadron never did fly the F-80, although it has often been reported that they did so). The "Kansas Coyotes" were partially equipped with Shooting Stars, but never received enough aircraft to reach squadron strength nor became proficient enough to reach combat readiness status. Most of their training operations were flown in conjunction with the 127th FIS during this period. They flew F-80Cs until the Spring of 1958 when they were replaced by B-57s and they became a tactical reconnaissance squadron.

Based at Des Moines, Iowa, the 132th Fighter Wing was activated on April 1, 1951. Included in this order was the 124th Fighter Squadron, also at Des Moines, the 173rd from Lin-

The "B" on this F-80s fuselage reflects its position for the upcoming Rick's Trophy Race. The 174th Fighter Squadron at Sioux City only flew the F-80 for three years. (via Menard/Isham)

Taxiing out for a training mission from the Air National Guard summer encampment base at Casper, WY. Stars of the 132nd Fighter Bomber Wing prepare to take the runway. (132nd FBW)

48-365 was one of the first batch of TF-80C's/T-33s built by Lockheed, and it went to the 124th FS. The F-80 in the background, for those who like to follow an aircraft's assignments, originally served with the 62nd Fighter Squadron: After it left Des Moines it went to Oklahoma's 125th FS, Illinois' 169th FS, to a park in Aurora, IL, and now is at Robbins AFB, GA. (132nd FBW photo via Olson)

coln, NB, and the 174th Fighter Squadron at Sioux City, IA. At the time of activation, the 124th FS was flying F-51Ds; as mentioned the 173rd had F-80s, and the 174th was equipped with F-84Bs. The two jet squadrons surrendered their jets to the Air Training Command, and all three squadrons once again became equipped with Mustangs. After serving at Dow and Alexandria AFB's with the Mustangs, the Wing was released from Federal Control on December 31, 1952 and the squadrons were returned to their home fields to continue with F-51Ds.

During the summer of 1953 the 124th Fighter Bomber Squadron switched to F-80s, as did the 174th. Captain Robert Forney was the commanding officer of the 174th FS at

45-8305 started its career with the 94th FS and went to Alaska with them. At the time of the photograph, it belonged to the 124th Fighter Squadron, and is following their "follow me" truck onto their ramp at Des Moines. (132nd FBW photo via Olson)

the time. On July 1, 1955 both the 124th and 174th were redesignated as Fighter Interceptor Squadrons. In 1955 the 132th Fighter Wing placed first over-all during the last annual ANG Gunnery Meet. This was the swan song for the F-80, as this was the last such meet where non radar gunsight equipped fighters were allowed to compete. The 174th FIS also won the Spaatz Trophy on July 22, being rated as the best ANG unit in the nation. During August 1956 the 174th switched to F-84Es, and the 124th did the same the following month.

During this time, the third squadron of the 132nd FW, Nebraska's 173rd Fighter Squadron, transitioned back from F-51Ds to F-80s. Also, Major Fred Bailey had returned from Japan and resumed his duties as squadron commander. This re-equipping with F-80s brought a period of unhappiness within the 173rd, for when they initially received these aircraft in 1947 they were brand new aircraft received directly from the Lockheed factory, now the ones they were receiving were aged F-80As without ejection seats and they were in a fatigued condition.

On December 16, 1953 Captain Fritz Craig was killed when his F-80 disintegrated near Crete, NE. Its turbine wheel was never found. On January 24, 1954 Lt. Alden Ike also lost his life. Again the turbine wheel had come apart and severed the control rods to the empanage. As a result of these accidents, all F-80s were grounded for inspection, flown to Lockheed and modernized to include ejection seats in the older versions.

Nebraska's 173rd Fighter Bomber Squadron was redesignated as a FIS in October 1953 and they started standing a fourteen hour alert during daylight hours on July 1, 1955 being one of the first ANG squadrons to commence these pro-

Arming a 181st Fighter Interceptor Squadron F-80 prior to a practice gunnery mission at Casper, WY. The ammo cans could be pre loaded, which permitted a minimum turn-around time between sorties. (Esposito)

A 181st FS F-80 prepared for a parade. A rather inglorious end for a fighter. (Esposito)

activated on February 1, 1951 and assigned air defense duties from Lockbourne flying F-84Cs. Upon release from Federal Control, the squadron moved to Youngstown Municipal Airport, Youngstown, OH and received F-51Hs and were redesignated as a FBS. In March 1954 the Mustangs were replaced by F-80s and the squadron was again recommitted to the Air Defense Command. Lt. Colonel James Poston was their commanding officer during this period. Ten months later, in January 1955 the F-80s were replaced by F-84Es.

F-80s were assigned to the 182nd FBS at Brooks AFB, San Antonio, TX in August 1956, replacing some of the last F-51Hs in the ANG. They were led by Lt. Colonel Nowell Didear. On January 1, 1957 the 182nd was designated as a Fighter Interceptor Squadron, but by the close of the year the F-80s had been replaced by F-86Ds.

Wyoming's 187th Fighter Squadron is based at Cheyenne Municipal Airport, Cheyenne, WY. They were one of the first Guard squadrons to receive Federal Recognition, in August 1946. Initially equipped with F-51Ds, they retained them

grams. Their operations continued with the F-80 until January 1957 when the Shooting Stars were replaced with F-86Ds.

Florida's 159th Fighter Interceptor Squadron was returned to State Control on July 10, 1952 after their tour of duty in Japan and Korea. Initially re-equipped with F-51Hs, the 159th was the first of the ANG squadrons released from Federal Service to be assigned to the ADC, but six months later in a twist of circumstances, they were committed to the Tactical Air Command and designated as a FBS. As this was taking place, they received first F-86As, then F-80As that had been modified to F-80C standards, becoming operational with them by December 1954. In July 1955 they were once again transferred to the Air Defense Command. On July 1, 1956 the squadron expanded and the 125th Fighter Interceptor Group was formed. The following month the Shooting Stars were transferred out and replaced by F-86Ds.

Two Ohio squadrons were equipped with F-80Cs for a short period, with the 166th Fighter Interceptor Squadron being assigned to the Air Defense Command between March 1954 and July 1955. The 166th, originally based at Lockbourne AFB, OH (Now Rickenbacker AFB.), had been

Wyoming flew F-80s between September 1953 and the Summer of 1957. Although designated as a Fighter Bomber Squadron, most of their F-80s were uprated A models without ordnance carrying capabilities. (WY-ANG photo)

Arming the .50 caliber machine guns in a New Mexico ANG F-80C-12, a F-80B-1 than had been modified to F-80C standards. (Air Force Museum)

44-85327 started its career as a fighter with the 71st Fighter Squadron, and was later modified to a RF-80 and assigned to the 105th TRS. The 105th was the last squadron to carry the Lockheed lightening flash as a part of their squadron's paint scheme. The 105th had previously flown RF-51Ds, and in 1961 they changed roles and mission aircraft, converting to KC-97s and becoming an aerial refueling squadron. (Esposito)

as a mission aircraft through their Korean War activation and until September 1953 when they were replaced by F-80s. During the summer of 1957 the squadron transitioned to F-86Ds.

The last Air National Guard squadron with an Air Defense Command commitment was the 188th FIS at Kirkland AFB, NM. They flew F-51Ds both prior to and after their Korean War activation, and switched to F-80As and Bs in August 1953. As with the other ANG squadrons, these aircraft had to be replaced by refurbished F-80s that had been brought up to F-80C standards. In April 1958 the 188th FIS switched to F-100As, being the one ANG unit to have flown the F-80 longer than any other.

Tactical Reconnaissance

As expected, the role of tactical reconnaissance is a necessary one. As also may be expected, it is a solitary role where

the "recce" pilot is assigned a target to photograph and has to go out at do it "Alone, unarmed and unafraid." He does all of his mission planning alone, too, as he is the one responsible for the successful completion of the mission. He selects the best altitudes and routes in and out of the targeted area for optimum photography, avoiding obstacles as radio transmission towers, power lines and mountains. In wartime this role is compounded by the enemy's attempt to discourage his efforts. Low-level work is the key to good work, and survivability. It is dicey arduous work and the pilots flying in this role are a far different breed of cat than the average interceptor or fighter bomber pilot. A select and unheralded group.

Prior to the Korean War there were no tactical reconnaissance units in the ANG, although many of the squadrons had a pre WWII heritage of observation squadrons. With the activation of most of the ANG squadrons, several where then assigned the role of reconnaissance while on active duty with the USAF. Post Korean War, 14 of these squadrons retained

The "Old Hickory Squadron," the 105th Tactical Reconnaissance Squadron was one of the ANG's longest serving RF-80 squadrons, flying recce Stars from September 1954 until 1961. (Esposito)

The 153rd Tactical Reconnaissance Squadron was based at Key Field, Merdian, MS and they had some of the prettiest markings ever applied to a Shooting Star. (Leo Kohn)

Arkansas's 154th Tactical Reconnaissance Squadron converted from RF-51Ds to RF-80As in the Fall of 1954. This particular recce Star had previously been utilized in developing standardized tip tanks for the F-80. (Olson)

44-85225 of the 185th FS , Oklahoma ANG, came to grief at Casper, WY after a landing gear failure. The pilot escaped, but the Star was broken in two and became scrap. (Arnold via Esposito)

this mission when they were returned to state Control. The majority of them first received RF-51Ds that were brought back from Korea, and then RF-80s as they became available. (A few reconnaissance committed ANG squadrons flew RB-26s during the Korean War and retained them afterward, while others, as the 155th, switched from RF-51Ds to RB-26s).

In squadron numerical order, the RF-80 squadrons were the 105th Tactical Reconnaissance Squadron at Berry Field, Nashville, TN. RF-80As replaced their recce Mustangs in September 1954 and they flew them until the Spring of 1961 before switching roles and becoming a transport squadron with C-97s. They had the distinction of flying the Shooting Star longer than any other ANG unit and were the last operational ANG F/RF-80 unit.

Mississippi's 153rd TRS switched from RF-51Ds to RF-80s in June 1955 while based at Key Field, Meridian, MS.

44-85160 was another ex-1st Fighter Group F-80 that had been converted to a RF-80. Note the bulbous nose, in contrast to the standard RF-80's nose. When the 160th TRS converted to RF-84Fs, this RF-80 went to Kansas's 127th FIS in a pilot proficiency role. (Besecker)

However, as at this time the runways at Key Field were to short to permit jet operations and were in the process of being extended, most flying operations were conducted from Gulfport Field, Gulfport, MS. In October 1956 the RF-80As were replaced by RF-84Fs, before the squadron was able to resume flying from Key Field.

The 154th TRS was returned to Adams Field, Little Rock, AR in July 1952 after flying missions over Korea with the 136th FBW. At this time they received a switch in assignments from fighter-bomber to reconnaissance and received RF-51Ds. In December 1954 they converted to RF-80As, and these were replaced by RF-84Fs in May 1957.

The 160th TRS had been based at Sumpter Smith Field at Birmingham, AL when activated during the Korean war emergency on October 10, 1950 when they were one of the first ANG squadrons to be activated. Initially they had been equipped with F-51Ds, but when they were activated they first received RF-51Ds, and then converted to RF-80s in June 1951 at Lawson AFB, GA. In January 1952 they took their recce RF-80s to Germany, first being stationed at Furstenfeldbruck, and then Neubiberg, and then Toul-Rosieres Air Base, France. Upon return to State Control on January 1, 1953, they gave their RF-80s to the 10th TRW in France and were then permanently reassigned to Dannelly Field, Montgomery, AL with RF-51Ds. They again received RF-80As in June 1955 and flew them until they were replaced with RF-84Fs in May 1956.

The 184th TRS was a relative new comer to the ANG, not receiving Federal Recognition until October 15, 1953. Based at Ft. Smith Municipal Airport, Ft. Smith, AR they initially were allocated RB-26s and they flew them until they were replaced by RF-80As in June 1956. In January 1957 the 184th TRS converted to RF-84Fs.

Oklahoma's 185th TRS had been so designated on February 1, 1951 when they switched from F-51Ds to RF-51Ds. Two months later they were activated into the USAF and even-

Fifty caliber armament cans being loaded into a 185th FS Shooting Star. It was only took a few minutes to re-arm a F-80's machine guns if the ammo cans were prepared in advance. Note the residue from the guns having previously been fired. (via Esposito)

A nice flight line view of 185th FS F-80s at Will Rogers IAP, Oklahoma City, after an atypical Oklahoma thunderstorm. (Rich Lindsay)

tually were relocated to Shaw AFB, SC. In January 1952 their recce Mustangs were sent to the 67th Tactical reconnaissance Group in Korea, along with many of their pilots, while the remainder of the squadron became equipped with RF-80As. Upon return to State Control on January 1, 1953 the 185th was redesignated as a Fighter Bomber Squadron and given F-51Ds once again. In the Spring of 1953 they re-equipped with F-80Cs and became TAC -gained. In May 1958 the 185th became a FIS with F-86Ds and several of their F-80s were given to the Federal Aviation Agency for various purposes.

Tactical Air Command

Shooting Stars assigned to the ANG, prior to the Korean War were as mentioned, all assigned to squadrons with air defense commitments. Post Korean War saw the remaining non reconnaissance or ADC committed F-80 equipped squad-

rons assigned to the Tactical Air Command in their primary role as fighter-bombers. However, in November 1953 the primary mobilization assignments for all ANG squadrons was shifted from TAC to the ADC. Between 1955 and 1957 all of the F-80 squadrons were all redesignated as fighter-interceptor, but their primary assignment remained with TAC and not ADC. In order by squadron these were as follows:

The 110th Fighter Bomber Squadron at Lambert Field, St. Louis, MO. The 110th, "Lindberg's Own," started out with Mustangs, but switched to B-26s when they were returned to State Control on December 1, 1952. In January 1953 they started to receive some F-80Cs and were designated as a Fighter Interceptor Squadron, although they never became operational as such. The 110th continued to operate with the disparate F-80 and B-26 until late fall 1957 when both types of aircraft were replaced by F-84Fs.

Indiana's 113th Fighter Bomber Squadron had been activated at Stout Field, Indianapolis, IN February 1951. When they were returned to State Control on November 1, 1952 they squadron was relocated to Hulman Field, Terre Haute, with F-51Ds. On July 1, 1955 the 113th was redesignated as a FIS, and during the summer they converted to F-80Cs. In March 1956 conversion to F-86As commenced.

The 120th Fighter Bomber Squadron is probably the best known Air National Guard F-80 unit, because of their superlative aerial demonstration team, "The Minutemen." After being returned to State Control on January 1, 1953 the 120th FBS received F-51Ds, and then in July they switched to F-80As. Under squadron commander Lt. Colonel Walter Williams, the 120th, along with pilots from the 188th and 187th FBS's, represented the 140th Fighter Bomber Wing during the 1954 ANG gunnery meet, and placed 1st in the jet class. On July 1, 1955 the 120th FBS was redesignated as a FIS. Also in 1955 Lt. Colonel Williams was promoted to Group Commander of the parent 140th FBW, and he was replaced first by Major Warren Harvey, and then in 1956 Major Wynn

"Lindberg's Own." Charles Lindberg had once been a member of the Lambert Field, St. Louis, MO based 110th Fighter Bomber Squadron. In the mid 1950s the 110th flew a mixed batch of B-26s and F-80s before switching to F-84Fs. (Menard)

Coomer became squadron Commander.

"The Minutemen" began, unofficially, in 1953 with the receipt of the F-80s and with Williams in the lead. As their proficiency and exposure to the public increased during the following years, they became more and more in demand for airshows. Maneuvers as the "squirrel cage break" and the "corkscrew roll" characterized them as superior to any other team flying at the time, much to the dismay of some of the politicians within the Air Force. In October 1956 Secretary of the Air Force, Donald Quarles officially sanctioned them as the ANG Demonstration Team. In March 1958 the 120th switched to F-86Es, and "The Minutemen" continued with the Sabres until June 30, 1959 when they were told that there were no more official funds available for their services. "The word was" that the funding had been denied because there

When the Air Training Command at Williams Field reequipped with F-84s and F-86s, their F-80s were transferred to the Air National Guard to replace their aged Mustangs. In all, during the period, the ANG was a hand-me-down step sister of the Air Force to begin with. This example belonged to the 113th Fighter Squadron that was based at Hullman Field, Terre Haute, IN. (Martin via Isham)
10.45

F-80s of the 120th FS not specifically assigned to the "Minutemen" bore standard ANG markings. (Leo Kohn)

were more requests for "The Minutemen" to appear at airshows than for the official USAF team, "The Thunderbirds," which was causing political distress.

The 122nd FBS was Louisiana's tactical squadron. Based at New Orleans Airport, New Orleans, LA, the 122nd flew B-26s from Federal Recognition on December 5, 1946 through their Korean War activation, and until the Spring of 1957 when they received F-80Cs. On June 1, 1957 the 122nd was redesignated as a FIS and the "Coonass Militia" flew the Shooting Stars until conversion to F-86Ds in the fall of 1959.

Oklahoma's other F-80 squadron was the 125th FBS, which is located at Tulsa. Activated with F-84Bs in October 1950, they served at Alexandria AFB, LA until July 1952. Upon return to Tulsa, they flew F-51Ds until 1954 when they obtained F-80Cs, and they flew the Shooting Stars until the Summer of 1957 when they switched to F-86Ds and were assigned to the ADC.

The 144th Fighter Bomber Squadron was the last of the ANG squadrons to be Federally Recognized from the original Post WWII allocation of ANG units. They were constituted at Elmendorf AFB, Anchorage, AK in September 1952 and were officially Federally Recognized on July 1, 1953. Colonel Lars "Larry" Johnson was their squadron commander. Their first aircraft were three T-6s, three LT-6s and a T-33, but by February 1954 they had gained 14 F-80Cs.

On November 16, 1954 the 144th lost a T-33 and two crew members. On the same day in a separate accident, Lt. Albert Kulis was killed in a F-80. On July 1, 1955 the 144th was redesignated as a FIS and moved to the newly constructed Air National Guard Base at Anchorage International Airport, which was named the Kulis ANGB in honor of their first fighter pilot lost. During the 1955 summer period the 144th FIS also converted to F-86Es.

South Carolina's 157th FBS had been based at Congaree Field, Columbia, SC prior to their Korean War activation. Upon call-up, on October 10, 1950 the 157th became a TRS and obtained RF-51Ds for training. In June 1951 they switched to RF-80s and then relocated to Furstenfeldbruck, Germany were the recce version of the Shooting Star. They returned to State Control on July 10, 1952 and received F-51Hs as a

This F-80 was the personal Shooting Star of Brigadier General Joseph Moffitt, commanding officer of the 140th Fighter Bomber Wing, the parent unit for the 120th FS. (Menard)

FIS. On December 1, 1952 they were redesignated as a FBS, and the following June started to receive some F-86As. In March 1954 the Sabres were partially transferred and they started to receive F-80Cs, retaining the last of the F-86s until January 1955. In February 1958 F-86Ls commenced to arrive and transition into the All-Weather fighters was completed by the end of Spring of 1958.

The 163rd Fighter Bomber Squadron is based at Baer Field, Ft. Wayne, IN. Activated during the Korean War call-up, the 163rd remained at Baer, although many of their people were assigned to the 113th FIS and stationed at either Sioux City, IA or Scott Field, IL. Initially equipped with F-51Ds, they retained the Mustangs during this period, and on until September 1954 when they switched to F-80Cs. In October 1957 the 163rd, now designated as a FIS, converted to F-86As.

The second Ohio squadron to receive F-80s was the 164th FBS at Mansfield-Lahm Airport, Mansfield, OH. In 1949 the 164th FBS was one of the first ANG squadrons to replace their F-51Ds with the newer F-51H. They flew these Mustangs until September 1953 when they received their first F-80Cs. Under Major Albert Line from 1951, the 164th enjoyed the fact that they were one of the few ANG fighter squadrons not activated during the Korean Emergency. In October 1954, after flying the Shooting Star for only one year, they were replaced by F-84Es.

Illinois 169th Fighter Bomber Squadron at Peoria, IL had a limited experience with the F-80. Under Lt. Colonel Harold Norman, the 169th was not activated during the Korean War, but exchanged their F-51Ds for F-51Hs. In 1954 they were the top scoring ANG unit in the all-ANG Gunnery Meet at Gowen Field. In 1955 the F-51Hs were replaced by F-51Ds, and these were replaced in turn by pathetic T-28s in 1956, as the runways at Peoria were too short for jet aircraft at the time. Intending to receive F-84Fs when they became available and the runways were lengthened, the 169th FBS initially received a pair F-80Cs from Oklahoma's 125th FIS in 1957 and flew them until August 1958 when the Thunderstreaks finally arrived.

The 181st Fighter Squadron is based at Love Field, Dallas, TX. Flying F-51Hs during the Korean War period, the 181st was not federalized. In January 1955 the Mustangs gave way to F-80Cs, which they flew until August 1957 when they were replaced by F-86Ds.

One more time to the Rockies. General Moffitt's F-80 in its natural element. (120th FS)

49-1849 of the 144th FBS bears an unusual "buzz number" for the 1954 period, since an "A" had been added to the "NG" in 1950 in all other ANG units. It too had a combat history, as it had been assigned to the 25th Fighter Interceptor Squadron in Korea. On January 25, 1951 it had been damaged by flak, and again on January 30. The damage the second time was enough to see its withdrawal from combat. Repaired, it was assigned to Wyoming's 187th FIS, and then the 144th. (USAF)

Assigned to the 125th Fighter Bomber Squadron at Tulsa, Oklahoma, this F-80B-1 reflects some of the changes to F-80C standards. A new canopy and a relocation of the pilot tube from the vertical fin to the bottom of the aircraft's nose, along with bomb racks under its wings. (J. Geer via Isham)

Colonel Lars Johnson, commanding officer, 144th FBS, congratulates the ferry pilots that have just delivered the first F-80s to the 144th in 1954. (AK ANG)

Photographed at Boise, ID during the 1954 All Air National Guard Gunnery Meet. The 144th placed 10th, out of the fifteen participating teams, which wasn't too bad for a first showing. (Paulson via Menard)

After having served with both the 8th and 35th Fighter Bomber Squadrons in Korea, 49-717 finished out its service life with the 144th FBS. (Olmsted)

One of four F-80 pilots to have an Air Base named for them, (all posthumously). Lt. Al Kulis was killed in November 1954 in a 144th FBS F-80 accident. (AK ANG)

49-873 had been known as the "Homesick Angel" when it served with the 36th Fighter Bomber Squadron in Korea. Battle damage on December 3, 1951 was sufficient to declare it a combat write-off, but FEAMCOM rebuilt it, and it finished its service life with Alaska's 144th FBS. (USAF)

The same 49-1849 after application of an Arctic Red paint scheme for service in the wild's of Alaska with the 144th FBS. (USAF)
10.53

Based at Baer Field, Ft. Wayne, IN, the 163rd Fighter Interceptor Squadron kept their F-80s in immaculate condition, atypical of the pride the ANG had in their aircraft. (IND-ANG photo)

Chapter XI: The Korean War

When the Korean War began on June 25, 1950 the Far East and Pacific 5th, 13th, and 20th Air Force's F-80 assignments showed the 18th Fighter Bomber Group at Clark Field, Republic of the Philippines, with the 12th, 44th, and 67th Fighter Bomber squadrons; the 51st Fighter Interceptor Wing at Naha Air Base, Okinawa with the 16th, 25th and 26th Fighter Interceptor Squadrons; the 49th FBG at Misawa Air Base, Japan with the 7th, 8th and 9th FBS's. (The 8th FBS actually at Yokota on TDY at the time); the 35th FIW at Yokota Air Base, Japan with the 39th, 40th and 41st FIS's; and the 8th Fighter Bomber Wing at Itazuke Air Base, Japan with the 35th, 36th and 80th FBSs. Assigned directly to Headquarters 5th Air Force was the 8th Tactical Reconnaissance Squadron that was based at Yokota.

At this time there were no longer any F-51 fighter groups remaining in the Theater, although most Wings still had a few left for proficiency flying by non jet qualified pilots and for service as target tugs.

The 8th Fighter Bomber Wing, under Colonel John Price, was the first unit to be notified of what was then called "The Korean Emergency." Happenstance saw Colonel G.L. Mason replace Colonel Charles Stark as 8th FBW Deputy Commanding Officer this same date, June 25. The 8th FBW was tasked with providing logistical and administrative support to the 35th and 49th Wings at this time, along with the responsibility for all tactical operations. This included the attachment of the 3rd Bomb Wing (Light) at Iwakuni with B-26s.

Colonel Price immediately ordered all of the commanders of these units to prepare for action. Colonel Samways was ordered to make all the 8th Fighter Bomber Group F-80s combat ready and keep them available for immediate takeoff during daylight hours. The 7th FBS was told to place twelve on constant strip alert. The 9th FBS, at Komaki, was put on fifteen minute alert and was directly assigned to the control of Headquarters 5th Air Force. Price also reactivated the 347th Fighter (All-Weather) Group (Provisional). This brought the 4th Fighter (All-Weather) Squadron to Japan from Okinawa and the 68th and 339th F(AW)S's from the 35th FIW and 8th FBW under one command, and they would be the first to see combat in Korea. At this time intelligence was so lacking of the North Korean Air Force that the 8th Tactical Reconnaissance Squadron was first ordered to take stereo photographs of all North Korean airfields.

On June 26 United States Ambassador John Muccio ordered the evacuation from South Korea and the 347th F(AW)G (P) started flying their first Combat Air Patrols (CAP's) over Seoul and Inchon to cover the withdrawal by sea of these people with their F-82 Twin Mustangs.

The 8th FBW was ordered to take aggressive action against the North Korean forces on June 27 by President Harry Truman's authorization to provide support to the Republic of (South) Korea when it became apparent that this Korean Emergency was not a minor border incursion. Immediately thereafter the 8th FBG started patrols over South Korea, along with the 3rd Bomb Wing, and Lt. William Hudson, 68th Fighter (All-Weather) Squadron, drew first blood in aerial combat by shooting down a North Korean aircraft with his F-82G.

To provide optimal tactical support for this Korean situation meant moving most of the F-80 units to airfields in Japan where their limited range would be the most effective. At the moment there were no known airfields in Korea that were suitable for jet fighter operations, nor logistical support available for them had they been known. A decision had to be

Wartime quickly brings an attempt at personalizing a pilot's mount. This photograph, here in its original form, did not get past the censor. (O'Donnell)

"The Wolf" lost a wing tip when its tip tank tore off while on a ground attack mission on July 2, 1950. The original "Misawa" tip tanks did not have internal baffles, which permitted the fuel to slosh back and forth inside the tank, which created an overstress of the wing tip and a hazardous situation. (USAF)

49-537 belonged to the 49th Fighter Bomber Group and was written-off on July 10, 1950 after being hit by North Korean ground fire. In the upper photograph the pilot is making a controlled bounce off a rice paddy, hence what appears to be smoke is actually muddy water. (USAF)

Major Richard McNess was the commanding officer of the 36th Fighter Bomber Squadron. He was killed right after this photograph was taken, on July 18, 1950, when his 49-658 lost a tip tank and wingtip while on a ground attack mission. (O'Donnell)

made, also, as to which squadrons to commit, and which to hold back for the air defense of Japan, as Russian intentions in the matter were unknown.

The 9th Fighter Bomber Squadron, under Major Charles Williams, was relieved of assignment to the 49th FBG and attached to the 8th FBG for operational duty on June 27. They immediately moved to Itazuke and flew twenty-four combat sorties in six combat missions before the day was over. The 8th FBS, on TDY at Yokota, was moved to Komaki for air defense duties over the Kanto Plain, around Tokyo, while the 7th FBS remained at Misawa with the 49th FBG Headquarters for the moment.

On this date, too, the F-80 proved that it could do what it had been originally designed for. Captain Raymond Schillereff, Operations Officer 36th FBS, and three wingmen encountered a flight of seven heavily armored IL-10s that were trying to interfere with the evacuation of personnel from Kimpo Airfield at Seoul. Schillereff shot down one, Lt. Robert Wayne shot down two, and Lt. Robert Dewald got the fourth.

The following day, June 28, the 8th Fighter Bomber Wing flew its first combat strike against the North Korean interlopers at Seoul. The 8th FBW's attached 3rd Bomb Group flew their first combat missions on June 29 with eighteen B-26s

attacking Heijo Airfield at Pyongyang, North Korea's capital city. They destroyed twenty-six aircraft in the process.

Also on June 29 1st Lt. William Morris shot down a La-7 and probably destroyed another for the 9th FBS's first kills. Although the enemy aircraft was seen to burst into flames after Morris and his wingmen made four firing passes upon it, and its pilot was seen to bailout, the claim was not credited to anyone because too many pilots had hit it with .50 caliber fire before it went down. The thing had truly proved to be a flying tank! During the same encounter, with a total of six LA-7s involved, Lt. Roy Marsh, 80th FBS, also drew first blood for his squadron.

The 36th Fighter Bomber Squadron scored their first kills on June 30 when Lt.'s John Thomas and Charles Wuster each shot down a Yak-9. It was also on the 30th that the Air Force

Major William O'Donnell, commanding officer of the 36th FBS, briefs Major James Buckley on the F-80. O'Donnell assumed command of the 36th upon the loss of McNess, who was his best friend. Right after this photograph was taken the 36th FBS switched to Mustangs, and O'Donnell named his "Mac's Revenge" in honor of McNess. In November 1950 O'Donnell probabled a MiG-15 while flying that F-51. (O'Donnell)

49-600 of the 8th Fighter Bomber Wing suffered this battle damage on July 1, 1950. Repaired, it was lost on July 19 when 1st Lt. Howard O'Dell was shot down by a Yak 9 over Taejon. (USAF)

first discovered what the F-80 could take in the way of combat damage.

1st Lt. Edwin Johnson was hit three times by 20mm antiaircraft (AA) fire while attacking a marshaling yard at Seoul, with the third hitting the canopy along side of his head. At this point Johnson shoved the stick instinctively forward, and dove the F-80 through some steel cables at an estimated 500 mph. He then climbed and headed for Japan while he and his wingman surveyed the damage. "Both wing tip tanks and the wingtips themselves had been torn off. Each wing had three or four deep gashes. Most of the canopy and windscreen were gone, while the upper half of the rudder and vertical stabilizer had been sliced off as had half the left elevator and horizontal stabilizer. Johnson climbed to 13,000 feet, and his wingman reported that the entire tail section was waving back and fourth as though about to fall off." As Johnson's particular F-80 did not have a working ejection seat, he was forced to bail out manually near Suwon. He hit the right stabilizer in the process, receiving painful, but not serious injuries. He

was picked up by friendly forces and airlifted back to Itazuke that afternoon.

Another F-80 of the 9th FBS had to be belly landed at Pusan as a result of attacking this marshaling yard. 1st Lt. Robert Olsen was hit by AA fire in the left wing, and also lost his airspeed pitot tube. After being escorted south by his wingman, Olsen tried to land at Pusan, only to discover that he had no brakes. He retracted his landing gear and completed the landing on his belly. The F-80 was a write-off, but uninjured pilot was flown back to Itazuke in a C-46 that evening.

On July 1 "Task Force Smith" landed in Korea to start assisting the South Korean Army. This was the First Battalion, 21st Infantry Regiment. The remainder of the 24th Infantry Division, behind Major General William Dean was airlifted into Taejon on July 3, and on July 5 "Task Force Smith" engaged the North Korean Army for the first time in what was going to be a long and painful "Police Action." In less than three weeks Dean would become a POW, and he would be the first member of the U.S. Army to be awarded the Medal of Honor for duty in Korea.

Just how painful this war was going to be in terms of the loss of aircraft and pilots and crews was forcibly brought home to the Air Force on July 3 with the loss of the first F-80 and its pilot in combat. Major Amos Sluder, commanding officer of the 80th FBS, was strafing a column of tanks northeast of Suwon when he was hit by ground fire, and with flames seen coming from his plenum chamber and tailpipe, he was forced to "stopcock" his engine. Sluder set the F-80 up for a glide south towards friendly territory, but just as he approached a line of low hills, his fighter nosed down into the hills and exploded. He was replaced by Major Harold Price as commanding officer.

A massive, and confusing movement of fighter units took place in late June and early July. On June 29 the 49th FBG's 8th FBS, under Major John Dugenne, had been ordered to Johnson Air Base, and upon arrival there, were immediately ordered to move on to Ashiya, arriving there on June 30. They flew their first combat mission from there on July 2, but on July 8 they had to move again, to Itazuke, to join with the 9th FBS. The 7th FBS, under Lt. Colonel Jack Brown, would remain at Misawa until August 14 when they too were committed to combat and moved to Itazuke.

The 35th Fighter Interceptor Group was committed to the "Police Action" on July 4 with the expectation of being assigned to Pohang, South Korea as the first USAF unit to be stationed in South Korea. But this was changed to Ashiya, and on July 7 the 40th Fighter Interceptor Squadron moved sixteen F-80s from Yokota to Ashiya to commence combat operations the following day. On July 9 the 39th FIS followed suite and also moved to Ashiya, while the 41st FIS would remain in Japan as a non-committed Operational Training Unit and air defense squadron. The 41st FIS did, however, send fourteen pilots, including their squadron commander, and ten enlisted men along with the 35th FIG.

49-526 of the 49th FBG takes off for a mission in August 1950. The Japanese laboring in the fields ignored the aerial activity as a matter of course, unless it involved a B-29, which always caught their attention. This particular F-80 was lost on April 25, 1951. (USAF)

Commonly known as JATO, RATO was the more accurate designation for Rocket Assisted Take Off, as they were not air-breathing engines. "Bashfull Bess" is from the 51st Fighter Interceptor Wing. (Note the bomb fuzes protruding from the bombs and the 35mm camera pods for photographing ordnance delivery. (USAF)

Among all this, on July 9 the Headquarters 35th FIG and Headquarters section 40th FIS moved to Pohang, along with this some ground personnel from the 39th FIS went along to help open the new base, and this group was reorganized as the 6131st Base Unit, (BASUT), to provide support functions at Pohang. The next day came the "big switch," as the 40th FIS was informed that since they had been the last USAF Mustang squadron in FEAF, they would be the first to revert back to the aged F-51Ds. Their first Mustangs actually arrived before the day was over, and some pilots flew combat missions in both the F-51 and F-80 before darkness fell.

This switch in tactical aircraft from F-80s to F-51s was brought about as the need for both additional aircraft and pilots became obvious with the increase of North Korean pres-

Wearing the markings of the early and pre-Korean War 8th FBG. 49-696 fought the Korean War, returned to the United States, and then went to Uruguay. It was returned to the U.S. in 1958 and restored to immaculate condition. (Air Force Museum)

sure and success in their drive to force the United Nations and South Koreans out of Korea, itself. The Pusan Perimeter was being established, but there was insufficient USAF resources in FEAF at the time to support an extended combat operation. More F-80s would have been ideal, but they were not available within the USAF inventory at the moment. Already 145 Mustangs had been gathered up from the Air National Guard and were on their way to Japan to supplement those precious few in FEAF. And these F-51s would have to do until more F-80Cs could be obtained from other units, but at the moment they had to be held back by these units, as there were no replacements available for them and the USAF did not dare weaken themselves any further by depleting these squadrons.

On July 11 the 40th FIS was advised that they would move to Pohang as soon as sufficient Mustangs were available, and this move was accomplished on July 14.

July 7 had proved to be a bad day for the 8th FBW, as they lost two pilots. 1st Lt. Donald Sirman, 35th FBS, was leading a flight of four F-80s when he hit by ground fire while making his second strafing run at Chonan and his F-80 caught on fire and he was forced to bailout. Radio Pyongyang made a big thing out of his capture, but he was declared as KIA on July 14, 1951.

That afternoon 1st Lt. Eugene Hansen, 36th FBS was hit by AA fire in the same area. He pulled up above a cloud layer and bailed out, but disappeared into the clouds still attached to his ejection seat. He was KIA on his 35th mission.

On July 9 the 35th FIS lost 1st Lt. Leon Pollard. During a mission led by their squadron commander, Major Vincent Cardarella, they had encountered a line-squall near Pusan and had to climb to 40,000 to get over the top of it. After letting down at Pyongtaek, they knocked out three tanks and four trucks, and then had to go back on instruments to get back to Japan. On the way back, Cardarella's radio failed, so he passed the flight lead over to Lt. Clark and assumed the number four position in the formation on Lt. Pollard's wing. Near Pusan Pollard went out of control and disappeared. Cardarella then had to go "lost wingman" and find his way back to Japan with basic flight instruments.

1st Lt. James Hughes, 8th FBG, became the first F-80 pilot to receive the Purple Heart on July 9. His F-80 received a direct hit by AA fire on the armored glass windshield and he was wounded by glass fragments. He also received the Air Medal and an Oak Leaf Cluster for bringing his damaged aircraft home. He returned to missions in a few days.

The bad weather continued through the following day and caused the loss of Lt. Schwartz, 8th Fighter Bomber Squadron. On the return leg of his mission Schwartz got separated the rest of his flight, became disorientated, ran out of fuel over the Tsushima Strait and disappeared. In spite of an extensive search by the Air-Sea Rescue people, no trace of his aircraft could be found.

On July 17 Captain Francis Clark, 35th FIS, shot down a Yak-9. While on a ground support mission, Clark was called by "Angelo Control" to the aid of "Mosquito Dog," a T-6 that was being attacked by a pair of Yak's. Clark shot one down and drove the other off.

On July 18 the 36th FBS lost its squadron commander. Major Richard McNess who crashed as the result of a situation heretofore not encountered. McNess's Shooting Star was carrying the Theater devised "Misawa" tip tanks, which had been developed in January to extend the F-80s range. Not foreseen was the fact that these tanks required internal baffles to prevent the fuel from sloshing forward when the aircraft was in a dive, and then sloshing to the rear of the tank under high gravity forces when the aircraft was pulled out. McNess had dove down on a rocket attack, and when he pulled out, the tip tank fuel rushed to the rear of the tank, creating an overstress of the wingtip, which failed under the load. The tip tank then tore off the horizontal stabilizer and the aircraft crashed. McNess was replaced by Major William O'Donnell, who just happened to be his best friend and had just arrived that morning in the Far East.

July 19 turned out to be one of the most memorable days in the history of the 8th FBW during the Korean War. A RF-80 of the 8th TRS had discovered a small grass airstrip at Pyongyang where some two dozen North Korean aircraft were parked. Colonel Samways immediately led seven F-80s on the attack, and they claimed fourteen single-engine aircraft destroyed and one twin-engine. Every aircraft that was there was hit, but if they didn't burn, they weren't claimed. Pilots awarded ground kills were: Samways three unidentified prop types; Lt. Robert Walsh, 80th FBS two unidentified prop types; Lt. Jack Watts, 80th FBS two unidentified prop types; Lt. Roy Marsh, 80th FBS, two unidentified prop types; Captain Homer Hansen, 36th FBS, two unidentified prop types; and Lt. Ralph Ellis, 36th FBS, two unidentified prop types; 1st Lt. Charles Wurster, 36th FBS, one Yak-9.

49-650 was "Saggon Dragon" and was assigned to the 16th Fighter Interceptor Squadron. It crashed on takeoff at K-2, Tague, on March 7, 1951. (McLaren collection)

In aerial combat a flight of 36th FBS F-80s intercepted a flight of Yak-9s near Taejon and 1st Lt. Robert McKee and 2nd Lt. Elwood Kees each claimed one. 1st Lt. Charles Wurster claimed a probable. (Three days earlier, Wurster had flown into a cable stretched across the Han River and lost most of his rudder and vertical stabilizer, and barely made it home. On August 18 he would be wounded in action in a F-51 crash. He was a busy, and lucky pilot). This encounter proved costly to the 36th FBS, although the North Korean pilot was probably not aware of it. 1st Lt. Howard O'Dell, 36th FBS Engineering Officer, had been hit by Yak fire and headed for Taejon for an emergency landing. He almost made it, but while turning base-leg in the traffic pattern his F-80 dove into the ground.

On July 20 Yaks were again encountered near Taejon. Lt. David Goodnough, 35th FIS, and Captain Robert Lee, 36th FIS, each destroying one. Lee was leading the flight of F-80s when he spotted some unidentified aircraft below then, and then two Yak's were seen in their six O'clock high position. Lee pulled up, while Lt. Robert Meade, his wingman, dove down, and a Yak foolishly followed him. Lee gave chase and

49-668 of the 49th Fighter Bomber Group was heavily damaged by flak on April 7, 1951 and was stripped for spare parts as a result of the damage. (USAF)

"The Dregs" was the personal F-80 of Colonel Irwin Dregne, commanding officer of the 51st Fighter Interceptor Wing. It was written-off as a result of a takeoff accident at Tague on May 7, 1951. (Air Force Museum)

fired and the Yak started to come apart, rolled over and crashed. The second Yak made a turn to the right and was chased by Captain Clark and Goodnough, and Goodnough peppered him from below and it burst into flame and its pilot bailed out.

Another F-80 pilot was lost to the Misawa tip tank problem on July 21 when 1st Lt. Ralph Ellis, 36th FIS Squadron Adjutant, crashed while making a strafing pass on Taejon.

Lt. Colonel William Samways destroyed an IL-2 on the ground on July 24. This gave him a final total of four enemy aircraft destroyed, and made him the highest scoring F-80 pilot. Lt. Colonel Harold Price destroyed an unidentified propeller type the following day for the last F-80 claim until September.

The last F-80 and pilot lost in July was on the 30th when 1st Lt. John Netterbald, 80th FBS, was leading an early morning weather reconnaissance mission with two other aircraft. In the dark they penetrated an unobserved thunderstorm and it was believed that Netterbald's electrical system failed, as he was known to be a good instrument pilot, yet the flight was led into a uncontrollable spiral and the other two pilots went "lost wingman" and recovered on their own. Netterbald crashed on the island of Tsushima.

The wayward press was calling the Korean War the "breakfast war" at this time, and Netterbald's loss goes to show just how wrong this statement was. During this early phase of the war, many of the pilots had their dependents with them in Japan, and did have the luxury of being with their families when they were not flying combat missions. But all was not as it appeared, as quite soon the USAF sent all these dependents back to the United States, as it was hard upon these families to have breakfast together, and then discover that their pilot would never be home for dinner again. Some pilots flew their first mission of the day with the intention of having breakfast upon their return, and they never returned.

The first combat missions of the day were launched from Itazuke and Ashiya at 0430, and by the time the reporters got to the flightline to take their photographs and get their interviews, the second mission of the day was in the pattern for landing. In the evening the flacks headed for dinner and drinks at the "O Club" at the normal dinner hour, yet the last mission of the day did not return from Korea until 2200.

The ground crews were originally slated to work six days, with the seventh off, on a rotational basis, but as the war intensified, they had to work straight-through. Then they gave 10% of the men a three day pass at a time, and then it worked out to a three day pass every six weeks, if they were lucky.

Living and flying conditions in Japan were jammed in tight. Ashiya had a five thousand foot runway, with no overrun. In the pre Korean War period it had been utilized as a training base for one squadron at a time. Now four squadrons were located there in tent cities. Itazuke was jammed even tighter, as Mustang squadrons were passing through there, along with the All-Weather squadrons and F-80 and other tactical groups.

Most of the actual time spent in combat amounted to a bare ten minutes. The duration was limited by ordnance and fuel available. The F-80 could barely lift off of Ashiya's short runway with a full fuel load and four 5" High Velocity Aircraft Rockets, HVAR's. It could get off Itazuke's 7,000' runway with napalm tanks or bombs, but the weight penalty still reduced the time over target, (TOT). Pre-briefed missions were few, as the fluidity of the ground situation and poor communications between Korea and 5th Air Force Headquarters in Japan, changed things so rapidly that the pilots could never be sure that what they would find was what they had been told to expect, and an error could be fatal to UN forces.

The missions were staged 150 miles from their targeted areas, which resulted in only 25% effectiveness. If they had airfields closer to the front lines, the estimate was that they could have been at least 90% effective. The weather, as noted,

49-838 of the 16th FIS. Napalm tanks are hung under the wings and its crew chief is in the process of attaching JATO bottles. Captain Gerald Brose was killed in this F-80 on August 11, 1951. (USAF)

"Brock Buster" with the extended 265 gallon tiptanks. Assigned to the 16th FIS, she was lost on October 12, 1951 with 1st Lt. Richard Borschel being killed while attempting to bail out. (Remington via Isham)

contributed to many losses. Navigation had to be by time, speed and distance. The pilots were not familiar with how to fly the aural-null quadrants of the existing radio ranges, and had little knowledge of how night effect affected low frequency radio aids. Direction Finding, DF, worked okay, if a pilot had the time and fuel to work with a DF station. The radar sites were too saturated with targets and the F-80s at this time did not have IFF, Identification, Friend or Foe. and the poor "skin paint" of the F-80 made the radar useless to the pilot.

Most of the missions were ordered to contact a designated airborne Forward Air Controller, FAC, in a T-6 "Mosquito" aircraft and follow his instructions. If he could not be contacted, they then had to seek out a target of opportunity north of the established bomb line to expend their ordnance. They could not carry it back to Japan, for the weight curtailed their range and they wouldn't have the fuel left to get home, nor could they land with it, for safety's sake.

Just contacting their "Mosquito" was a challenge, as they only had four radio channels available, and all were congested beyond comprehension with the constant flow of chatter of

45-8379 was a RF-80 assigned to the 15th Tactical Reconnaissance Squadron. Attacked by MiG-15s on August 28, 1951, its pilot managed to get it home with this damage. (USAF)

pilots attempting to contact each other. And when they did make contact and were able to locate their target, they then had to contend with further difficulties.

The .50 caliber ammunition was old and either had a tendency to misfire or not fire at all. Gun barrels ruptured and exploded, either through faulty rounds or because a nervous pilot held the trigger down too long and overheated his guns. Bomb and napalm tank fuzes were old and they often failed to detonate, which made the entire effort worthless.

Then there was the problem with the rockets. When the war started few of the pilots had ever fired the ineffective 2.5" rocket, and none had ever fired the 5" HVAR. Weather and combat conditions dictated that the pilot start his rocket firing pass at altitudes below what had been the minimum peacetime minimum safe recovery altitude to begin with. Inexperience with this resulted in many F-80s becoming damaged as a result of being hit by their own rocket fragments before the pilots learned by experience that they could not fire them any closer that 1,200 feet slant range, and pull out immediately to preserve themselves. The 80th FBS, alone, had twenty-two F-80s damaged by their own rocket blasts.

In the first five weeks of the war the 8th Fighter Bomber Wing and associated combat committed units lost a total of seventeen F-80s. (The USAF stated that only nine had been lost). Parts of several others were cannibalized for spare parts. The Wing averaged over one hundred combat sorties per day. Seven pilots were missing in action, one was known to be killed at the time. One was wounded. Two of those carried as MIA's were squadron commanders.

During August 1950 the 8th Tactical Reconnaissance Squadron was attached to the 8th FBW for all operational purposes. Due to an economy drive within the USAF in 1949 the role of tactical reconnaissance was all but abolished. Thus in 1950 there was only the equivalent of one tactical reconnaissance group, three squadrons, remaining in the USAF. And, only the 8th TRS was in the Far East. "All of the remain-

F-80s of the 8th Fighter Bomber group enroute to Korea after they had adapted new identification markings for their aircraft. They are armed with two 500 pound General Purpose bombs. 49-675 was involved in a mid-air collision over North Korea, but its pilot brought it home to be repaired and reassignment to the 45th TRS. 49-491 was lost on November 9, 1951 while 49-846 was downed by flak on December 14, 1951. (USAF)

der of those highly skilled people of the inactivated units either returned to civilian life or were scattered throughout the Air Force."

The 8th TRS and their RF-80As were beleaguered from the outset of the war for photographic coverage of anything and everything in Korea. Although all of South Korea and most of North Korea had been photographed and mapped prior to the withdrawal of the USAF from Seoul in 1949, none of the required coverage could be found in 5th Air Force files when it was needed.

During the press of the demands upon this unit, little was recorded of their early adventures in the Korean War.

On August 1, 1950 the 35th FIS lost their commanding officer when Major Vincent Cardarella, leading "Contour William" flight hit some wires strung across his path while strafing a railroad tunnel northwest of Chochiwon.

Indicative of what was to come, one of the other pilots of this flight of four would be killed in a F-51 in December. Major William Lancaster was selected as their new commanding officer.

The 39th Fighter Interceptor Squadron turned over their F-80s to the 41st FIS on August 3 and re-equipped with F-51Ds. This was done with some trepidation, as although they had two F-80s damaged in action, they had not lost any aircraft. The 39th FIS then joined the 40th FIS at Pohang.

The 9th FBS lost their first pilot on August 8 when Lt. William Morris was shot down. He had been strafing in the Chorni area when AA fire hit him.

On August 11 the 8th Fighter Bomber Group with the 35th and 36th FBS moved to Tsuiki and converted to F-51Ds, which they would fly until the end of December before returning to

F-80s. On August 14 the 8th FBG was joined by the 35th FIG and the 39th and 40th FIS's, and these units formed the 6131st Fighter Wing. Headquarters 8th FBW would direct this unit, along with the 6002nd FW (Provisional) until August 24 when Headquarters 5th Air Force assumed control of them. At this time the 8th FBW was left with controlling the 49th FBG and 77 Squadron, Royal Australian Air Force (With Mustangs). The 49th FBW continued with the 8th and 9th FBS's, along with having the 80th FBS as an attached squadron.

Thus at mid-August there remained but three F-80 and one RF-80 squadrons committed to combat in Korea. The 7th FBS (49th FBG) and 41st FIS (35th FIG) being non-committed units. But on August 14, the 7th FBS "Screamin Demons," under Lt. Colonel Jack Brown, exchanged roles with the 9th FBS going back to Misawa for a little rest. The 9th FBS, with Major Frank Ellis commanding, would return to combat on September 4.

Numerous combat losses occurred during this period without documentation as to the cause, presumably because the historical officers were just too busy flying combat missions to record the events transpiring around them. The 80th FBS lost 1st Lt. Orrin Fox on August 2, (Fox having shot down two IL-2s on June 29 while flying a "Bout One" F-51.) 1st Lt. Warner Siber on August 4, and 2nd Lt. Glenn Payne on August 10. Captain Peterson, 80th FBS, was hit by AA fire at Tangyang on August 14. With flames consuming his left wing, he flew the burning F-80 back to Japan for a crash landing. The F-80 had been named "Flame Out."

There were no more pilot losses until September 5, although two F-80s had been lost in the previous five days. On September 5 1st Lt. James Petty, 7th FBS, was killed. On September 14 Lt. Irving May, 8th FBS, was killed, and on September 15 Lt. Richard Bartly, 7th FBS, and Lt. Paul Kearns,

8th FBG F-80s. 49-817 was lost on January 3, 1953. FT-547 was the subject for the decals for the original Monogram 1/4" scale plastic model kit, and it survived the war to be assigned to the AFRES in Texas. FT-811 also survived the war, while FT-531 was shot down by a Mig 15 on November 27, 1951 with 1st Lt. Rafael Dubrevil being killed. (USAF)

Assigned to the 15th TRS, 67th TRW, 45-8477 is prepared for a mission in somewhat hazardous conditions. Several typhoons effected combat/recce missions during the course of the Korean War and these storms cost the USAF over a million dollars in damages to ground installations. (USAF)

On September 25 the Lt. Colonel Harold Price's 80th FBS was assigned to the 51st FIW for tactical purposes, which brought them up to the standard three-squadron tactical group-strength, and established the 49th FBG similarly. Also attached to the 51st FIW at this time was the 68th Fighter (All-Weather) Squadron with F-82Gs. All of the congestion over Itazuke resulted in a rather unfortunate incident, as there was a mid-air collision over the field with one of these Twin Mustangs and a F-80 of the Group. The F-82 crew was killed, but the F-80, minus four feet of wing, got down okay.

The next day, on September 26 the 543rd Tactical Support Group was established. Assigned to it was the 8th TRS, along with the 45th TRS (Which would not receive any aircraft or personnel until December 3.), the 162nd TRS (Night Photo) with RB-26s, and the 363rd Reconnaissance Technical Squadron for photo interpretation. On October 2 the 8th TRS would be attached to the 6149th Tactical Support Wing at Taegu for logistical purposes.

8th FBS were both killed. The irony was that all four pilots had graduated in Pilot Class 45C.

On September 6 the North Korean Army had mounted a major offensive against Taegu, South Korea. This proved to be an unfortunate decision on their part, as coincidentally the 49th FBG had decided to start carrying eight 5" HVARs at the same time. In the first day's efforts, the 49th FBG destroyed thirteen tanks, and damaged thirteen more, along with all sorts of other enemy targets.

Lt. Colonel Price, 80th FBS, caught Colonel Samways in F-80 scoring on September 12 when he destroyed three Yak-9s on the ground.

The 51st Fighter Interceptor Wing at Naha, Okinawa was alerted for duty in Korea on September 6, and the air echelon's of the 16th and 25th Fighter Interceptor Squadrons arrived at Itazuke between 12:00 and 13:30 on September 22 with 61 F-80s. At this time the 51st Fighter Interceptor Wing was commanded by Colonel John Weltman, the 51st Fighter Interceptor Group by Colonel Cellini, the 16th Fighter Interceptor Squadron by Major Evans Stephans, and the 25th FIS by Lt. Colonel Clure Smith.

With the arrival of the 51st FIG, the first missions, commenced that afternoon by elements of the 25th FIS, and they were flown with members of the 49th FBG for combat orientation under "realistic" conditions. As the 49th FBG was scheduled for deployment to Taegu, South Korea, the 51st FIG was assigned to the 8th FBW for immediate logistical purposes and the intention was for them to remain at Itazuke for the duration.

Effective September 11 Major Walter Selenger became the commanding officer of the 7th FBS, replacing Major Jack Brown. Selenger had previously been Director of Flying at the Advanced Training School at Williams Field, AZ and was the last active duty member of the original Acrojets.

Happy pilots. Left to right: Ben King, John Fraizer, Bill Smith and Larry Leggitt. All four flew their 100th combat mission together and got to go home. King was the commanding officer of the 8th FBS at the time. (Esposito)

The "Monstrosity" was a F-80C that had been modified by FEAMCOM in an attempt to increase its firepower. Aerodynamically, it was a failure, as the proximity of the external stores to each other created too much buffeting, and the additional weight reduced the fighter's range too much. (USAF)

On September 28 the 7th FBS moved to Taegu, followed by the 8th FBS on the next day, and the 9th FBS the succeeding day. The 49th FBG and Wing would remain in Japan until late fall, providing administrative support and rear echelon maintenance.

As September closed the 51st FIG had flown 507 effective combat sorties. Captain Earnest Fahlberg, 80th FBS, had destroyed three unidentified prop types on the ground on the 30th, which helped them look good and it appeared that they were off to a good start.

For a period in late August and early September worthwhile targets for the fighter bombers had been hard to find, as the North Koreans had learned the hard way that it was not wise to attempt to move by day. Yet after the Inchon Invasion on September 17 they began a daylight panic escape attempt to the north and tactical targets again became plentiful. In addition, with the recapture of Seoul, the 51st FIG sent an advance party to Kimpo on October 5 to clean up the mess, and the 16th FIS moved there on October 22, the 25th FIS on October 24 and the 80th FBS the following day. This made every worthwhile target in Korea accessible to F-80 operations.

In the meantime combat losses continued: On October 2 Captain Thomas Myers, 16th FIS, was on a mission to Singasan when hit by AA fire. He bailed out successfully, but became entangled in a tree when he landed. He was captured and killed.

The next day 2nd Lt. William Carter, 25th FIS was lost on the return from his sixth mission. Carter's flight had landed at K-9, "Dogpatch," for fuel and then made a night takeoff for the remainder of the trip home to Itazuke. Apparently he lost sight of his flight leader along the way and spun-in, as his body and the wreckage of his F-80 was found the following week near Pohang.

The 8th FBS lost unidentified pilots over Pyongyang on October 7 and 8.

1st Lt. Alfred Breitkreutz, 16th FIS, had a lucky escape in a crash landing thirty miles north of Taegu on October 11 after his engine's oil system failed. He was uninjured. 1st Lt. Alfred Lang was equally lucky on October 18 when he crashed on the runway at Itazuke during a night landing on the return from a mission. He too was uninjured.

The 25th FIS lost another pilot on October 19 when 2nd Lt. Theon Eason was shot down by flak fifteen miles north of Pyongyang while strafing an enemy position. The North Koreans had buried his remains, which were found three weeks later when the UN forces gained the area. Captain Calvin Roraus, 25th FIS was also lost while strafing, on October 20. While north of Pyongyang his aircraft was seen to explode in the air, but the cause could not be determined. His grave was also found later.

Further attrition involved 2nd Lt. Edward Ormsby, 16th FIS, on October 29 when he had an electrical failure on a combat mission. He was uninjured in the ensuing forced landing. The 25th FIS lost two other aircraft as a result of self-inflicted rocket damage, and one due to an engine failure. The two to rocket damage involved Lt.'s Hanson and Strother while they were attacking under a low cloud base and when their rockets exploded against their targets, the debris came up in their faces. The engine failure occurred over Kaesong at 28,000' and Lt. Hass dead-sticked his F-80 to Kimpo to land hot and long and then his F-80 went off the end of the runway and flipped over on him. Fortunately he only suffered a broken right wrist.

November 1950 proved to be a very active and exciting month. On November 1 the 21st Infantry Regiment, 24th Infantry Division, reached a point only eighteen miles from the mouth of the Yalu River at Sinuiju. Some Army patrols even got to the Yalu, but they did not attempt to hold any positions at this time, as their supply lines were extended far to thinly. During that night the first engagement between the UN force and the Chinese Communist Forces, CCF, took place, but no one believed their reports. The following night the Seventh Marine Regiment had a similar encounter south of Chosen Reservoir, but then the CCF disappeared for three weeks.

Even though the U.S. Army was almost within cannon range of Sinuiju, it was up to the Air Force to hit the heavily defended port. On November 1 Captain Frank Van Sickle, 16th FIS, was hit by flak over the Sinuiju airfield and he crashed straight into the ground on the southeast corner of the field.

The 7th FBS lost Captain Frank Doyle while he was making a rocket attack in the Unsan area. His tip tanks and other parts of his aircraft were seen to come off his F-80 before it crashed, but what actually caused it to go in was unknown.

1st Lt. Frederick Wysocki, 26th FIS on detached service to the 16th FIS, was killed on takeoff at Kimpo on November 6. He crashed into a truck doing repair work to the runway and died of burns that afternoon.

1st Lt. Thomas Wadsworth, 80th FBS, died the following day while enroute to Japan on a ferry flight. He ran low on fuel and decided to land at Ohiba, Japan but then changed his mind and attempted to bailout, but he was too low at that point for his parachute to function.

November 8 became a day in history for the USAF as President Truman allowed 79 B-29s to bomb the Yalu River bridges at Sinuiju. It was also the first day that the elusive MiG 15 was taken on in force by Mustangs and F-80s. Although three MiG's were damaged by Mustang pilots on November 1 and many claim that Kendall Carlson shot down the first one on November 7, with another probable by Lt. Colonel William O'Donnell, along with two more being damaged by Mustang pilots that day: November 8 was the first encounter by F-80 pilots with the MiG, and they did well for themselves.

1st Lt. Russell Brown, 26th FIS on detached service to the 16th FIS, was a part of a flight CAPing Sinuiju, "Sunny Joe," while other 51st FIG F-80s were attacking the airfield. Brown's flight, led by Lt. Colonel Stephens, had been warned to expect Yak's, but as Stephens' led the flight upwards to 18,000 feet, they could see MiG's cavorting north of the Yalu.

Brown: "Suddenly, all hell broke loose. An instant later two flashing enemy jets dove on me out of the sun. As they shot by, I locked on to one of them, hoping to get a good angle on him . . . Suddenly, he veered to the left and that is where he made his mistake. I cut him off and fired four short bursts with my fifties . . . I was about 1,000 feet behind him when I gave him four more short bursts. Black smoke spouted from the right side of his fuselage. I gave him one more long burst and, suddenly, the MiG exploded in mid-air." (The correct serial number of Brown's F-80 was 49-713, and not 49-737 as usually stated).

Additional encounters with MiG's: Major John Kropenick, operations officer, 25th FIS, when his flight of three F-80s chased seven MiG's to the Yalu River, but had to break off the pursuit to avoid a boarder violation. Squadron commanding officer Lt. Colonel Clure Smith closed in on four MiG's and hit one while in a climbing turn, getting credit for a damaged. Lt. Garland Hanson, 25th FIS supply officer, was initially credited with one destroyed, but his claim was not upheld.

Lt. Colonel John Duganne, CO of the 8th FBS, and wingmen Lt.'s Decust, J. W. Smith and Dalman encountered the Yak-9s that came in behind Lt. Smith. Duganne and Dacust dove on two of them that were chasing Smith, and Smith circled-up to come in behind one of them, which he "disintegrated." Duganne and Decust bracketed the other Yak and sent it down smoking. Both were credited as probables, however.

1st Lt. Charles Boone, 80th FBS, was lost on November 17 at Seoul. Boone was coming back from a mission when his engine lost power, and in the ensuing attempt at an emergency landing he overshot the runway, hit the ground and bounced three times before rolling inverted into the Han River.

One of the first pilots to score an air-to-air kill in the Korean War was killed on November 25 when 1st Lt. Harry Sandlin, 80th FBS, was making a strafing run on a North Korean target. The left tip tank came off his F-80 for some reason, and the Shooting Star rolled into the ground. Sandlin had destroyed a La-7 on June 29 while flying a F-51.

Administrative changes on November 25 brought Lt. Colonel Charles Williams in to command the 9th FBS, while Major Selenger took his place as 49th FBG operations officer. It was a full circle move for Williams, as he had been CO of the 9th FBS on June 25. Major Frank Ellis, former CO of the 9th FBS moved to 49th FBG S-4. Lt. Colonel John Duganne, having been the commanding officer of the 8th FBS for two years, was transferred to Headquarters 5th Air Force. He was replaced by Major Benjamin King. Lt. Colonel Jack Brown remained as CO of the 7th FBS.

The last F-80 loss for November occurred on the 26th when 2nd Lt. Richard Scott, 7th FBS, was lost in the area of Taichon. While on a strafing mission Scott's F-80 went into a series of rolls and crashed on the third one.

What the GI's called a "bug out," while the brass titled it an "armed withdrawal" started on November 27 and marked the major change in the complexion of the Korean War. The CCF encircled the U.S. Seventh Infantry Division's "Task Force McLean/Task Force Faith" east of Chosen and annihilated them. Only 385 men out of 3,200 survived. The First Marine Division found themselves encircled at Chosen, too, and had to start fighting their way towards Hungnam in temperatures that reached forty below zero. Their courage has rarely been recognized. While this was going on, the 32nd Infantry Regiment, Seventh Division, actually attained the Yalu at Ch'osan, but on the 29th General Walker ordered their withdrawal to Pyongyang. Between November 29 and December 1 the U.S.

49-873 was "Homesick Angel," and here she is headed to a Korean target with 500 pound GP bombs. In December 1951 she was heavily damaged by flak, but after repairs she served with Alaska's 144th FBS.

Second Infantry Division was decimated while covering this withdrawal.

With winter weather now upon them, the maintenance people were having more that their share of difficulties at Seoul. Due to the logistical problems in obtaining 100 octane fuel for starting the F-80s, they tried to stay with the standard JP-1 fuel, which resulted in" balky and/or hot starts," which placed abnormal stress upon the J-33 engines.-Major Clyde Good had his plenum chamber explode while starting his engine, which blew the top of his fuselage right off the aircraft.

The F-80s were getting more than beat-up while operating off the pierced steel planking, PSP, taxiways and runways. Two F-80s of the 49th FBG being lost due to landing gear material failure as a result of the roughness of the PSP in November. HVAR's were another problem, as they were mis-wired. In one flight of four F-80s with four HVAR's each, thirteen out of the sixteen rockets failed to fire. Not only was this dangerous to the pilot setting up an attack against a Russian-built T-34 tank for naught, the effect upon his morale was beyond frustration. Nonetheless, the 49th FBG flew 1967 effective combat sorties in November and earned a Distinguished Unit Citation for their part in the Korean War.

On December 1 the unheralded 8th TRS lost a RF-80A and pilot near Sinuiju. 1st Lt. H. B. Shawe and wingman, Lt. C. R. Ritchie were taking photographs when Shawe's engine quit. He couldn't get an airstart, nor could he release his canopy for a manual bailout. (The RF-80A's did not have ejection seats). Shawe bellied in twenty miles south of Sonchon on a coastal mud flat, but after sliding only fifty yards, a wing tip dug into the mud and the aircraft flipped over on its back. Air-Sea Rescue was alerted, but it got dark on them and the could not locate the crash site, and Shawe was given up for lost. He was rescued, however, by enemy forces, and became a POW.

MiG-15 activity was limited during the last weeks of November, but on December 4 Lt. Markette, 8th FBS, was providing a fighter escort for Lt. R. R. Hudspeth, piloting a RF-80A of the 8th TRS near Sinuiju when they were attacked by five MiG's. Markette fired at one MiG, with possible damage to it, while another clobbered his F-80. He got back to Kimpo for a successful emergency landing, and the unarmed Hudspeth escaped.

On December 9 Captain Richard Moore, 8th FBS, was killed on a combat mission, but the details of his loss were unknown.

The failure to hold the line at Pyongyang and the continuing press southwards by the North Korean Army and CCF caused the Headquarters section of the 51st FIG to be withdrawn from Seoul back to Itazuke via 21st Troop Carrier Squadron C-54s on December 10. The 51st FIG's squadrons would remain at Kimpo until January 3, 1951. The 8th Fighter Bomber Group, at Pyongyang, "Pingpong," until December 3 with F-51s was evacuated south to K-16, Seoul City Airport, where they remained until December 10. At this

40th FIS Mustangs and 41st FIS F-80s on strip alert at Johnson Air Base, Japan. Normally each squadron placed four of their aircraft on alert at a time to fulfill air defense duties for Japan while their other fighters were used to train pilots for service in Korea. (Chard)

time the 8th FBG and the 35th and 36th FBS turned over their Mustangs to the 18th FBG and the 35th FIG and were evacuated back to Itazuke with the expectation of being re-equipped with F-80s.

On the following day, December 11, the 8th FBS had Lt. Mathewson downed behind the enemy lines. His F-80 exploded as he was starting an attack on the Pyongyang East airfield, and luckily, he was thrown clear of the tumbling hulk. Immediately a RESCAP was set up by his wingmen, as Mathewson was seen to be surrounded by enemy troops. When the F-80s ran short on fuel, they were replaced by Mustangs of 77 Squadron, RAAF, who capped him until dusk. Then a L-5, flown by Lt. John Michaelis struggled in and landed on a dry spot alongside a rice paddy and picked Mathewson up. He was the first of the 49th FBG pilots to be plucked from the enemy's grasp by a courageous liaison pilot.

"Sunny Joe" remained a major target for the fighter bombers, as this was a key transfer point for communist supplies coming into Korea from Manchuria. On December 12 the 25th FIS lost 2nd Lt. William Kimbro while strafing Sinuiju's airfield. His F-80 was hit in the tail by flak and the fighter spun in.

On December 15 a flight of four F-80s from the 8th FBS was jumped by ten MiG's. Lt. John Fraizer and Captain Sandborn, in the first element, found that they could not drop their tip tanks, for more speed and maneuverability. Lt. Buihmer, in the second element, could drop only one, and he slung the other one off in combat. Neither side managed to score a hit on the other, however.

Air traffic saturation accounted for the next 51st FIG loss, over Kimpo on December 20. The 25th FIS lost 1st Lt. Richard Hass as he was returning to land from a mission in low visibility and hit the F-80 flown by Lt. Charles Perry, 16th FIS that was also returning from a mission. Both pilots were killed, and an additional 25th FIS F-80 was destroyed when the wreckage of Hass's aircraft fell upon it.

The last 1950 51st FIG F-80 loss occurred on December 27 and was due to a MiG 15. 2nd Lt. Harrison Jacobs, 25th FIS, was over Kwaksan making a rocket attack and found himself jumped by a pair of MiG's. He reported that an aileron and a part of a wing were shot away, and that he was over water and was bailing out, but no trace of him or his aircraft was ever found.

The last 49th FBG F-80 lost during the month was on December 29 when Lt. James Clayberg, 8th FBS, disappeared over North Korea.

On December 20 the 80th Fighter Bomber Squadron with 21 F-80s returned to the control of the 8th Fighter Bomber Group. They were operational on the 22nd, and on the 29th 1st Lt. Bertram Wilkins was killed while attempting an emergency landing at Itazuke with a full load of armament and fuel. He hit short of the runway and exploded. On December 30 the 36th and 80th FBS's flew their first combat missions to represent the "new" 8th FBG. The 35th FBS would become combat operational with the F-80 the following day. The 8th FBG was still led by recently promoted Colonel Samways, while Major James Buckley took command of the 36th FBS.

The ground war saw Seoul abandoned on January 4, 1951, and Inchon the next day. The fighter bomber groups thus had an abrupt change in their mission, as they were directed to the Seoul-Suwon-Inchon area to destroy UN material that had to be left behind. During the week between January 7-15 the enemy forces were finally halted, and then forced to a defensive position that roughly paralleled the original 38th Parallel demarcation line, but bending south to below the Han River. It would not be until March 14 that Seoul was regained.

Thus as 1951 began the three combat operational F-80 fighter groups were stationed as follows: the 8th FBG and the 51st FIG at Itazuke AB, Japan, and the 49th FBG at Taegu AB, South Korea. Strength was: 8th FBG with the 35th, 36th and 80th FBS; the 51st FIG with the 16th and 25th FIS's; and the 49th FBG with the 7th, 8th and 9th FBS's. On January 20-22 the 51st FIW moved to Tsuiki, with Colonel Weltman becoming the base commander. This move was made in anticipation of the 49th FBW withdrawing from Taegu, which they did on January 26. Then the 51st FIW became a tenant organization, and the 49th FBW, under Colonel Aaron Tyer, the controlling organization.

Combat operations in January 1951 showed that for the first time since they had entered combat, the 51st FIG had no combat losses, however they did have 1st Lt. Robert Davis, 16th FIS, injured on January 4 when he had to make a belly landing. On January 31 1st Lt. Robert Darnell, 25th FIS, was wounded by a .30 caliber round that smashed through his canopy, creased his neck and struck him in his jaw. The wounded pilot had to fly 150 miles to land at K-2 for treatment.

The 49th FBG continued to use Taegu as a staging base to support their combat operations, although their squadrons had been pulled back to Japan late in January. Thus opera-

A fly-by of 41st and 40th FIS F-80s and Mustangs over Johnson Air Base in 1953. While not generally recognized, Japan was every bit the sanctuary for the United Nations as Manchuria was for the communists during the Korean War. An unstated fear was that if UN pilots were permitted to cross the Yalu River, there was little to deter the communists from over-flying Japan in retaliation. (Chard)

tions were not far removed from what they had been during the fall of 1950. The early morning missions would depart from Tsuiki to fly a strike, then land at Taegu to rearm and refuel, fly another mission, return to Taegu to repeat the process, fly a mission and then head home to Tsuiki that evening. This operation was obviously efficient, but the stress upon the pilots and the ground crews again was tremendous. On January 23 their role was changed from striking tactical targets to that of flak busting to support B-29 missions out of Okinawa.

The 49th FBG lost six aircraft and two pilots during January. On January 21 a flight of three F-80s was returning from a mission when late afternoon ground fog settled in at K-2, along with low ceilings, and the flight had to search out a suitable forced landing site along the Tatkong River for belly landings when low fuel would not permit them to search any longer for the airfield. Preceding this event was the loss of 1st Lt. Joe Dalman, 8th FBS, who was the number four man in this flight that had encountered MiG 15s while escorting a RF-80. A MiG caught him unawares, and shot him down while the others depleted their fuel in fighting off the MiG's. The 8th TRS recce pilot, unidentified, was also shot down.

The 8th Fighter Bomber Group lost two F-80s in accidents on January 9. One a flight test, and the other while returning from a combat mission after dark. Both pilots were uninjured. But on January 23 the 80th FBS lost 1st Lt. Ralph Jacobs through a rather unusual incident. While in the process of making a strafing run, a tip tank collapsed and folded over the leading edge of his wing. Jacobs climbed to 2,000 feet to try and shake it off, but lost control in the process and spun-in.

On January 29 the 36th FBS lost 1st Lt. Arthur Hutchinson in another unusual incident. While flying a radar CAP mission, his F-80 flamed-out twenty miles north of Iki-Shimi, some seventy miles north of Itazuke. He was attempting an airstart when he descended into a cloud deck, and although his flight leader dove through the deck to join up with him, no trace of Hutchinson or his aircraft could be found.

On February 3 the 35th FBS lost a pilot through drowning. 1st Lt. John Adkins was up on a two-ship routine strip alert scramble mission, and when his flight leader started a turn, Adkins started a cross-under maneuver under his leader, below and behind him. When next seen, his aircraft was in the process of disintegrating and was falling in pieces into Fukouka Bay. Adkins parachute was seen to open and he was apparently alive when he hit the water, yet although the crash boat was to him within minutes, he had perished in the cold water.

Hard luck continued to plague the 8th FBG into February. On the 7th Captain Cecil Ware, 36th FBS, took off on "Cousin Victor" flight from Itazuke at 0635 hours. Something went wrong, and Ware salvoed his tip tanks, napalm and rockets just off the end of the runway, climbed and jettisoned his canopy and then fired his ejection seat. But he was still too low and his parachute did not have time to open.

On February 13 Captain Thomas Symington, 36th FBS, started his second combat mission and while he was attacking an enemy troop position near Seoul he took a direct hit from a 40mm AA battery. His F-80 partially disintegrated and crashed before he could eject.

1st Lt. Harry Peyser, 36th FBS, was seriously injured in a crash landing in the Naktong River bed on February 19. AA fire had knocked out his electrical system and Peyser was unable to obtain fuel from his leading edge and wing tanks. He headed towards K-2, but flamed out from fuel starvation. He then tried to bail out, but he couldn't get his canopy open, and was forced to make a belly landing in the river bed, from which he was rescued by a helicopter crew.

On February 22 1st Lt. Ray Van KenBelt was forced to make a belly landing at Itazuke when his nose wheel shimmy

F-80s of the 41st FIS takeoff on a practice scramble from Johnson Air Base as a part of their garrison duties. As they were a noncommitted squadron, pilot and aircraft losses incurred by the 41st FIS, as well as the 26th FIS and 44th FBS, which also served as Operational Training Units, were not considered to be Korean War losses. (Chard)

damper failed and the nose wheel "cocked." Four days later his luck ran out when he received a direct hit from a 40mm round while making a napalm run at Hengchon. The tail section was blown off his F-80, and the remainder of the aircraft and the trapped pilot tumbled into the town.

The 51st FIW had a little better luck with their combat operations in February, only losing one pilot. On February 12 1st Lt. Edward Flemming, 25th FIS, was hit in the left wing while making a rocket attack, and the wing folded-up on him before he could get out. Previously, two pilots had narrow escapes. On the 8th 1st Lt. Herbert Pickett, 16th FIS, lost his oil pressure while returning from a mission. Then his engine started to vibrate, and then exploded. Pickett bailed out forty miles north of Taegu in the midst of a snow storm, but suffered only a bruised knee. On the 15th Captain William Searby crashed on takeoff from Tsuiki on a combat mission. His F-80 would not become "unstuck" and piled-up 800 feet off the end of the runway. Searby suffered back injuries.

Several administrative changes effected the 51st FIW during February. The main portion of the 49th FBW returned to Korea in February, so the 51st FIW became the parent organization at Tsuiki, (While also starting to use K-2 as a staging base on February 1.) while the 49th FBW became the tenant organization. Lt. Colonel Stephens was transferred to Headquarters 5th Air Force, and Lt. Colonel Benjamin Warren became the commanding officer of the 16th FIS. Lt. Colonel Clare Smith left the 25th FIS for Headquarters 51st FIW, and was replaced by Lt. Colonel Charles Appel. Colonel Irwin Dregne was transferred from 51st FIG operations officer to the Headquarters Squadron, 51st FIW.

All but the most essential people of the 543rd Tactical Reconnaissance Group had been withdrawn from Taegu on January 12 and relocated to Komaki Air Base, Japan. On February 24 the 543rd TRG was deactivated and replaced by the 67th Tactical Reconnaissance Wing the next day. Colonel Karl Polifka, "The father of modern photo reconnaissance." was wing commander, while Colonel Jacob Dixon retained control of the redesignated group. Coinciding with this move, the 8th TRS was redesignated as the 15th TRS, presumably because there were too many units with a 8 designation within FEAF at the time. The 162nd TRS (NP) became the 12th TRS, still with RB-26s, and the 45th TRS was just starting to get bonafide RF-51s to supplement their regular F-51s. The 363rd TRS was redesignated at the 67th TRS on March 1. The 8th TRS lost one RF-80 during the course of a recce mission during the month.

The 49th FBG's 8th FBS lost 1st Lt. Jack Brock on February 23 while he was flying his fourth combat mission. Two other F-80s of theirs had been lost two day's earlier as a result of their pilots receiving bad approach instructions in instrument weather. Taegu needed a good DF station! One pilot was injured, the other unscathed. Three other 49th FBG F-80s were lost on combat missions, but the involved pilots could not be ascertained.

After the 40th FIS was relieved of their combat assignment in Korea in 1951, they served as an OTU for Korea bound Mustang and Shooting Star pilots, along with being tasked with providing air defense for Japan. The pilot of 49-1826 was Major James Stewart, commanding officer of the 41st FIS, a U.S. Military Academy graduate, whose squadron assisted the 40th FIS in this role. (Chard)

Going into March 1951 the 49th FBG was encountering even more problems at Taegu with their F-80s. 47% of them were found to have cracked main landing gear fulcrums from operating with heavy loads on the rough PSP. An additional problem was that the main fuel pumps were failing at an abnormal rate, which was found to be from corrosion because of contaminated fuel. Four F-80s were lost to accidents at Taegu, while five more were lost either enemy action or an operational cause while on a combat mission.

In spite of the problems, the 49th FBG concentrated upon providing fighter escort for B-29s or RF-80s, even though it was recognized that the F-80 was no match for the MiG 15. In addition, they experimented with Operation Tunnel, a study on exactly what was the best armament and technique to be followed to close a North Korean railroad tunnel. They tried it all, including 11.5" "Tiny Tim" rockets borrowed from the U.S. Navy. Also, an aborted experiment was run with Headquarters 5th Air Force called Operation Rice Krispies. This was to determine the best way to pollute North Korean rice crops with JP-1 fuel. They never did find out the results of this project, but as the communist radio broadcasts were already making a big propaganda stink over supposed germ warfare, the entire effort was aborted.

The 7th FBS did not lose any pilots in March, but two of their F-80s were among those written off. The 8th FBS lost Captain Robert Cannon on March 4, and Captain Thomas VanKipper on March 23, both killed in action by flak. The 9th FBS lost Captain Kenneth Grangerg on March 30. Again the cause was flak. It was becoming apparent that the communists were quite serious about defending themselves with antiaircraft equipment, and before the war was over it was said by all that the that targets in North Korea were far more heavily defended than any in Europe had ever been.

Something of probable interest happened within the 8th FBG on March 3 and March 20, but whatever transpired remains classified by the Privacy Act.

On March 12 the 36th FBS sent a flight of four F-80s on an armed recce mission, and at Namsi-dong they found a train to attack. This flight, composed of Lt. Arthur Walton, 2nd Lt. Charles Blomberg, Captain Paul Carlisle and 1st Lt. Richard Baldwin split into elements, with one attacking the rolling stock, while the second element provided top cover. The number four man called an attack by four MiG's out of the sun, and he and his element leader turned into them, while the lower flight climbed to join them. Then, four more MiG's dove in on them from the north. After about two minutes of violent maneuvering with neither side being able to get a bead on the other, four additional MiG's joined the fray from the southwest, and two of these MiG's collided in mid-air at 8,000 feet while attacking Blomberg and exploded.

Baldwin's gun camera film showed a MiG pilot in a parachute, but it could not have come from one of those involved in the collision. Baldwin was initially credited with one MiG destroyed after an assessment of his gun camera film, but then it was taken away. Then, a claim to be shared by the four F-80 pilots was entered, as all had fired on one MiG or another during the course of the battle. But an award was not given to anyone.

The 36th FBS lost 1st Lt. Clarence Slack on March 14. While on a mission led by Major E. Burnett in the area of Sunan, Slack reported that he was diving on a selected target. Moments later the wreckage of his F-80 was seen on the ground.

March 17 turned out to be a momentous day for the 8th FBG. A flight of four F-80s of the 35th FBS took off from Itazuke on a mission, but three of them had to abort for various reasons. The number four man, 1st Lt. Donald Jenkins, got as far as Pusan before encountering heavy weather and he too decided to abort. He reported that he was returning and would be back at Itazuke in twenty minutes and asked for a DF steer, and disappeared. No trace of his aircraft was ever found.

The 36th FBS sent three F-80s to Sunchon, and while they were down on the deck looking for worthwhile targets they were jumped by four MiG's. The MiG's made a look-see pass on them and climbed up into a cloud deck. Bases at 5,000 feet, tops at 7,000 feet. The F-80s went up after them, and when 1st Lt. Ralph Hopkins tried to fire on a MiG, his guns wouldn't shoot. A gun heater had burned out. His wingman, 2nd Lt. Lloyd Smith, was lining up to fire on the MiG, when it broke and collided with the F-80 flown by 1st Lt. Harold Landry head-on. Landry was on his second mission of the day, and had flown 112 previously. He was given posthumous credit for downing the MiG.

The 80th FBS suffered their losses on March 20 and 21. On the 20th Captain William Yoakley was strafing enemy troops near the Chosen Reservoir when he got too low and bounced his F-80 off of the top of a mountain ridge. He managed to get his battered F-80 as far as Wonsan Harbor before it gave out on him and Yoakley bailed out. He was rescued from the cold water by a U.S. Navy H-5 within ten minutes and was back on flying status within a week. On the 21st, however, it did not go as well for 1st Lt. William Wall. Wall was strafing enemy troops and supplies near Inchon when his F-80 was seen to partially disintegrate. It was believed that his tip tanks were torn off in a high G pullout and they tore off his horizontal stabilizers in the process.

The 51st FIG was averaging 26.5 combat sorties per day during March with operations out of Tsuiki and staging from Taegu. They were sending one F-80 per day to Far East Air Material Command, FEAMCOM, for modification and overhaul, which included the new larger 255 gallon tip tanks and bomb pylons.

On March 18 the 25th FIS lost 1st Lt. Alfred Bull. He was flying an armed recce mission over Hamhung when hit by random flak. His F-80 burst into flames and Bull was killed. The 16th FIS lost 1st Lt. Albert Ware on March 23 while he was testing a F-80 ten miles north of Tsuiki. Sixteen other 51st FIG F-80s suffered combat related major or minor damage in one form or another during the course of the month. Six of these pilots being injured critically, most through forced landings upon their return that resulted in back injuries.

The 49th FBG got some new squadron commanders in April. Major Irving Boswell took over the 8th FBS, and Major Paul Hall got the 9th FBS. Lt. Colonel Jack Brown was transferred to Headquarters 49th FBG. Seven other 9th FBS pilots were transferred elsewhere, and two of them became better known later on as ace Sabre drivers; Lt. Ralph Parr and Captain Frederick Blesse.

There was no let up in air-to-ground action as the U.S. Army attempted to establish the Kansas Line that cut across the 38th Parallel to the infamous Iron Triangle. The 8th FBS lost 2nd Lt. John Thompson on April 7 went he went down into enemy waters after being hit by flak. The 9th FBS lost 1st Lt. James Towle on April 25 and 2nd Lt. Kenneth West on April 28. Six other 49th FBG F-80s were written off as a result of battle damage.

An evaluation of the 51st FIG effectiveness was conducted in April and showed that their two squadrons were operating at 75.5 combat effectiveness, scoring 384 out of the base-line 460 possible points. This gave them an "excellent" rating, as their dive and skip bombing techniques were particularly noteworthy. Their evasive tactics after bombing were observed to be "weak," however. The 51st FIW thus established a training flight to bring new pilots up too combat proficiency and discontinued sending the replacement's to the 26th FIS for this training.

As the CCF Spring Offensive was in full swing, the 51st FIG had their hands full with ground support and interdiction missions, both of which were hazardous enough in their own way. On April 4 Captain Richard Hale, 25th FIS, was hit by small arms fire, which caused his engine to catch on fire. He made a successful crash landing on the mud flats near

Chinnampo, and was rescued a hour later by an ARS helicopter. The 25th FIS lost 1st Lt. Robert Lempke on April 8 after he was hit by AA fire southwest of Songdong-ni. His F-80 burst into flames and Lempke bailed out. He was seen by his wingmen on the ground and carried as MIA. Lempke became a POW and was returned in Operation Big Switch in September 1953. 1st Lt. Edward Alpern, 25th FIS, was not as fortunate. He was orbiting Lempke as a CAP while awaiting word on a possible rescue attempt when his F-80 was hit by AA fire over Yongyori. Alpern's F-80 burst into flames and exploded when it hit the ground.

The following day 1st Lt. Douglas Matheson, 25th FIS, could not get his tip tanks to feed after taking off from Taegu on a mission. He headed to the bomb disposal area to drop his tanks and ordnance, but his F-80 went into a violent snap roll when the load came off asymmetrically and he crashed in the disposal area.

The 16th FIS lost two pilots on April 23 when 1st Lt. Lee Schlegal was hit by ground fire at Chorwon and crashed. 1st Lt. Cornelius Scott was hit by AA fire at Chokhyon-dong and his F-80 burst into flames before crashing. Both were KIA.

The 8th FBG damaged a F-80 on April 2 when Captain William Alden hit a dog while taking off on a combat mission. The impact bent the landing gear doors and the gear could not retract, so Alden had to abort the mission. The dog was awarded 100% of the blame for the accident. Highly unusual, as accident boards just love to blame a pilot for at least something if they have any possible chance to do so.

The MiG's were back on April 3 and a F-80 from the 36th FBS was hit in the left wing's fuel tank by a 30mm round and it exploded, but the pilot managed to bring his ship back. This pilot was unidentified. The flight of four near Sinuiju had been jumped, and 1st Lt. Willis Jones, 35th FBS, hit one of them head-on with .50 caliber fire and it was initially claimed as a kill, but the claim was not upheld.

July 25, 1950 and "Hybrid I" was accomplished by the joining of a RF-80As nose with the fuselage of a F-80C at Itazuke Air Base. They are in the process of installing a K-18 camera, and the aircraft would serve with the 8th Tactical Reconnaissance Squadron. (Air Force Museum)

The 36th FBS lost neither pilot or aircraft during April, which was certainly exceptional. The group's other two squadrons caught their proverbial lunch. On April 4 1st Lt. Ben Carnell, 35th FBS, was flying his 100th mission when he flew into cables strung between hills north of Pyongyang. The cables tore up the nose, wingtips and fuselage of the F-80, but he did make it back to Itazuke okay. On April 8 1st Lt. Robert Loeffler, 35th FBS, took off on a test hop from Itazuke when his engine flamed out. Loeffler salvoed his tip tanks and bellied-in a rice paddy. He was uninjured, but the F-80 was written off.

On April 8 Captain William Munson, 80th FBS, was attacking an enemy troop concentration near Sukchon when he was hit by flak in the right wing. The flak burst exploded the napalm tank that he was carrying, and the burning tank folded across the wing. Munson headed for Kimpo for an emergency landing, but hit a Mustang that had just been wrecked, slued off the runway, and demolished the F-80. His luck held, however, and he only suffered a wrenched back.

1st Lt. Richard Briggs, 35th FBS, was killed after taking off on a local flight at Itazuke on April 14. After a flameout just after he made it to 1,000 feet, Briggs tried to turn back to make an emergency landing, but a F-82 had already taken the runway for its own takeoff, so Briggs tried to put his F-80 down on the grass along side of the runway. It didn't work, and the F-80 exploded. Since this incident took place in Japan and was not related to a combat mission, Briggs is not considered a Korean war casualty.

The following day, 1st Lt. John King, 35th FBS, was the number four man taking off on the first morning mission from Itazuke. Just after becoming airborne, King lost sight of the rest of his flight in the early morning fog and haze, became disorientated, then his F-80 also flamed out and he crashed into Fukuoka Bay.

The cause of all of the 35th FBS engine failures was found to be JP-1 fuel getting into the water-alcohol tank, and the fuel then floated to the top of the tank, and was sucked into the engine just at the time that the water/alcohol combination would have been consumed. Effectively, the additional JP-1 flooded the engine and caused the flameout.

On April 25 1st Lt. Direck de Rhee Westervelt, 35th FBS, aborted a mission while heading north from Seoul. In one of the more tragic incidents, he could not drop one of his napalm tanks, and when he tried to make an emergency landing into the short runway at Seoul City airport, the heavy laden aircraft hit short of the airstrip directly into a AA gun emplacement.

2nd Lt. Horace Martin, 35th FBS, was lost on April 26 as he was making a napalm attack on an enemy troop position at Inje. He was seen to drop the napalm tanks, then roll twice and crashed while inverted.

On the 30th 1st Lt. Samuel Hoffman, 80th FBS, was hit personally by ground fire that shattered his canopy and wounded him in his right arm. He was also temporally blinded, but with the assistance of his wingman, he managed to get back okay.

Many administrative changes were now taking place within the F-80 units as their commanders had all surpassed their maximum number of combat missions, spent too many months in the Theater, or their experience was needed elsewhere. (Now) Major Ray Schilleref, operations officer 35th FBS, finally got to return to the States in May. Colonel William Samways was transferred to Headquarters FEAF. Colonel Richard McComas came from Hq. FEAF to replace him as 8th FBG CO. Deputy commanding Officer of the 8th FBG, Lt. Colonel Wilbur Grumbles, was transferred to become the commanding officer of the 49th FBG vice Colonel John Murphy, who had been the 49th FBG commander since October 20, 1950. Murphy went to Hq. FEAF.

On May 9 the largest jet mission of the war to date was flown with 97 F-80s from all three groups, along with U.S. Navy jets, to hit Sinuiju. In a rare instance, not a single F-80 was damaged.

The 8th FBG had another tragic incident at Itazuke on May 10. F-80s flown by 1st Lt. Harry Compton and 2nd Lt. Joseph Dunaway were scrambled by the Itazuke Air Defense Control Center, and shortly after breaking ground one of Compton's tip tanks came off and he momentarily lost control of his F-80. He got too low before recovering and hit a telephone pole and wires and tore off six feet of wing before being able to recover it and land. Dunaway, attempting to maintain formation, flew into the side of a house, killing himself and ten Japanese that were living there.

During the course of combat missions on the 10th 2nd Lt. Frank Bay, 36th FBS, was strafing near Kumchon when his F-80 crashed and exploded. Two days later 1st Lt. Lewis "Bud" Haefele, 36th FBS, was leading a flight of F-80s on an armed recce mission. Near Paeksong-ni antiaircraft fire from the village hit his engine, and Haefele tried to belly his F-80 in, but it hit a dike and exploded. He had been a member of the "Florida Rockets" aerobatic team and was one of the recalled ANG pilots.

On May 14 1st Lt. Carl Celeschig, assistant operations officer, 36th FBS, was killed. His flight had spotted an abandoned airfield and were circling to see if there was anything worthwhile there to report when his F-80 was hit by small arms fire. He radioed that he was going to bailout and then ejected, but he did not clear his seat and his parachute did not open. In those early type ejection seats, the pilot had to kick himself clear of it before opening his parachute manually. There were many instances of pilots ejecting themselves and then maintaining a death grip upon the seat handles and riding the seat all the way down in the terror of it all.

On May 23 Captain Charles Chenault, 80th FBS, was hit by ground fire while on a close air support mission, (CAS). With his fuel system damaged, he tried to get back to Taegu, but his F-80 flamed out. He hit short of the runway and demolished the F-80, and suffered a broken back.

1st Lt. Herbert Byers, 36th FBS, was wounded in action on May 29 while strafing Pyongyang airfield, but he managed to get back to Itazuke okay.

The 51st FIG, operating from Tsuiki, was faced with flying 335 miles to reach enemy territory, and with the new 255 gallon tip tanks now in use, operations from the short runway were proving hazardous. On May 18 the operations of the Group relocated to K-13, Suwon, South Korea. There they had a concrete runway that was 5,800 feet long, which wasn't much better that at Tsuiki, but since they were now only sixty miles from the front lines, their fuel loads could be reduced. In addition, they were now using the water/alcohol injection systems for more thrust, and were starting to get JATO bottles to assist them in taking off with heavier combat loads.

Regardless of the distances being flown to enter combat, the attrition remained high. On May 3 2nd Lt. Charles Andrews, 25th FIS, was hit by ground fire near Surnan. His F-80 immediately caught fire and the tail section was blown off his F-80. That afternoon the 25th FIS lost Captain Louis Christensen when he crashed into a hill northwest of Munsarni while on a strafing run.

On May 12 1st Lt. Robert Spragins, operations officer 16th FIS, was making a rocket attack when the napalm tank under his right wing was hit by AA fire. The tank exploded and took off the F-80s right wing in the process, and the aircraft rolled and crashed. That afternoon 2nd Lt. Robert Gillespie, 26th FIS, but attached to the 16th FIS on TDY, said "I'm hit," and "a flash was seen on side of hill near target." Since the 26th FIS was considered to be a noncommittal squadron, Gillespie was not considered a Korean War loss.

The following day, May 13, the 16th FIS lost 1st Lt. Adrin Christensen. He too stated "I'm hit," and then said that his F-80 had flamed out. He was attempting an air start when his F-80 crashed into a clump of trees northeast of Hwachon Reservoir. While flying a CAP over Christensen, 2nd Lt. Frank Frey, 16th FIS, disappeared. His flight leader reported a flash and explosion north of the reservoir.

Once again it was proved that being a squadron commander was not a safe position. On May 21 Major Thomas Harrison had made a pass over an enemy troop position when his F-80 was seen to catch on fire and then the tail section blew off. Harrison managed to bailout, and radio contact was established with him on the ground near Kwakson, but the communists got to him before a rescue attempt could be started. He was killed on his first day as commander of the 16th FIS. (Captain Royal Koons had been CO prior to Major Harrison's arrival in the squadron, and he got the position returned to him after Harrison's loss).

1st Lt. Donald Torstad, 25th FIS, was killed on May 23 while making a napalm attack. He told his flight leader that he had been hit, and was told in return to bail out, but Torstad stated that he could not. He attempted a belly landing near Murdurni, but the F-80 burned before he could get out of it.

On May 17 Captain Cecil Wright had to belly in at K-46 after his F-80 sustained battle damage. Uninjured, Wright was scheduled for a mission from Suwon on May 23, but crashed on takeoff and was killed.

The 49th FBG's historical records were less than poor for May 1951, but the most notable loss, IF THERE IS SUCH A THING, was on May 16 when their former Group executive officer and operations officer, Lt. Colonel Walter Selenger and Lt. Colonel Leland Molland were killed in a T-33 crash south of Pusan while on a weather reconnaissance flight. At the time of this incident, Selenger had flown 223 combat missions, had over 7,000 flying hours, of which 2,000 were jet time, and this was believed to be more than anyone else in the USAF. He was a charter member of the Acrojets. Molland was a WWII ace with eleven kills in the Mediterranean Theater and had temporally served as the 49th FBG's commanding officer the first part of the month.

2nd Lt. Alfred Alverson, 8th FBS, was killed while pulling a stint as a forward air observer in May. 1st Lt. Edwin Reeser was killed on May 25 in a takeoff accident. Two other 8th FBS pilots were critically injured during May in takeoff accidents: 1st Lt. William Pedro and 2nd Lt. Kent Linderman. In all, the 49th FBG lost ten F-80s in combat or combat operational incidents.

On May 25, 1951 the 35th Fighter Interceptor Wing was transferred "Less Personnel and Equipment" from Pusan to Johnson Air Base, Japan where they absorbed the personnel of the 6162nd Air Base Wing. The 40th Fighter Interceptor Squadron went to Misawa to join the 6163rd ABW, and the 39th FIS was detached from the 35th FIW to the 18th Fighter Bomber Group. (This move gave the 18th FBG four Mustang squadrons, the 12th and 67th FBS's, 2 Squadron Republic of South Africa, and the 39th FIS, which refused to give up their designation as fighter-interceptor. In June 1952 they would be assigned to the 51st FIW, which was by then flying F-86s, and they would resume this role). At Misawa the 40th FIS would fly a combination of F-51s, F-80s, and later F-86s and serve as an operational training unit for the 39th FIS.

The 41st FIS, under Major Harry Fletcher, and not touched upon here for awhile, was relieved of OTU duties and assumed the fighter-interceptor role with F-80s. One of their first actions was to send six F-80s to Niigata, Japan, J-30, for air defense purposes. (The 334th FIS, 4th FIG, was supposed to have fulfilled this role, but did not as they were occupied over "MiG Alley." One of the first things they did was shoot down a C-119 that had been abandoned by its crew, but failed to go down on its own. In June 1951 Major Besby Holmes became their squadron commander.

On May 24 the 49th FBG had been notified that as soon as Pusan's runways could be repaired they would convert from F-80Cs to F-84Es. In the meantime, 24 F-80s had to be based at Tsuiki, as there wasn't enough room for them at K-2 with the construction going on. On May 26 the 49th FBG sent six pilots to the 27th Fighter Escort Wing to commence Thunderjet training.

F-80 operations in the 49th FBG continued hot and heavy until June 26 when the 7th and 8th FBS's were relieved of combat assignment for F-84 training. On June 13 the 8th FBS lost 1st Lt. Warren Polk while he was flying an armed recce mission. On June 24 they lost 1st Lt. James Kinner on a training flight. 2nd Lt. Ernest Dunning was shot down on a reconnaissance mission on June 23 when his flight was jumped by a dozen MiG's. Captain Edward Miller was lost from the 7th FBS in mid June. He was serving as their operations officer at the time.

Administrative changes in the 51st FIG moved Lt, Colonel Charles Appel to deputy Group commanding officer and executive officer from squadron commander of the 25th FIS. His replacement was Major Edward Sharp. Sharp having been the 51st FIG operations officer, and he was replaced in that role by Captain Robert Ryan. Then, effective June 23, Appel, now Wing Deputy for Operations, was placed in charge of the 51st FIG operations operating out of Suwon.

The 16th FIS was joined at Suwon by the 25th FIS on June 27, which left only the Wing and support elements at Tsuiki. With the summer heat, water/alcohol injection had to used on all missions, and JATO on most. The normal combat load for the hot weather period being 165 gallon tip tanks, the use of the larger capacity tip tanks having been discontinued, four 5" HVAR's, and somewhere between two 90 gallon napalm tanks up to 1,000 pound General Purpose bombs, depending upon the mission. Approximately 1/3 of the missions were close air support, and the rest were interdiction, railroad cutting, or flak suppression.

The 16th FIS lost no pilots, but did use up four F-80s. On June 6 2nd Lt. Francis Johnson was shot down by a MiG 15, but he made for the coast and managed to be one of the few F-80 pilots to successfully ditch a F-80. He was able to evade capture with the assistance of a specially trained Escape and Evasion team, and got a trip back to the U.S. as a successful evader. The air battle had lasted ten minutes and ranged from down on the deck up to 6,000 feet. The MiG's tried to fight the F-80s on the F-80s terms instead of using their own speed and rate of climb advantages, and four MiG's were claimed as damaged in the process. The 25th FIS lost one pilot, 1st Lt. Sherman Black, who happened to be flying a 16th FIS airplane, but since he was not assigned to them, they did not consider his loss as one of theirs.

Black was shot down by enemy ground fire and killed. On June 6, 1951 another milestone in the history of the F-80 and aerial combat was attained with the flying of the first air-refueled combat mission. As an end result of "Project Collins," RF-80 pilots of Colonel Jacob "Jake" Dixon's 67th TRG, 15th TRS, had been trained by Captain H. E. "Tom" Collins to fly RF-80s equipped with Fletcher 265 gallon tip tanks that had probe refueling kits installed.

Their tanker, a KB-29M piloted by Captain Harry Huggard, took off from Yokota AB and refueled at 25,000 over Wonson Harbor, with this aerial refueling taking place over enemy air-space. The RF-80s were flown by Major's Clyde East and Jean Woodyard, and 1st Lt. Henry Ezelle. After the refueling was accomplished, the recce pilots departed the area to accomplish their own separate missions. Unfortunately, wartime security prevented any acknowledgment of their accomplishments at the time, and it became generally believed this these type of missions did not occur until the following year, with F-84s.

The 8th FBG relocated from Itazuke to Kimpo on June 25, and to celebrate the action, 1st Lt. Robert Loefflar, 35th FBS operations officer, was selected to fly the Group's 20,000 combat sortie. While still flying out of Itazuke one of the 80th FBS pilots had a real, albeit unusual scare. 1st Lt. Wallace McCaffarty was the number two man in his flight and he was following his leader down a narrow ravine to attack some enemy troops hiding there. Lead dropped his napalm, and McCaffarty flew directly into its smoke, which was enough to deprive his engine of enough suitable air to cause it to flame-out. He had to execute a drastic pull-up to avoid the ravine's sides while blinded by the smoke and get himself an air-start before he ran out of airspeed to do so. He was successful.

After moving to Kimpo the 8th FBG's fortunes went down hill in a hurry. On June 26 2nd Lt. Robert Lauterback, 35th FBS was hit by flak near Sunchon and his F-80 started to burn. He was told, then ordered to bailout, but did not. His F-80 turned away from the target, nosed over sharply and crashed.

The 36th FBS had two losses on June 28: 1st Lt. Arthur Johnson was last seen by other members of his flight near Sunchon at about 500 feet while they were encountering intense and accurate AA fire. 1st Lt. Talmadge Wilson in the same flight had major damage from flak at the same time and barely got back to Kimpo.

That afternoon 1st Lt. John Murray was hit by flak while leading his flight on a napalm run against a village near Singosan. They had been sent up on a four-ship Joint Operations Center scramble to work with "Pistol Control" on a CAS mission, but then discovered that the U.S. Navy was coming in to work over that particular target, so they went looking for targets of opportunity. As they found this one and made their napalm attacks, Murray's F-80 was hit by AA fire. His wingman, 1st Lt. Wilbur Thompson, advised him to bailout, and Murray jettisoned his tip tanks and napalm in order to gain some altitude to do so, but the F-80 burst into flames, and Thompson told him to get out, now!, but Murray did not acknowledge the call as he was in the process, and the F-80 rolled over and crashed from 300 feet. Murray's parachute was seen to be fouled on the F-80s vertical stabilizer as the aircraft went down.

The next day 1st Lt. Will C. White, 36th FBS, was in a flight attacking troops in a valley near Sutzae-ri when his F-80 struck the top of a ridge while he was climbing back up from a napalm run. He almost made it, as he managed to get up to 1,000 feet to bailout, but the F-80 snapped and dove into the next ridge.

As the 49th FBG was in the process of switching from F-80s to F-84s in June, with a scheduled completion date in July, their F-80Cs were being sent to FEAMCOM in Japan for Project Rebirth. The process involved an almost total rebuilding of the Shooting Star from the tires up, and was the most extensive aircraft overhaul program outside of the United States. At the end of the rebuild, the F-80s were "zero timed," and started their total flying time from scratch. These rebuilt fighters were then assigned to either the 8th or 51st Fighter Groups to continue their combat career.

The 49th Fighter Group pilots did not enjoy either the respite or the overhaul. The F-80 pilots nearing the completion of their combat tours were given two choices, either transfer to another F-80 group, or extend their missions and transition into F-84s. The low total mission pilots went directly into transition training. In either case, the opinion on the switch to the F-84 was up in the air, as although it had been touted as being a far better fighter-bomber than the F-80, being able to carry heavier loads and more able to deal with the MiG because of its higher speeds, it was basically unproven in combat.

On July 21 the former commanding officers of the 8th and 9th FBS's, Lt. Colonel Irving Bosewell and Major George Irving, respectively, were allowed to rotate back to the United States. The 7th FBS started operations with their new F-84s on July 23, and the 9th FBS was withdrawn from combat at this time for their own conversion training.

While carrying the load for the 49th FBG in July, the 9th FBS had flown 513 effective combat sorties. On July 3 their "Bully Charlie" flight, led by 1st LT. Richard Imming, with Captain Herbert Williams, 1st Lt. John Starck and 1st Lt. William Plumm caught a concentration of approximately 200 vehicles out in the open some twenty miles northeast of Pyongyang. Many of these vehicles were horse-drawn. Regardless, all were destroyed or damaged.

On July 14 the 49th FBG lost Major Marlyn Ford, their Deputy Group Commander and Executive Officer when his F-80 went down over North Korea. 1st Lt. John Starck, was their last F-80 pilot lost, on July 18.

The emphasis for the 8th FBG changed almost entirely from CAS to interdiction type missions in July. And July 1951 was a period of miserable weather over Korea with low ceilings and heavy rains. It made missions all the rougher, and life on the ground the tents all the worse. There was no dust, but everything became either muddy or mildewed: Including their historical reports.

On July 1 1st Lt. John Flornoy, 36th FBS, was hit by flak and crashed. On July 7 the 35th FBS lost 1st Lt. Charles Blomberg while bombing the airfield at Sunen. He went straight into the ground while still carrying his bombs.

July 10 marked the date of the first armistice talks at Kaesong. The diplomatic palaver would continue for two more years.

On July 11 Lt. Colonel William Betha, CO 36th FBS, led twenty-six F-80s to attack the airdrome at Sinuiju, and they were attacked by about thirty MiG's. Calls for help brought in the F-86s of the 4th FIG, and they knocked down two or three and damaged another in the process of driving them off. That afternoon twenty-four F-80s went to attack the bridges at Sinanju and Lt. Cecil Mohr, 36th FBS, flew his F-80 into a hillside and 1st Lt. Irwin Taylor, 80th FBS, was hit by AA fire. His F-80 simply rolled over and dove in. Four more 8th FBG F-80s were lost during July, but neither the pilots nor the causes could be identified.

The 51st FIW busied themselves during July by moving from Japan to Suwon, K-13. There may be more to say about this someday, but presently portions of their history in July remain classified.

Captain William Brockmire, 16th FIS, was killed while flying with the 25th FIS on July 2. Their F-80s had gone up on an Operation Ratkiller mission, to strafe North Korean guerrillas trapped behind the lines in South Korea. His tip tanks came off while pulling high G's, and one tore off his horizontal stabilizer. 2nd Lt. Harvey Roundtree, 25th FIS, was killed on a practice mission over the Omura gunnery range on July 24. Apparently his aircraft had been overstressed, for it came apart in the air and multiple splashes from wreckage hitting the water were observed by his wingmen. A partially opened parachute was also found. Two other 51st FIG F-80s were lost two operational incidents, but their pilots emerged unscathed.

On July 29, while returning from a dive bombing mission against bridges in North Korea, six F-80s were jumped by a dozen MiG 15s. Three of the F-80 pilots were on their first combat mission, but they acquitted themselves well. Lt. W. W. McAllister probably destroyed one of the MiGs, with pieces of it being see falling off as a result of being hit by .50 caliber fire. McAllister's F-80 was the only one damaged by the MiG's return fire, but he got back ok. Film assessment later verified that he had actually destroyed the MiG, and McAllister was credited with the last air-to-air victory for the F-80.

The 51st FIG completed its move to Suwon on August 4. Almost all of their operations at Tsuiki were now terminated, pending the arrival of the 51st FIW at Suwon in October when their facilities were expected to be available.

Combat losses for the 51st FIG in August included Captain Gerald Brose, 30th Weather Squadron, who was attached to the 51st FIW as their weather officer, with further attachment to the 16th FIS for flying. While in the area of Sunan on an armed recce mission, his flight encountered intense automatic weapons fire and heavy flak, and Brose's F-80 was seen to be pulling up off the target just before it exploded.

August 20 was a tough day for the 51st FIG. While on a flak suppression mission over Sariwon, 2nd Lt. Edwin Tabaczynski, 16th FIS, was flying as the number two man with two 1,000 pound bombs with instantaneous fuzes under his F-80s wings. At 5,500 feet his F-80 was apparently hit by flak, as it simply evaporated in the air.

That afternoon Captain Emmett Long, was the number four man in his flight on another flak suppression mission near Chongnyon when his F-80 flamed out at 15,000 feet. His attempts at an airstart were unsuccessful, and Long settled for a belly landing. The aircraft was demolished in the process, with no indication of his possible survival, and Long was killed.

On August 24 the weather finally cleared after weeks of hampering fighter bomber operations. The 16th FIS dispatched five flights of F-80s to attack rail targets in the area of Kunu-ri. After bombing and cutting railroad tracks, they then went off to seek targets of opportunity and found a convoy being ferried across a river. Two flight expended all of their remaining ordnance, and called for two more flights to be launched. The squadron accounted for forty trucks, twenty railroad cars, several barges, a supply dump and many smaller targets.

The 25th FIS lost 2nd Lt. Robert Lacey on August 29. While on an armed reconnaissance mission a group of camouflaged vehicles was spotted near Mason-ni and his flight went down to strafe them. Lacey's F-80 passed over them and mushed into the ground on the north side of the road. It slid for several hundred feet before it burst into flames and disintegrated.

Colonel Harvey Case replaced Colonel McComas as the commanding officer of the 8th FBG on July 31. Then in August Lt. Colonel Edgar Beam was transferred to the 8th FBG and Major Carlos Dannacher became commanding officer of the 35th FBS. Major John Tulloch became commanding officer of the 36th FBS, with Lt. Colonel Betha going to the 8th FIW. All of these later changes taking place during a move from Kimpo to Suwon.

The 8th FBG officially moved to Suwon on August 24, which was their eighth and final move of the Korean War. Their unofficial motto had become "The Spirit of Hobo" in 1950 with the first of these many moves, to recapitulate: From Itazuke to Tsuiki August 11, 1950; (And conversion to F-51s.) to Suwon October 7; to Kimpo October 28: to Pyongyang November 25; to Seoul City December 3; back to Itazuke December 10; (And to switch back to F-80s.) to Kimpo June 25, 1951; and back to Suwon again on August 24. So far "Hobo" had flown 24, 287 effective combat sorties.

At Suwon, the 8th FBG shared the field with the 51st FIG, and there was a massive congestion problem created by two fighter groups attempting to fly scheduled missions at the same time from the single runway, and even worse problems when the aircraft returned from North Korea, particularly for those that were "hurting for fuel," or with battle damage. This was eventually resolved by staggering scheduled mission times for the two groups.

On August 10 there was very poor weather, but the 8th FBG had to go up anyway on interdiction missions. 1st Lt. Mark Castellno , 80th FBS, couldn't get his heavily laden F-80 airborne and crashed a half mile off the end of the runway at Kimpo. He died two hours afterwards as a result of sustained injuries. While on this mission 1st Lt. James Kiser, 36th FBS, flying as "Merrimac Victor 3," was hit by the blast from his own bomb. His F-80 caught on fire, and Kiser bailed out east of Namsi-dong. He remains one of the 8,100 Korean war MIA's. Upon return from this same mission 1st Lt. Henry Nielson, 36th FBS, "Merrimac Victor 4," had a flame out because he had run out of fuel. He stated that he was going to bail out, but he was never heard from again. Rescue combat air patrols, RESCAPs, were launched for the missing pilots, but they could not find anyone, and upon return a rainstorm moved across Kimpo. One F-80 pilot made three unsuccessful attempts to get down, and on the fourth, the luckless pilot ran off the runway and demolished his aircraft.

Attrition remained high during the rest of the month, also. On August 18 2nd Lt. Bruce Wilson, 36th FBS, was launched as the spare aircraft, in case one of the regularly scheduled four aircraft had to abort the mission. As he wasn't needed, he headed back to Suwon, but hit a high tension line fifteen miles north of Seoul and crashed. His body was recovered the next day.

On August 20 1st Lt. Billy Dixon, 80th FBS, was hit by flak over Songchon. He managed to get his burning F-80 as back as far as Inchon Harbor when his wing burned through, and he bailed out. He was rescued by a H-5. On August 24 the 80th FBS lost another F-80, and its pilot. 2nd Lt. Robert Martin was strafing at Haeju, and he got as far as the sea, but he didn't have a chance to bailout before his F-80 crashed.

The MiG's came back to harass the F-80s of the 8th FBG on August 31. "Uncle" flight of the 36th FBS and "Billy," "Charlie" and "Dog" flights of the 80th FBS were jumped by fourteen MiG's that made four firing passes on the F-80s, while the F-80s turned it around on them and made three attempts to get at the MiG's. The F-80 pilots claimed no hits as being made, and the MiG's downed 1st Lt. Jack Henderson, "Merrimac Uncle 3," 36th FBS, who reported to his flight leader that he was on fire and was heading for the coast. He didn't make it.

Captain Robert Vantrease was "Merrimac Uncle 1," and he was having his own problems with the MiG's. One was on his tail, and he broke hard into it, and the MiG's avoided him by climbing straight up. Vantrease continued out to sea with another MiG on his tail, and he broke hard into him, and the MiG overshot, so he was able to return fire, but scored no hits. "Merrimac Uncle 4," Henderson's wingman, was 2nd Lt. Travis Etheridge, and he was jumped by two MiG's at 5,000 feet. Both overshot him, and then he got in the dogfight of his life. The MiG's came back down on him and made a total of six firing passes on his F-80, all without success. Etheridge was firing back, but without success, either.

The role of the 8th FBG in September 1951 continued to be primarily rail interdiction. "Our target for today will be the railroad lines from YD 5094 to YD 4578." (Map coordinates.) The Group was fortunate in that they only lost two pilots during the course of these hazardous missions during September.

On September 11 it was the MiG's again that caused a loss, and not the constant AA fire they usually had to contend with. 1st Lt. Sterling Bushroe, 35th FBS, and his flight were dive bombing railroad tracks when they were cut off by six to eight MiG's that had been south of them at 25, 000 feet. As they were climbing off their target and started to reform to head for Suwon, the MiG's bounced them, and Bushroe was not seen again.

The 36th FBS had their "Merrimac Mike" flight jumped at the same time. The MiG's dove through the two F-80s that were flying as top cover and attacked the pair that were bombing, and then climbed back up to attack the top cover again. Lt. Casey made two firing passes on a MiG, without effect, and then the low flight fired at another MiG, but it was out of range. The F-80s, out of ammunition, and the MiG's, apparently out of fuel, broke off the engagement at the same time.

The 2nd Infantry Division began an assault on "Heartbreak Ridge" on September 13. It would take them a month to capture this location, and cost them 3,700 casualties in the process. The ground war in Korea had become WWI all over again.

The 36th FBS lost 1st Lt. William Pugh on September 23 to small arms fire. After making a strafing attack on a small village, his F-80 was hit and started burning profusely. Pugh headed for the Chinnampo Estuary and climbed to 8,000 feet, but as the F-80 continued to burn, he shut down its engine and set it up a 300 fpm gliding descent while his flight leader, Lt. Ventrease, called for Air-Sea Rescue. Descending through 12,500 feet, the F-80 rolled to its right, skidded, and Pugh's guns started to fire, and they continued to fire as the aircraft dove into the water.

The 51st FIG was also heavily involved in railroad interdiction during September, in fact, all but two RESCAP missions were flown against rail targets. The 16th FIS flew 872:40 combat hours in 595 combat sorties, the 25th flew 779:40 combat hours in 522 combat sorties during September.

During this period the 51st FIG was suffering heavy morale problems, as the majority of their pilots had flown all of their required 100 combat missions, but they could not be relieved from combat missions because there were no replacement pilots available for them. And, in addition to facing enemy flak, they found themselves placed in an almost equally hazardous situation at Suwon. The single taxiway had given way and had to be closed. This meant that when they landed they had to taxi back down the side of the runway to their parking ramp head-on with aircraft that were attempting to land. As this was obviously dangerous, they balked, and the method was changed to either taxi through the 8th FBG ramp (Which was not appreciated.), or wait at the end of the runway for everyone to get back down. (And pray that no one's brakes failed). To solve part of this congestion problem, the 4th FIG was moved to Kimpo from Suwon, which got them out of the fighter-bombers way.

The 25th FIS lost a F-80 on September 6 when Captain Robert Ryan had a flameout and got to the Chinnampo Estuary before he was forced to bailout. He was rescued the next day by the rarely acclaimed Air Rescue Service.

Two weeks later, on September 23 the 25th FIS lost 2nd Lt. Lewis Pleiss while he was dive bombing railroad tracks near Sukchon. Flying in a flight of three F-80s, Pleiss disappeared after making his attack, and although his wingmen searched the area for fifteen minutes, no sign of him or his aircraft could be found.

On September 29 the 51st FIG lost 2nd Lt. Eugene Class as he was returning from a R&R trip to Japan. The C-119 he was riding on crashed near Izehorz, Japan. Since he was not on a combat mission at the time, he is not carried as a Korean War casualty.

The following day the 16th FIS lost 2nd Lt. William Grammer over Pyongyang. While making a strafing pass on a vehicle, Grammer called his flight leader and said that he had been hit personally -- an antiseptic way of officially stating that he was wounded. His F-80 went into a steep dive and crashed just southeast of the capital city.

During September the F-80 units had only 53% of the number of F-80s authorized to a unit. Under normal conditions, a fighter squadron would be equipped with twenty-five aircraft, and use sixteen of them for their usual combat operations, while the remainder were expected to be down for maintenance or utilized for other purposes.

The F-80 attrition rate so far during the war was indicating that there was a monthly average loss of eighteen F-80s. Effectively, the loss of an entire squadron each month.

Even though Project Rebirth was rebuilding F-80s at a steady rate, it could not keep up with the demand rate for replacement fighters. The non-committed 16th FIS, 41st FIS and 44th FBS's were pressed to sent their better F-80s to Korea in exchange for the more war-weary aircraft that were not quite ready for Rebirth, but there just were not enough of these F-80s available. Coupled with the lack of combat qualified F-80s, FEAF was beginning to have real problems that were not publicly admitted.

A puzzling situation also occurred on September 5 when there was the first appearance of red-nosed F-80s over North Korea that were not United Nations aircraft. The reports of the pilots that were bounced by these F-80s were poo-pooed by USAF intelligence, as it was not believed that the communists could, or would, bother to repair recovered F-80s from North Korea and then fly them against the USAF. But then, why not? as the Germans did similarly during WWII. The red-nosed F-80s were again encountered on November 1, and then FEAF believed the pilots that encountered them, but there wasn't much to be said about it beyond be careful of your aircraft recognition. Before the war was over there were reports of rogue Sabre's being flown, also, that cannot be discounted. Any power that had the technology to build an aircraft as complex as the B-29 was into their own version, the Tu-4, would certainly be capable of assembling wrecks into an whole, and they were getting plenty to choose from.

The 51st FIW officially moved from Tsuiki to Suwon in October, while maintaining a Detachment at Tsuiki for rear echelon maintenance. At Suwon, the 51st FIG continued to be attached to the 8th FBW for administrative and logistical purposes, while at Tsuiki AB, the 8th FBW also maintained a detachment for their Rear Echelon Maintenance Organization, (REMCO), which fell under the control of the 51st FIG's detachment commander. During September this REMCO unit worked on 82 F-80s, 41 from each unit, repairing battle damage and repairing the stress damaged landing gear fulcrums.

On October 12 the 16th FIS lost 1st Lt. Richard Borschel while on a dive bombing mission. His F-80 flamed out at 2,000 feet, and attempts at airstarting it were fruitless. Borschel told his flight leader that he could not get his canopy open, and then fought it open and bailed out manually. By then he was too low for his parachute to have time to open and he perished in a reservoir south of Chareyong.

1st Lt. Vernon Wright, 25th FIS, had some narrow escapes on October 25. Hit by ground fire in the fuselage fuel tank while making a strafing run his F-80 started to burn and Wright tried to eject, but he had on so much winter survival clothing that he could not get his arms back far enough in the cockpit to reach the ejection seat handles. So he had to bailout manually. A helicopter came in and picked him up, but then it too was shot down. The next morning another chopper came in and rescued them all.

On October 30 1st Lt. Bradford Martin, 25th FIS, was hit by ground fire while strafing, which sheared off his throttle linkage and caused his engine to flame out. At first Martin said he was going to ditch his F-80, but then settled for a belly landing. The forced landing fractured his pelvis, but he was rescued by troops of D Company, 1st Medical Battalion.

Captain Howard Wilson, 25th FIS, was lost on the 30th, too. He was the Number 3 man in his flight, and before he had a chance to strafe the targeted trucks, his F-80 was hit in its left wing. His wingman saw pieces fly off of Wilson's aircraft, and then its left wing folded in half and the F-80 spun-in.

On October 2 the 8th FBG took on the MiG's with serious intent. The MiG's, flying in a "V" formation in two flights of four aircraft, attacked the F-80s by elements of two out of the sun at 7,000 feet. The F-80s were just climbing off a railroad interdiction attack at the time. The MiG's attempted to attack "Merrimac Victor" flight, but overshot the tighter turning F-80s, and couldn't do it, mushing-out in the process. The F-80s turned into them, firing without scoring, while the MiG's fired into the open air between "Victor" three and fours, Lt.s Augsberger and Delancey. The MiG's came up scoreless, while Major John Tulloch, 36th FBS CO, and Lt. Edwin Faulconer each claimed a probable and Group CO Colonel James Tipton, claimed a damaged.

The 8th FBG lost its adjutant on October 4 when Captain Donald Akers crashed into the water near the Groups bombing range. The cause remains unknown.

The peace talks that had begun at Kaesong in July were moved to a more permanent location at Panmunjom on October 7, but they would not start until October 25.

On October 9 the 35th FBS lost 1st Lt. Sidney Mullikin while he was making a strafing pass. Apparently he was hit by small arms fire, as the F-80 flew into the side of a small hill and exploded.

Captain James Treester, 36th FBS, was shot down by flak south of Kumuri on October 11. His F-80 suffered a direct hit in the center fuselage section by a 40mm round and the aircraft exploded.

On October 13 Major Carlos Dennacher, CO 35th FBS, led a flight of four F-80s to cut the rail lines south of Kunu-ri. Colonel Tipton, was along on this flight, and he, being the high ranking officer on the mission received credit for flying the 8th FBW's 25,000 combat sortie.

1st Lt. Louis Esposito, 35th FBS, was downed on October 22 when his F-80 was hit by a high explosive round. He was killed.

The 35th FBS lost another pilot on October 29 when 1st Lt. David Warfield had to bailout over the Chinnampo Estuary on the return leg of a mission. His parachute did not completely open.

In order to improve the combat capability of the F-80, the 8th FBG conducted an experiment with modifying the F-80s rocket rails into bomb racks to carry either 100 or 265 pound General Purpose bombs. It worked, but the resulting weight and drag reduced the F-80s speed and range so much that it was not feasible to use the extra ordnance.

During the later portion of October the 51st FIW was notified that they would be switching to F-86Es , and by the end of the month they had started to send some of their maintenance people to the 4th FIW at Kimpo to learn the new aircraft's idiosyncrasies. On November 1 Colonel Cellini was relieved from the 51st FIW to rotate home, being replaced by Colonel William Linton. Colonel Linton departed Itumi, Japan that same day to check out the 51st FIW interests at Tsuiki, and disappeared enroute. Again, as his loss occurred in Japan, he is not considered a Korean War casualty. Colonel George Stanley was then named 51st FIW commander on November 2. Two days later Colonel Francis Gabreski was transferred to the 51st FIW from the 4th FIW to take over the Wing. On November 13 Lt Colonel George Jones came in from the CO's position of the 334th FIS to relieve Lt. Colonel John Thacker as 51st FIG commanding officer. Thacker was transferred to the deputy wing commanders position, which had originally been held by Linton. Major Royal Koons stayed with the 16th FIS into the F-86 era, while WWII ace Major William Whisner would take over the 25th FIS from Major Edward Sharp.

The 16th FIS lost 1st Lt. Henry Batease on November 4 on a ferry flight to Tachikawa, Japan where his aircraft was to go through Rebirth. Apparently he attempted to land without flaps and touched down a third of the way down the runway, discovered that he was not going to get stopped, and tried a go-around. The F-80 hit a fence, and then smashed into a clump of trees three hundred yards off the end of the runway.

The last 51st FIG F-80 loss in Korea occurred on November 10 when Captain Gerald Gill, 16th FIS, returned from a mission that had been recalled because of deteriorating weather. Suwon was covered in fog, and all of the alternate airfields were also obscured with bad weather. In the poor visibility he touched down short of the runway and suffered an injured back.

The last F-80 combat mission flown by the 51st FIG was on November 19 with seventeen F-80s. At this time the F-80s were either sent to Rebirth or towed across the field and given to the 8th FBG. The short time F-80 pilots were also sent to the 8th FBG, while the others transitioned into F-86s.

During the period September 22, 1950 - November 19, 1951 the 51st FIG claimed five MiG 15s destroyed, eleven damaged. Fifteen conventional aircraft destroyed, eleven damaged. 952 vehicles destroyed, 822 damaged. 70 bridges destroyed, 129 damaged. An estimated 17,621 enemy troops killed. Nineteen camels were also claimed as killed! Their F-80s had fired 14,372,004 rounds of .50 caliber ammunition. Fired 2274 rockets, dropped 1525.7 tons of napalm and dropped 2946.3 tons of bombs. Sixty-three F-80s had been lost to one operational cause or another, and ten more were lost through accidents, for a total of seventy-three. This equated to an entire Group's complement of aircraft.

Just after the 49th FBG converted to F-84Es, the mobilized Air National Guard 116th and 136th Fighter Bomber Wings arrived in Japan. The 136th FBG took over the F-84Es of the 27th FEW, which returned to the United States, and the 136th FBW moved to Taegu from Itazuke to commence fighter-bomber operations. For the immediate period, the 116th FBW remained at Misawa AB, Japan to pull air defense duties, but soon they were also employed as a F-84E fighter bomber unit. This left the 18th FBW to provide ground support and interdiction with Mustangs, and the 8th FBG to do the same as the last operational F-80 FBW.

8th FBG operations were now hampered by the onset of winter. The troops broke out their "long Johns" and began to endure the ice and snow while launching 2024 combat sorties in November. Administrative changes in the Group saw Major Herbert Mann become the commanding officer of the 80th FBS when Major Burnett became the 8th FBG's operations officer. Lt. Colonel Robert Tyler bumped Major Tulloch to 36th FBS operations officer when Tyler joined the 36th FBS.

On November 4 the 36th FBS lost 2nd Lt. Michael Kovalish while on a rail-cutting mission that went on a recce flight after bombing their assigned tracks. Between Youngyang and Sengi, the flight spotted some trucks and as Kovalish was making a second strafing run, his flight leader announced that flak was being thrown up at them. Kovalish acknowledged it with a "roger," but then his F-80 was seen to start trailing smoke, rolled over and crashed.

1st Lt. Jerome Volk, 35th FBS, was killed on November 7. As a part of a flight of three F-80s on an interdiction mission attacking between Chorwon and Kaesong, Volk discovered that his tip tanks would not feed fuel to his engine. In spite of now being encumbered by the heavy tanks, Volk made a napalm attack, dropping one napalm tank on his first pass,

and the other on a second pass. At the completion of this second pass, his F-80 became uncontrollable and went into a series of rolls before crashing. Volk Field (Now Volk Air National Guard Base.) at Camp Douglas, Wisconsin was named in his memory. He was the first of four F-80 pilots to have an Air Force Base named in his honor.

On November 8 a flight of two F-80s led by Captain Charles Brower, 35th FBS, was on an interdiction mission north of Sunchon when they were jumped by twenty-four MiG's. In spite of being out numbered twelve to one, in the battle that lasted for ten minutes, Brower managed to damage two of the MiG's and the F-80s made good their escape.

2nd Lt. Thomas Hadley, 36th FBS, went down on November 9 while on an interdiction mission. His F-80 was seen to snap-roll at 500 feet and then go in.

Also on November 9 the 80th FBS was conducting a rail strike at Kunu-ri when they were jumped by a flight of MiG's. Although unidentified 80th FBS pilots claimed two MiG's shot down and three damaged, none were awarded claims.

The 36th FBS's "Merrimac Victor" flight was flying as top cover for the rest of the squadron on November 27 when they were bounced by eighteen MiG's from 9:00 o'clock high. The MiG's came down in two-ship elements, and the F-80s dropped their tip tanks and turned into them. It was a bit of a ploy, as often they dropped their tips to make the MiG pilots believe that they had jettisoned their ordnance, and then the MiG pilots would think that they had accomplished what they had come for, in forcing the F-80s to needlessly expend their ordnance, and then they would fly off and leave the F-80s alone.

In this case, the MiG's did not leave, and one shot down 1st Lt. Rafael Dubreuil. 2nd Lt. Travis Etheridge, the number 3 man in "Victor" flight did sort of even up the score, however, as he got either a damaged or a probable claim out of the conflict.

The weather had forced the cancellation of all missions during five days in November, and in December it had not improved. There were six days where there was no flying at all, and five with limited missions. Regardless, the 8th FBG flew 2348 effective combat sorties. On December 16 Lt. Edward Moore, 35th FBS, flew the 30,000 combat sortie for the 8th FBG. As a part of Operation Strangle, the 8th FBG was tasked with flying most of their interdiction missions against the railroads between Kunu-ri and Sunchon. They flew 1835 sorties out of the 2348 against this heavily flak infested twenty-five mile stretch of track.

On December 1 the MiG's were back to try and hamper fighter-bomber operations. While south of Pyongyang, near Sin-mak, the 35th FBS's "John Peter" flight was jumped from behind by two MiG's that closed on them to a bare 100 foot range. The F-80s broke to the left, and the MiG's broke to the right in a climbing turn and were not seen again. But they had done their damage. 2nd Lt. Thomas Mounts was shot down to become a POW.

Mounts was seen to bailout, and his parachute was spotted on the ground, so Lt. William Womack started looking for him, in case a rescue mission might be attempted. Running himself out of fuel in the process, Womack climbed to 30,000 feet and shut down his engine and set up a glide for Suwon. With only forty gallons of JP-1 remaining, Womack restarted his engine and elected to land at Seoul. After refueling, he made a night takeoff in order to get his F-80 back to Suwon for the next day's mission, but for an unexplainable reason, Womack crashed soon after takeoff and was killed.

On December 11 2nd Lt. Richard Cronan, 35th FBS, was flying his first mission on a close air support strike. After making his first pass, he was seen to pull up, roll over and crash inverted.

The 36th FBS lost 1st Lt. Edgar Grey on December 14 as he was leading "Merrimac Mike" flight. He was hit by flak while conducting an armed recce mission between Sunchon and Pyongyang. Four days later, on the 18th, the 36th FBS lost 1st Lt. Regie Sellers as he was leading "Merrimac Victor" flight. They had made a dive bombing run on some railroad tracks and Sellers stated that he had an AA battery in sight and was going to attack it, and he was not seen again.

The 80th FBS's loss occurred on December 16 when Lt. Lawrence Kelly crashed while on a flak suppression mission. Kelly was making a dive bombing attack as the number three man, and disappeared near Kunu-ri after he pulled off the target.

The 35th FBS came close to loosing 1st Lt. Joseph Jordon while strafing on December 27. Jordon's F-80 was hit by ground fire while on a strafing run and it caught on fire. He headed for the coast of Korea to bailout while being escorted by Lt. Russel Ryland, but the fire burned itself out, and they were able to land at K-18 successfully.

January 1952 was a miserable and the most costly month for the 8th FBG thus far in the war. Eight pilots were lost while conducting combat missions. The primary mission continued to be rail interdiction, first on the lines south of the Chongchong River, and then north of the river from Kunu-ri to Huichon, where they got more than 200 cuts. Then, the targeted area moved back to between Kunu-ri and Sunchon again. While they were attempting to destroy between five and seven miles of track each mission, it was observed that the damage was always minimal, which was believed due to the frozen soil that reduced bomb impact damage.

Administratively, 35th FBS CO Major Dannacher was promoted to Lt. Colonel. And, on January 22 Colonel Levi Chase came from Headquarters 51st FIW to replace Colonel Case as Group commander, with Case rotating home.

The first loss for the new year occurred on January 2 when 1st Lt. Robert Toony, 80th FBS, was hit by flak east of Sunchon. Toony bailed out and was captured as he touched the ground to become a POW.

On January 5 2nd Lt. Charles Maultsby, 35th FBS, was making a dive bombing run north of Kunu-ri when he was hit by flak. "He peeled up from a dive bomb run, jettisoned the canopy, and ejected himself from the aircraft. He also became a POW, and he and Toony were returned on August 31, 1953.

On January 8 the 35th FBS's "Bluster Mike" flight was jumped by supposed enemy F-80s that were heading west. One of these, dark colored, made a firing pass on Lt. Henry, who broke left into the rogue F-80 with his flight leader, and then Henry lost sight of Lt. Jones, his leader. All alone, Henry was attacked three more times by this F-80 before it disappeared. Two more rogue F-80s, one with a reported solid red vertical stabilizer, and the other with a red striped tail, attacked "Whippit Roger" flight at the same time. Not being exactly sure of the action they should take, some of the friendly F-80s only feinted attacks and did not fire. (Post War reports by some pilots in this incident stated that they knew all along that these F-80s were friendly, but that several of the pilots panicked and saw things that were not actually the case.)

January 8 saw the loss of two pilots. Lt. Leo Nicaise, 80th FBS, flew into his target while dive bombing. On the way back from the rail cutting mission, Lt. Colonel Lewis Webster, executive officer, 35th FBS, was hit by flak. His F-80 started flying erratically just as they were approaching the bombline on their way home. From 2,000 feet it climbed to 15,000 feet and its guns started firing. The tip tanks came off, and the F-80 dove to 500 feet, only to climb back up to 10,000 before it entered a hammerhead stall and crashed. Webster had been on his ninety-seventh mission.

On January 11 the 36th FBS lost their executive officer when Major John Tullock was hit by small arms fire while strafing trucks east of Sinanju. His F-80 was seen to roll over and crash with its guns still firing.

The 80th FBS lost Lt. Richard McNulty on January 16 as he was flying the number four position in his flight. While conducting an armed recce mission, he disappeared after making a strafing pass on some trucks. The 80th FBS lost a second pilot on January 24 when Lt. Jerry Bingaham was attempting to make an instrument let-down over North Korea in order to reach his targeted area. He became separated from the rest of his flight in turbulent clouds and went "lost wingman." His flight leader gave him instructions on how to locate the rest of the flight under the clouds, which Bingaham acknowledged, but he was not seen again.

On January 26 1st Lt. Vincent DiPalermo flew into the blast from his flight leader's bombs while bombing near Huichon. The canopy came off his F-80 in an attempt to bailout, but he did not get clear of his aircraft before it crashed. He remains one of the MIA's. The 15th TRS also lost a RF-80 on the 26th, but its pilot and the circumstances are unknown.

Winter weather continued to hamper operations in February, with only 1587 combat sorties being flown. Also slowing things down was the lack of serviceable F-80s. The 8th FBG possessed sixty-five, but twenty-five of them had to be rotated through REMCO for maintenance each day.

As far as losses were concerned, February was exceptional, particularly after January. On February 2 1st Lt Robert Bull, 80th FBS, was killed over North Korea. On February 6 1st Lt. Robert Martin, 35th FBS, was downed southeast of Huichon after pulling up from a look-see of a possible target while on a recce mission. As he climbed, his engine flamed out, and although he attempted two airstarts, they were both unsuccessful. His F-80 was then seen to roll over from 1500 feet and crash into the side of a mountain. Unseen was the fact that he was able to bailout, and Martin became a POW. Only one other F-80 was lost during the month, which crashed on takeoff at Suwon. Blamed on pilot error, this pilot was relieved of his wings.

The number of combat sorties increased to 2,433 in March, with 3260 combat hours being flown. Although the winter weather was abating, there were three days when there was no flying at all, and five when only a few missions could be dispatched.

On March 6 2nd Lt. George Robey, a brand new pilot assigned to the 8th FBG's provisional training detachment, was killed while enroute to the gunnery range. The cause was undetermined. He was the 8th FBG's only pilot loss in March.

A maximum effort mission was flown on March 11 when the 8th FBG went after an enemy troop concentration near Nuicaeri. This was a dawn to dusk effort with the Group flying 254 sorties with fifty-one F-80s. Each carried four 500 or 1,000 pound General Purpose bombs, the F-80s being sans tip tanks for the short ranged mission. They dropped 155 tons of bombs, fired 63,500 .50 caliber rounds, dropped 33,660 gallons of napalm, with each F-80 averaging five sorties. Although they were put in for a Distinguished Unit Citation for this effort, it was not approved.

One of two morale damaging instances to hit the USAF in general and the 8th FBG in particular was President Truman signing an Executive Order in April that extended, involuntary, all enlistments an additional nine months beyond their normal discharge time. The other was the return of the specter of death over the Group, as they lost seven F-80s and five pilots during the month. Fortunately, not all of these losses turned out to be as severe as they first appeared to be.

On April 8 Lt. Ward Tuttle, 36th FBS, was hit by flak while flying through an intense concentration of communist AA fire. Tuttle stated that his engine had flamed out, and then his wingmen observed him make a crash landing and run from the cockpit of his F-80. He became a POW.

"Whippet George 3," a Lt.Winberg, 35th FBS, was "observed making landing on a well wooded ridge, and moved to higher ground," after a forced landing in enemy territory on April 20. While attempting to set up a RESCAP, Lt. Maxey Wall "was hit in the right wing by small arms fire that set his wing ablaze." Wall bailed out at 800 feet and established radio contact with Lt. Keller, who was leading "George" flight. At this point, Keller and his wingman were running low on fuel and had to depart the area, however, a flight of Mus-

tangs came in to continue the RESCAP, and they strafed the communist troops that were seen in the area. The end result was that Winberg managed to evade capture and make his way to friendly territory, and Wall became a POW.

On April 24 1st Lt. James Ure was leading a flight of four F-80s on a CAS mission. When his F-80 was hit by AA fire it snap rolled several times. Ure recovered and slowly made a climb to a safe altitude while assessing the damage to his aircraft. Suddenly the entire tail section of the F-80 disintegrated, and Ure, who had been hit in the leg was forced to bailout. He came down in friendly territory and was sent to a hospital in Japan where the wounded leg had to be amputated.

Two more F-80s were lost on April 30. Captain Victor Duer was flying his second combat mission with the 35th FBS when he became lost while breaking off from a target in marginal weather. He called for a DF steer, but ran out of fuel before it did him any good, and the wreckage of his F-80 was found on Cho-do, a small island off the coast of Korea that was held by friendly forces for use as an emergency landing site. 1st Lt. John Zwiacher, 36th FBS, was on an interdiction mission when his flight was jumped by MiG 15s. He was hit on their first firing pass and was seen to successfully bailout. Afterwards radio contact was made with him on the ground via his URC-4 survival radio, but then there was silence.

As April closed Lt. Colonel Tyler, CO 36th FBS, completed his missions and was replaced by Major Jack Wilson, their former executive officer. Representing the 36th FBS as an example in May, they had 38 assigned pilots who flew 588 combat sorties during the month. This averaged to 1.5 missions per day per pilot and meant that each pilot might complete his tour of 100 missions in 66 days, weather and other factors permitting.

The 15th TRS, during April had flown a record (for them) 51 sorties. During this period they were 87% effective on their photographic missions, photographing 50% of their assigned targets, which averaged 1826 objectives per month during this period. At this time it was also hoped by Headquarters FEAF to be able to convert the 45th TRS from their combination of F and RF-51Ds to RF-80s. At this time, also, the 67th TRW had twenty-seven RF-80s on board, and were expecting fifteen more, and these forty-two RF-80s would be all that would ever be available to them.

The 80th FBS lost their commanding officer on May 8 when Major Arthur Faunce was hit by flak over North Korea. Faunce told his wingman that he was going to bailout, but he did not make it. That afternoon the 80th FBS lost 1st Lt. Robert Coffee in the same area. His F-80 was seen to snap-roll violently and then explode in the air.

The 36th FBS did not lose a pilot or F-80 during May, but the 35th FBS lost 1st Lt. William Slade on May 12. Slade had been on a rail cutting mission and when he pulled up off his bombing run his F-80 burst into flames, climbed to 4,000 feet, rolled over and dove into the ground.

In June 1952 the 8th FBG switched roles from rail cutting to making maximum effort bombing strikes against North Korean electrical power plants, industrial targets and pin-point attacks against enemy supply dumps just behind the front lines. These were in addition to the usual CAS missions being flown.

It was on June 1 that the 36th FBS suffered the only pilot loss for the Group during that month. 1st Lt. Carl Washburn was working with a FAC, "Anaconda 5," and was leading "Bluster Queen" flight on a CAS mission when he was hit by small arms fire. The F-80 snaprolled twice and plunged into the ground. The FAC pilot reported that there was no sign of a parachute.

The 45th TRS was now flying a mixed bag of reconnaissance aircraft. In February they had received several of the "Project Ashtray" F-86A to RF-86A conversions. In June they received five RF-80As and four F-80s to go along with their twenty RF-51Ds. On June 26 the 45th TRS lost their squadron commander, Jack Williams, while flying one of the RF-86s, known as "Honeybucket." He was replaced by Lt. Colonel Thomas Hudson.

As the Korean War entered its 1952 summer doldrums, apparently the 8th FBW historian also fell into a stupor, as for a six month period he reported little of historical value. In July the 8th FBG lost three F-80s, but no pilots were reported as lost. However, this may not necessarily have been the case, as many pilots who were downed over North Korea were not declared as killed until after the fighting was terminated in July in 1953. These particular pilots, of which at least three of them were from the 35th FBS, were declared as KIA in December 1953 and March 1954 without verification of the date they were shot down.

As a matter of some historical interest, the 8th FBG did fly 1509 combat sorties in 1933 combat hours during July. In August they flew 2054 combat sorties in 2573 combat hours.

During this period, the supporting F-80 squadrons in Japan, Okinawa and the Philippine Islands went about their business of training pilots as OTU's. Although few pilots were now being pulled from the 16th FIS and 44th FBS for service with the 8th FBG, the 41st FIS still had a major role in supporting the 8th FBG's operations in this respect. In addition, the 41st FBS continued its air defense role and took on the task of providing simulated air cover for military training exercises conducted in Japan prior to the ground troops being transferred to Korea.

As an example of their activities, in July 1952 the 41st FBS flew three air-control missions for the U.S. Navy. On July 9 and 25 they flew simulated CAS missions against an abandoned airstrip north of Johnson Air Base for air-ground training, and also the FEAF survival school. On the 20th they had gone to Atsugi Naval Air Station for air defense exercises, where they "shot down" a PBM in a simulated interception.

The 15th TRS remained busy during this period, also. In July the weather, with rain and low ceilings, curtailed so many missions that the requests for photography became backlogged. When the weather did improve, two RF-80s had to be sent out at a time to catch up on the reconnaissance demands. (During this time the RF-51s of the 45th TRS were doing mostly visual reconnaissance work while they were trying to jet qualify their pilots in the RF-80s. The 15th TRS RF-80s were accomplishing all of the photography.

Between July 1 and December 31, 1953 the 15th TRS lost 6 Shooting Stars. Two of these by enemy action, and four through accidents. Three pilots were missing in action, but the only one that could be identified was Lt. Milton Wiseman that was declared KIA in December 1953. One of the contributing factors to these losses may have been the low experience levels of these pilots. The replacement pilots assigned to the 15th TRS at this time averaged a bare 400 hours flying time. Interestingly enough, all of the aircraft lost by the 15th TRS during this period were F-80s, and not RF-80s. The 45th TRS during this same period lost one RF-80 in a mid-air collision, but its pilot made a successful bailout.

Identifiable pilots lost by the 8th FBG during this period were: Lt. Wilbur Spradling, 35th FBS, on July 22; Lt. William Conlon, 36th FBS. on August 1; Lt. Allen Olsen, 35th FBS, September 9; Lt. James Roberts, 80th FBS, on November 22.

Also lost on November 22 was Major Charles Loring, 80th FBS operations officer. While leading a flight of four F-80s on a CAS mission, Loring was directed by a "Mosquito" T-6 to attack an enemy gun emplacement that was firing at friendly troops. Loring pressed his attack in spite of heavy ground fire, and when his F-80 was hit by AA fire at 4,000 feet, he elected to dive his F-80 into one of the gun emplacements. There was no doubt in his wingmen's minds that this was a deliberate action on his part, as his F-80 was under control at all times. Loring posthumously received the Medal of Honor and the now closed Loring AFB at Limestone, Maine was named in his honor.

There were no additional known combat losses of F-80 pilots in Korea in 1952. However, on December 22 a F-80 on a ferry flight into Suwon hit a C-47 in a mid-air collision that killed the F-80 pilot and all thirteen aboard the transport. The F-80's pilot was not identified.

In January 1953 the 8th FBG participated in Operations Plan 100-53 which was an intensive day and night series of attacks back in their old stomping grounds between Sinanju and Pyongyang. The targets were all bridges between Sinanju and Yong-Mi-Dong, with secondary targets of a bridge across the Taeryong River south of Pakchon and two bridges across the Chongchon River east of Sinanju. This area was the proverbial area of antiaircraft fire, as intelligence sources indicated that there were 95 heavy AA guns and 40 automatic weapons batteries in the area when the attacks began on

January 10. At the termination of these missions, it was believed that the communists increased this number to 139 heavy caliber guns and 75 automatic weapons. The raids cost the USAF four pilots, and thirty-two additional aircraft were damaged.

The 8th FBG flew 112 sorties on January 13 to Yong-Mi-Dong. These were something unusual for the Group in itself, as several were flown by the F-80 pilots at night in an attempt to suppress the searchlights and to harass the enemy's railroad repair crews. These were not welcome missions for the pilots, as firing the nose mounted machine guns or firing the rockets just once effectively night-blinded the pilots and prevented them for making more than one attack.

These attacks brought about one 8th FBG pilot loss. On January 10 2nd Lt. Roy Ryden, 35th FBS, was flying a flak suppression mission when his F-80 was hit by AA fire in its right wingroot. Ryden climbed to 3,000 feet with flames seen emitting from both sides of his fuselage at the wingroot that extended fifteen feet beyond the tail of his aircraft. He leveled off momentarily, and then was lost to the sight of his wingmen until an explosion was seen on the ground.

Additional pilot losses in January showed that 1st Lt. Heath Glass, 36th FBS, was killed on January 3 as he was making a bombing run. Apparently he was hit by AA fire as he started his attack and after he dropped his bombs, Glass pulled up and punched off his tip tanks. But, his F-80 rolled over and crashed before he could get out of it.

On January 17 2nd Lt. Edward Sickles was attacking a front line position near Sinenjung-ni on a CAS mission. He was hit by AA fire as he started attack, and he pulled up and ejected from his disabled fighter-bomber. He managed to make one call on his URC-4 that he was safely on the ground, and has never been heard from again. Sickles remains one of the Korean War MIA's.

1st Lt. Robert Hallman, 36th FBS, went down on January 26 while strafing vehicles north of Suan. His F-80 was seen to be hit by AA fire in the nose and cockpit, and then it climbed, rolled over and crashed.

Colonel James Stone had become 8th FBW commanding officer on January 24, 1953, and in early February he announced to the troops that the 8th FBG would soon be converting from their weary F-80s to brand new F-86Fs. The time schedule was open-ended, as the 18th FBG was already in the process of converting from Mustangs to Sabres, and everything was depending upon the delivery rate of the new fighter-bombers, as The F-86F was the first Sabre to be designed for the dual role. On February 22 the 36th FBS was withdrawn from F-80 combat operations to commence conversion training.

The 36th FBS had lost their last F-80 pilot on February 5. 1st Lt. Robert Crosley was flying a single-ship night armed recce mission and was presumed to have been hit while attacking a target. His last radio transmission was that he had Cho-do Island in sight and was going to bail out, but he was killed in the process.

The 80th FBS lost Major Melvin Wood on February 16 when his F-80 was hit by a single burst of flak in its belly. His F-80 caught fire and Wood bailed out, but he never let go of his ejection seat handles and his parachute was seen to foul as a result and it never had a chance to open before he hit the ground.

1st Lt. Garfield Guyer was killed in a similar tragedy on February 22. Just after he had taken off from Suwon on a mission his bombs and left tip tank fell off his F-80. Guyer told his wingman that "His aircraft was going crazy." And, his wingman told Guyer to bailout when he saw flames coming from its left wing. Guyer ejected at 300 feet, but failed to clear his seat in time for his parachute to open.

On March 14 the 35th FBS was taken off operations for F-86 training. This left the 80th FBS to carry the remaining load for the 8th FBG with the F-80 for the duration. Until the end of the month the 80th FBS flew sixty-four armed recce missions and 139 interdiction strikes as a part of Operation Spring Thaw, a further attempt to disable the North Korean railroad system.

The 80th FBS lost 1st Lt. Douglas Smith on March 17 during a "Thaw" mission while on another of the hazardous night recce missions. Smith, apparently could not find his targeted area and was overheard attempting to call his "Parka" controller for instructions, but he could not establish radio contact. He then called "in the blind" for anyone that heard him to give him a bearing home, but was too far away and too low to receive anyone's instructions. He disappeared, and was declared as killed after the war was over. "Body not recovered."

The 80th FBS lost their Last F-80 on April 1 when 1st lt. Donald Dahl was hit by AA fire on a dive bombing run. He managed to get it back as far as seven miles north of Seoul before he had to eject. For a change it was a successful bailout.

The 80th FBS flew their most effective combat missions on April 24 when they not only broke their own 8th FBG record of ninety-six combat sorties in a single day, established on April 11, 1952, but that of MAG 33 of 117 sorties in a day set earlier in the year. On the 24th they flew 120 combat sorties with twenty-nine pilots participating. Two of these pilots flew six missions, ten flew five missions, four flew four missions, two flew two missions, and the rest got in one. In a fourteen hour effort they burned 59,932 gallons of fuel and dropped 228,000 pounds of bombs.

The last 80th FBS F-80 missions were flown on April 30. They attacked an abandoned airfield on the Haeju peninsula, and then returned to turn over their weary F-80s to the 35th FIW in Japan for garrison duties.

Although the F-80 was officially out of the fighter-bomber role, they continued to be used in combat operations through the end of the conflict and beyond with the 67th TRW. The 15th TRS had started the year with twenty-four F-80s which they used for armed recce and as their own fighter escorts for their twenty-five RF-80s. By the end of June, all but six of the F-80s had been transferred out, but these and the RF-80s were utilized to fly "Buffer Zone" reconnaissance missions until September when they were replaced by RF-86s and RB-26s. It should be noted that the last combat related F-80 loss occurred on July 10 and the last RF-80 was lost on July 27. It was flown by Lt. John Rhoads, and he was lost on this memorable day when the armistice agreement was signed and the cease fire went into effect.

The F-80 continued to be used in Japan, Okinawa and the Philippines until early 1954 when they were phased out in favor of the F-86. The 35th FIW had finally been able to re-equip their 40th FIS from Mustangs to Shooting Stars in April 1953 when the 8th FBG transferred them to Japan.

The 41st FIS, under Major James Stewart, commenced transition to F-86s in September 1953 and in November the last sixteen F-80s from the 41st FIS detachment at Niigata were returned from there and grounded pending overhaul and transfer back to the United states. The 40th FIS, under Major Max King, was scheduled to make a similar change in December, but the F-86 pipeline slowed down a bit and they continued flying the F-80 until the end of January 1954 when the era of the F-80 in FEAF was over.

Chapter XII: The Air Force Reserves

The United States Air Force Reserve, AFRES, finally entered the jet age in 1953, some five years after their contemporary older, and better cared for, sister service, the Air National Guard. Like the Air National Guard in the Post Korean War era, the AFRES received worn out or battle weary examples of the F-80 Shooting Stars, in two different shipments.

The first allocations of F-80s to the AFRES were F-80As and -Bs that were primarily used for jet training and familiarization training, and most of these came from service in the Air Training Command. By 1954 these older versions of the Shooting Star were replaced by F-80Cs, most of which were combat veterans.

In the Post Korean war period the AFRES numbered among their units six Fighter Bomber Wings and two additional Tactical Reconnaissance Wings that initially received F-51D Mustangs. As the Mustangs were phased out of AFRES service, one of the two TacRecce Wings converted to Douglas B-26s, nee A-26s, while the other received F-80As for a short period, and then it too was reassigned a light bomber role with the Invader. The six FBW's started receiving Shooting Stars in mid 1953, shortly after these units had been returned to the Reserve after being activated during the Korean War. For a period of approximately two years these Wings were considered operational with the Mustang, and in training on the F-80.

Finally, in 1955 the Mustangs were phased out and the six fighter wings became listed as operational in the F-80C.

During this short span, the mentioned TacRecce Wing switched to B-26s, but its place was taken by an additional fighter wing that was formed and accepted their aircraft.

Assigned to the 89th Fighter Bomber Wing at Hanscom Air Force Base, MA was 48-904, a F-80C-1. This Wing was composed of the 24th and 25th Fighter Bomber Squadrons, which bore no connection to the similarly numbered Fighter Interceptor Squadrons. (Tom Cuddy via Esposito)

The 349th Fighter Bomber Wing was one of the largest AFRES Wings and the largest operator of reserve F-80s. They were also the only AFRES unit to apply truly distinctive markings to their fighters. (Esposito)

The F-80A and TF-80As that were originally assigned to the AFRES in 1953 were considered by Headquarters USAF to be more obsolete than the F-51Ds they shared ramp space with. Very few of these were actually flown by AFRES pilots, as most did what they could do to avoid taking one up, thus they became maintenance trainer "ramp rats." They were quite unpopular for two reasons: they did not have ejection seats, and they lacked acceleration on takeoff. The F-80A-10 did have, by this time, modified J-33A-9A (Or -9B, -11A, -11B, -17A, or -21) engines, but these only delivered a rated thrust of 3,825 pounds (dry), 775 pounds less thrust than given by the J-33A-35 installed in the F-80C variants.

When the F-80Cs came on the scene they were looked forward to with great anticipation by AFRES personnel. Even though many of these aircraft had seen extensive use in Korea and were all "high time" aircraft. As far as the combat veteran aircraft were concerned, upon their return from the combat arena in 1953 or 1954 they had been sent through IRAN (Inspect and Repair as Necessary) at McClellan AFB for complete overhaul prior to being allocated to an AFRES unit. All of the other examples were given 100 hour inspections by the transferring agency, and received the same inspection again upon receipt by the effected AFRES unit, thus they were all in reasonably good mechanical condition.

A total of 177 F-80Cs were allocated to the nine AFRES wings, commencing in mid 1954. Yet in May of that year a re-evaluation of the AFRES mission requirement by Headquarters USAF concluded that the Shooting Star was too weary and obsolescent to continue as a viable mission aircraft and they would be replaced as soon as practicable. The new replacement aircraft was to be the F-84G, but circumstance gave them F-84Es instead. By December 1954 the

49-739 had belonged to the 25th Fighter Interceptor Squadron, 51st FIW in Korea and it had been hit by flak on March 1, 1951. Repaired, it finished its career with the 349th FBW. (Esposito)

A formation of 349th FBW F-80s over California. The 349th included the 312th, 313th and 314th Fighter Bomber Squadrons under the control of the 2346th AFRES Flying Training Center. (Esposito)

94th Tactical Reconnaissance Wing had already received ten Thunderjets to begin the phase-in of these aircraft. Before complete transition took place another decision rendered in Washington resulted in the 94th TRW being redesignated as a Light Bomber Wing and they were transferred to Scott AFB, IL as a B-26 unit. Coinciding with this, was the decision to furnish the AFRES with F-86H Sabres, which was more in line with giving them an actual first-line aircraft. The F-86H started to replace the F-80C in a few units in 1956, although none of the effected units ever reached combat operational status with them before yet another Washington decision took jet aircraft away from the AFRES entirely.

The AFRES F-80s were officially withdrawn in October 1957 with the 448th Fighter Bomber Wing being the last AFRES jet unit within that time frame. During the summer/fall of 1957 three of the AFRES FBWs were inactivated entirely, while the others had their mission changed to that of "trash haulers" with C-46s and C-119s. It was not until July 1970 when several of the AFRES units started receiving A-37s that some of those units again became tactically orientated.

AFRES Unit Assignments

All of the AFRES units during the 1950s were either assigned to a regular Air Force Base, or stuck off in the corner of a joint-use civilian/military field. These circumstances resulted in a very low profile for AFRES members, and few of the local public even knew that an AFRES unit existed in their own environs. The Air National Guard was the most visible to the public as citizen soldiers, because they had better press as a result of at least some State funding available to them and also highly visible modern construction programs that were taking place that utilized local construction firms and workers. At that time, too, the ANG had an open gate policy, and anyone that wanted to explore their aircraft and facilities could do so at their leisure.

The AFRES, on the other hand, was usually sequestered off somewhere to the side and out of the way and as far out of sight as possible on a regular USAF installation. AFRES operations usually were regarded as something that got in the way of the "real" USAF. On the joint use airfields, the AFRES got the use of ex full time military installations that either were rundown or allowed to deteriorate to that condition before being turned over to the AFRES. It was not until the late 1950s that finally funding came their way to improve things for them.

Reservist were regarded, at this time, as even less than "weekend warriors," a half derogatory term thrown at guardsmen. They didn't even get paid for their service like guardsmen did, only receiving "points" towards retirement, and most were looked down upon by their full-time contemporaries. And, unfortunately, during this period, all reservists were held in low esteem by the civilian population, some employers even going so far as to issue ultimatums against such activities. There was no Public Law in existence during this period to protect the interests of the reservist.

As in the case of the ANG, the AFRES also had a great difficulty in obtaining personnel. This was for several reasons, not all being parallel with the ANG's recruiting problems. There was a great amount of bitterness among the reservist in general as to the way they had been treated by the USAF in particular, and the government in general, during the Korean War. In most respects, young men knew that if they joined the ANG they were relatively secure from actual military service, as they could not be touched unless their entire unit was activated, and if the unit was called up, they would in all probability remain with it and their friends for the duration. Reservist could be called-up piecemeal at the government's whim, and even if their unit was activated, experience showed that they would in all probability be immediately yanked from it and assigned to some other unit. They knew, too, that if there was an actual shooting war, they would be thrown into

49-710 appears more than a little worse for wear, and it deserved better than this ill treatment. After fighting through the Korean War with the 8th and 80th Fighter Bomber Squadrons, it was assigned to the 439th Fighter Bomber Wing at Selfridge Air Force Base, MI. When the AFRES got out of the fighter business, she went to Alamogordo, NM as a display aircraft. (Esposito)

the brunt of it, as in 1952 80% of USAF forces in Korea were reservist. Again, reserve positions were not as lucrative as those in the ANG, as they could only receive their points for retirement, and they were not getting paid anything for their efforts. Also, there were limited slots available in the ANG, so if one elected to be around military aviation and still be a civilian for whatever reason, the reserve had to be their choice.

Reserve F-80 Units

All of the AFRES units received a four digit identification for their primary controlling unit, which was assigned to either the 14th or 10th Air Forces, which was then subordinate to ConAc. These units were then designated with a standard three digit group identification number, with squadron numbers assigned to them following the previous heritage of the parent group. This, in itself, has caused some confusion over the years as to which unit was where, and what their assignment was. Thus, some explanation is required here.

The normal sequence of a squadron or group assignment generally followed a traditional path. A fighter group that in the pre WWII era was designated a pursuit group, became a fighter group, and then a fighter-interceptor group, with their attached squadrons being identified accordingly. For example, the 51st Pursuit Group (Fighter), became the 51st Fighter Group in 1942, and the 51st Fighter Interceptor Group in February 1950. Assigned to the 51st FIG were the 16th, 25th and 26th FIS's.

However, a change in mission aircraft, role and function often brought about similarly identified units that were in no way related, but they did appear that way upon initial observation.

An example of this is the 2234th Air Reserve Flying Center that was based at Hanscom AFB, MA and supported the

89th Fighter Bomber Wing. The 89th FBW had been a troop carrier group during WWII, and the designation was transferred to the AFRES in May 1949. Activated during the Korean War, they continued as a TCG, and were inactivated in May 1951. The 89th was reactivated in the AFRES on June 14, 1952 with the 24th, 25th, and 26th Fighter Bomber Squadrons, some of their original troop carrier squadrons that were now equipped with tactical aircraft. What ads to the confusion, here, is that the 25th and 26th FIS's had previously flown F-80s in the Far East, and now squadrons with the same number were flying them in Massachusetts, but there is no actual connection to be made from this.

The 89th FBW initially received five F-80As and a T-33 when they were reactivated. In October 1953 the A models were replaced by C models. On January 8, 1957 the 26th FBS was transferred to Youngstown, OH with the intent of becoming a F-86H squadron, but this program was curtailed and the 89th FBG was inactivated on November 16, 1957.

The 2256th AFRES Flying Center was located at Niagara Falls International Airport, NY. It supported the 445th Fighter Bomber Wing and the 700th, 701st, and 702nd Fighter Bomber Squadrons. This group and its squadrons had the heritage of a WWII B-24 organization. Post Korean War, the 445th FBW originally was equipped with F-51Ds, and then in November 1954 they obtained their first T-33 and F-80A. In June 1954 they switched to F-80Cs, and on November 16, 1957 conversion to a troop-carrier mission took place and they commenced flying C-119s. It should be noted, that for almost all of their early period, only the 445th FBW and the 700th FBS actually existed, with the 701st and 702nd squadrons being only assigned "on paper" until they were activated on July 1, 1957.

At Hamilton AFB, CA was the 2346th AFRES Flying Center and the 349th FBW. The 349th had previously been a TCW and had been activated on April 1, 1951 for the Korean War emergency. A year later, after all of its personnel had been absorbed into the regular USAF, the 349th was inactivated. It was reactivated on June 13, 1952 within the AFRES as the 349th Fighter Bomber Wing, with the 312th, 313th and 314th Fighter Bomber Squadrons assigned. Initially they received F-51Ds and some T-28As, but received three F-80As and a TF-80A shortly thereafter. On January 13, 1954 they received F-80Cs and were the largest AFRES unit to fly the Shooting Star. (Actor Alan Ladd "flew" one of their F-80s in the Hollywood film "The McConnell Story".) On October 13, 1955 the Wing was dispersed with the 313th FBS relocating to Hill AFB, UT and they converted to C-46s on September 1, 1957. The 314th FBS followed suit, moving to McClellan AFB, CA October 15, 1955, and they also converted to C-46s on September 1, 1957. The 312th FBS, remaining at Hamilton, also switched to C-46s in September 1957.

The 2242nd AFRES Flying Center supported the 439th Fighter Bomber Wing at Selfridge AFB, MI. Initially the Wing's flying squadrons were designated as the 91st, 92nd and 93rd Fighter Bomber Squadrons, but as there were also two other

Based at the Minneapolis-St. Paul IAP, MN and assigned to the 2465th AFRES Flying Center was 49-676. The 2465th supported the 440th Fighter Bomber Wing and the 95th, 96th and 97th Fighter Bomber Squadrons, which, again, bore no relationship to the similarly number Fighter Interceptor Squadrons. (Esposito)

fighter bomber squadrons of the same numerical designations assigned to the 81st Fighter Bomber Wing on active duty within the USAF, the 91st and 92nd: and a 93rd Fighter Interceptor Squadron with the Air Defense Command, the AFRES squadrons were redesignated as the 471st and 472nd FBS's, respectively, while the 93rd FBS was inactivated. Initially equipped with F-51Ds, the 439th FBG received six F-80As and one TF-80A in early 1953, loosing one in an accident, and then October 1953 they re-equipped with 40 F-80Cs. On December 28, 1955 the 472nd FBS moved from Selfridge to Willow Run Air Force Station at Ypsilanti, MI. Their last F-80 left in November 1956 when it was programmed that they would convert to F-86Hs, but each squadron, physically, only received one Sabre before this program was canceled and the 439th FBW became a troop carrier unit.

The 452nd Tactical Reconnaissance Group was under the 2347th AFRES Flying Center at Long Beach, CA. Post WWII, the 452nd had been allocated to the AFRES as a Light Bombardment Group and given B-26s. They were the first AFRES unit to be activated for the Korean War, on August 10, 1950, and by the fall of 1950 they were in Korea flying combat missions. Inactivated in Korea on May 10, 1952, the 452nd designation was returned to Long Beach and reactivated with the AFRES once again, on June 13 under Colonel James Kemp. Initially, they received F-51Ds, but in February 1953 they received their first F-80A. By the fall of 1954 they had received 14 F-80Cs and six T-33s, but effective May 25, 1955 their role again reverted to that of a light bomber unit and the three assigned squadrons, the 728th, 729th and 738th, re-equipped with B-26s.

The 2589th AFRES Flying Center at Dobbins AFB, GA supported the 94th Tactical Reconnaissance Wing with the 331st, 332nd and 333rd squadrons. Activated on March 10, 1951 as a Light Bombardment Group, the 94th was immedi-

ately plundered of all personnel and equipment, and ten days later it was inactivated as a unit. The designation was returned to the AFRES on June 14, 1952 and F-51Ds were initially assigned. Their first F-80As arrived in September 1953 and their T-33s arrived in the Spring of 1954. In July 1954 they switched to F-80Cs, which they flew until May 1955. On May 14, 1955 the 94th TRW was redesignated as a Light Bombardment Wing and transferred to Scott AFB, IL to fly B-26s.

Replacing the 94th TRW at Dobbins AFB was the 482nd Fighter Bomber Group that was activated there on May 18, 1955 with the 812th Fighter Bomber Squadron being their only tactical squadron at that time. For a short period coinciding with their activation they had 4 T-33s, 14 F-80Cs and received 10 F-84Gs, but these aircraft were immediately replaced by B-26s and the 482nd became a Light Bombardment Group.

The 2596th AFRES Flying Center at Hensley Naval Air Station, Dallas, Texas was the supporting unit for the 448th Fighter Bomber Wing. This Wing was activated with the AFRES on May 18, 1955 with the 711th Fighter Bomber Squadron as their active unit, and the 713th Fighter Bomber Squadron assigned to them "on paper." (The 713th FBS had been intended to be based at Davis Field, OK but the intended improvements to the runways to permit jet operations was not accomplished to permit this action). The 448th FBW received the F-80Cs that had originally been assigned to the 94th and 482nd Groups. During the summer of 1957 members of the 448th FBW qualified in the F-86H, but this transition program was curtailed as soon as this occurred and the 448th FBW was inactivated in October 1957.

Based at Minneapolis, MN was the 2465th AFRES Flying Center and the 440th Fighter Bomber Group. Assigned to the 440th FBW were the 95th, 96th, and 97th Fighter Bomber Squadrons. And, here again, the historical lineage of the units tends to get muddled. The 440th FBG had originally been a Troop Carrier unit, and these three squadrons were also troop carrier units. On June 15, 1952 when the 440th FBG was reactivated with the AFRES and redesignated as a FBG, there also existed a 95th, 96th, and 97th Fighter Interceptor Squadrons that were assigned to the Air Defense Command, but there is no historical connection between the ADC units and those assigned to the AFRES, although both were flying fighter aircraft. In November 1954 the 440th FBG converted from F-51Ds to F-80Cs, and they flew the Shooting Star until September 1957 when they converted to C-119s. Two months later, the 95th FBS, now the 95th Troop Carrier Squadron, was transferred to Milwaukee, WI as their AFRES unit.

At Milwaukee's General Billy Mitchell Airport was the 2473rd AFRES Flying Center that supported the 438th Fighter Bomber Wing. Assigned to the 438th FBW was the 87th, 88th and 89th Fighter Bomber Squadrons. Once again, there is no historical connection to be made between the 87th Fighter Bomber Squadron and the 87th Fighter Interceptor Squadron. (The 88th and 89th FBS's existed only "on paper"). The

438th FBG began conversion from F-51Ds to F-80s in early 1954 with the receipt of 3 T-33s and their first Shooting Star. By the end of 1955 they had 6 T-33s and 11 F-80Cs, and, in the Spring of 1957 they received their first F-86H. After commencing transition training into the Sabre, the program was terminated, and the 438th FBG and the 87th FBS was inactivated on November 16, 1957, being replaced at that time by the 95th Troop Carrier Squadron.

The last AFRES F-80 unit was to be the 2584th AFRES Flying Training Center at Memphis, TN. Although this unit received some advance "documentation" on the F-80, there is no evidence that they ever actually received an aircraft. A revision to their mission aircraft changed them to F-84Es, and it is believed that they obtained some ten examples of the Thunderjet before being notified that they were tasked with training all of the AFRES units that were to transition into F-86Hs. By June 1957 the 2584th had some seventy-five Sabres on hand and the training program was underway when it was decided to get the AFRES out of the tactical fighter business altogether. A few of the AFRES units that managed to have their people trained in Sabre operations took a few of these aircraft home with them, until November 1957, when these units were either inactivated or changed roles. At this time the AFRES F-80s were on their way to the bone yard at Davis Monthan AFB, AZ and the F-86Hs were transferred to the Air National Guard.

49-1868 had been assigned to the 8th Fighter Bomber Wing in Korea, and during the course of the war it had been over-stressed in combat, so it was returned to the United States and assigned to the AFRES's 438th Fighter Bomber Wing at General Billy Mitchel IAP, Milwaukee, WI. (Esposito)

Chapter XIII: Foreign Service

The only F-80s to serve in the air forces of foreign counties went to member nations of the Organization of American States in South America. These were all F-80Cs that were delivered to six of these OAS member countries under the Reimbursable Assistance Program, which was similar to the lend-lease Mutual Defense Aid Program that supplied aircraft to members of NATO and SETO.

Military aviation history, in respect to South American countries, has always been one of the most obscure topics. None of these countries, for past, present or future reasons of their own, have ever been inclined to release any solid information on their military units. Thus little factual information on F-80 operations has ever been brought to light.

The first South American country to receive the F-80 was Ecuador. Their air force, Fuerza Area Ecuatoriana, had entered the jet age in 1954 with the receipt of Gloster Meteor's and English Electric Canberra's. In 1957 they started receiving the first of a total of sixteen F-80Cs, but delivery was sporadic, and the last of these did not arrive until 1960. They were flown by Escuadron de Caza-Bombardeo 2112 at Taura Air Base. Six were returned to the United States in July 1965, and four after that time: all of them then being given to the U. S. Navy for uses as targets on their China Lake gunnery range. They were replaced by the Anglo-French Jaguar.

The second South American country to receive the F-80 was Columbia. Their Air Force, Fuerza Aerea Colombiana, had obtained six T-33s in March 1954 for use as trainers, at this time their primary strength was F-47s, B-17s and B-25s. In 1956 Columbia received a mixed-batch of Canadair and North American Aviation built F-86s, and then in 1958 they received sixteen F-80Cs. These Shooting Stars were flown by 10 Escuadron de Caza-Bombardeo, a fighter-bomber squadron at Palanquero. At least nine of these F-80s were known to have been lost in operational accidents. One of the survivors was ex Nebraska ANG 47-215, which was returned to the United States and became the only civilian registered F-80 not in the service of the FAA.

Chile was one of the two larger users of the F-80C in South America. The Fuerza Aerea de Chile had flown surplus P-40s, B-25s and Catalina's until being upgraded with A-26s and Beech T-34s, along with Canadian surplus Vampire's in the mid 1950 period. The first eighteen of a total of thirty F-80Cs were delivered to FAC between January and March 1958. They were assigned to Grupo 7 de Caza-Bombardeo at Los Cerrillos until the mid 1970s when they were replaced by Northrop F-5Es. The surviving F-80s were then transferred to Grupo 6 at Punta Arenas for proficiency flying, and Grupo 12 at Carlos Ibanez for tactical use until replaced by Cessna AT-37s circa 1976.

Brazil started receiving the first of thirty-three F-80Cs on March 31, 1958. Their air-arm, Forca Aerea Brasileira, had flown F-47s, B-17s, B-25s and AT-6s as their primary strength until 1954 when they modernized with sixty Meteors. The F-80Cs were assigned to 4 Grupo de Aviaacao Caca and continued operationally with them until 1969/70. The last of those remaining in the FAB inventory were withdrawn from use on August 16, 1973 due to a lack of spare parts. Tragically, as the last of these was being flown to a museum on August 16, 1973 it exploded in flight, killing its pilot. Two remain in Brazil as display aircraft.

A pair of long-lived war horses in formation over Japan during the Korean War as a part of a salute to a French ambassador. The 8th Fighter Bomber Wing F-80C later went to Ecuador as their TF-809, while the F-82 finished its service life in Alaska. (USAF)

One F-80 that survived for posterity was 49-851. After serving with Ecuador's Fuerza Area Ecuatoriana as TF-851, it was returned to the United States for use as a target on the China Lake Gunnery Range. Later, along with parts of 49-1872, it was restored and placed on display at Pueblo, CO. (Esposito)

Peru's Fuerza Aerea del Peru was the first South American country to become totally jet equipped. In the middle 1950s they received F-86Fs, Hawker Hunters and Canberra's, along with sixteen F-80Cs. Assigned to Grupo de Casa-Bombardeo commencing in March 1958, the F-80s had to be withdrawn in 1973 because of a lack of spare parts.

The last Organization of American States country to fly the F-80 was Uruguay. Their Fuerza Aerea Uruguaya replaced F-51 Mustangs and B-25s with seventeen F-80Cs in June 1958. They were assigned to Grupo de Caza 1 and 2, along with T-33s and AT-6s and remained "on strength" until 1968, but the last individual F-80 was not retired until 1971. It should be noted that one of their aircraft, 49-696, which had previously been flown in the Korean War, was returned to the United States and now resides with the Air Force Museum at Dayton, Ohio. Atypical of their display aircraft, it is in pristine condition.

One of the last South American F-80s in operational use was FAB 4200 of Forca Aerea Brasileira, and it was assigned to 4 Grupo before becoming a display aircraft. (via Esposito)

Chapter XIV: The End of the Line

A "Captivair" F-80A at Williams ("Willie Air Patch") Air Force Base, AZ. It could do anything a normal F-80 could do but fly. It was used to instruct fledgling pilots in how to start the Star, check its electrical and hydraulic systems, retract the landing gear and flaps, etc. (via Barry Nichols)

Not really an unusual transposition of this F-80s "buzz number" from "FT" to "TF," with the exception that these same codes were also found on F-51s, with "FF" also changed to "TF." This change indicated that the fighter had been modified to meet training standards. Usually this meant that the armament systems, guns, gunsight and bomb/rocket racks had been removed and the aircraft was assigned to a training role, but this particular airframe still is carrying its machine guns and K-14 gunsight. At the time the photograph was taken it was assigned to Williams AFB, after previously serving with the 57th Fighter Group. When the Air Training Command was finished with it, it went to Ellington Field and the 111th FIS. (Esposito)

45-8552 was assigned to the 3550th Combat Crew Training Wing at Moody Air Force Base, Valdosta, GA. The 3550th CCTW was tasked with teaching all-weather flying techniques and ran the Air Defense Command's Instrument Flying School. (L. Paul)

Retaining the normal F-80 "buzz number," this F-80A-11, a F-80A improved to F-80C standards, was assigned to Williams AFB. (Leo Kohn)

Williams Field F-80C-1s on graduation day. To celebrate the event, the entire class would take to the air for a fly-by formation, to show their stuff to the undergraduates. (USAF)

Las Vegas AFB graduates in a similar formation. The lead F-80 was one of the recalled ANG F-80s that rejoined the USAF inventory after its ANG squadron was activated during the Korean War emergency. (Isham)

Pulling off the target at the Indian Springs Gunnery Range, NV after a strafing pass. Note the dust behind the target. (USAF)

44-85123 in its first paint scheme. On January 26, 1946 Lt. Colonel William Council set a new speed record from Long Beach, CA to LaGuardia, NY in this P-80. After serving as a display aircraft at Lackland AFB, TX for many years, it was moved to the Test Pilots School at Edwards AFB, CA. (Leo Kohn)

Towards the end of the line: In 1959 Oklahoma's 185th FIS turned over to the Federal Aviation Agency a half dozen of their F-80s for use in high altitude flight inspection of navigational aids. (Esposito)

An inglorious fate. Ex-Air National Guard F-80s at the Davis-Monthan AFB, AZ salvage yard await the chopping blade like chickens with their heads on the block. (Olson)

On the range at Indian Springs, a 3595th CCTW F-80 shows its stuff. Note in the first photograph that the .50 caliber cartridge ejection doors are open as the pilot is firing his machine guns. (Isham)

Lockheed F-80 Specifications

	XP-80	P-80A	P-80B	P-80C	TP-80C
Span	37"	39'11"	39'11"	39'9"	38'11"
Length	32'10"	34'6"	34'6"	34'5"	37'9"
Wing Area	240'"	234'8"	234'8"	234'8"	234'8"
Height	10'3"	11'3"	11'3"	11'3"	11'4"
Empty Weight	6,287	7,920	-	8,240	8,084
Max Gross Weight	8,620	14,500	14,500	16,856	11,965
Max Speed	502 mph	558 mph	560 mph	580 mph	543 mph
Rate of Climb	3,000 fpm	4,580 fpm	4,580 fpm	6,870 fpm	-
Service Ceiling	41,000	45,000'	45,000'	42,750'	47,500'
Range (@ 5,550')	421 sm 560 sm	360 nm 540 sm	360 nm 1380 sm	920 nm	900 mn
Armament	- cal. M-2	6 .50 cal. M-2	6 .50 cal.	6 .50 M-3 cal	2 .50 M-3
Ordnance	-	to 2,000	to 2,000	to 2,000	to 2,000
Rockets	-	-	-	8 5" HVAR	-
Normal Fuel	200 gal (max 285)	481 gal	481 gal	755 gal.	-

Engine Data

Thrust

HB-1 (XP-80)	3,000 lbs @ 10,000 rpm (engine limited to 9,500 rpm, giving 2,460 lbs)
I-40 (XP-80A)	4,000 lbs (J-33-GE-5)
J-33A-9A, 11A 17A (P-80A)	4,000 lbs (J-33A-9B, 11B, 17B were retrofitted to the P-80A-10 series: all were interchangable. The later "B" series engines featured water injection, which was disabled on the P-80A aircraft)
J-33A-19, 21, 23 (P-80B, R)	5,200 lbs
J-33A-25, 35	5,400 lbs with water injection: 4,600 dry, (P-80C/TF-80C) 3,900 normal thrust.

Serial Numbers

XP-80	44-83020 "Lulu-Belle"
XP-80A	44-83021 "Grey Ghost"
XP-80A	44-83022 "Silver Ghost"
YP-80A	44-83023, -83025/-83035
XF-14	44-83024
P-80A-1	44-84992/-85199, -85202/-85336 (-85000 to USN as BuAer 29667, -85005 as BuAer 29668)
P-80A-5	44-85337/-85491
XP-80B	44-85200, modified to P-80R
XFP-80A	44-85201
P-80A-5	45-8301/-8363
FP-80-5	45-8364/-8477
P-80B-1	45-8478/-8565 (-8557 to USN as BuAer 29690)
P-80B-5	45-8566/-8595 (Series to 94th FS).
P-80B-1	45-8596/-8717
P-80C-1	47-171/-224 (Series to ANG except for 47-218/224 to USN as BuAer33821/33827.)
P-80C-1	47-525 (To USN as BuAer 35828)
P-80C-5	47-526/-600 (Series to Alaska)
P-80C-1	47-600/-604 (To USN as BuAer 33829/33832)
P-80C-1	47-1380/-1411 (To USN as BuAer 33833/33847, 33849/33864)
TP-80C	48-356/-375 (-356, -357 to YF-94
P-80C-1	48-376/-396 (-376/-381 to USN as BuAer 33865/33870. -382 as BuAer 33848
P-80C-1	48-863/-912
TP-80C	48-913/-920
P-80C-10	49-422/-878
TP-80C	49-879/1006 (-934 to USN as BuAer 124570)
P-80C-10	49-1800/-1899
P-80C-10	49-3597/-3600

Note: Out of the P-80A-5 and P-80C series, many were later modified to FP-80 standards without serial number discrimination. Likewise, post Korean War surviving P-80s were modified to, or close to, P-80C standards with activated ejection seats, newer engines, water injection, cockpit cooling, etc.

Bibliography & Acknowledgements

Arnold, Rhoads, Shooting Star, T-Bird & Starfire, Tucson: Aztex Corporation, 1981

Chilstrom, Ken & Leary, Penn, ed. Test Flying at Old Wright Field. Omaha: Westchester House, 1993.

-Colorado Pride: Dallas: Taylor Publishing, 1989.

Davis, Larry, P-80 Shooting Star in Action, Carrollton: Squadron/Signal Publications, 1980

Densford, James T. ed. 111th Squadron. 1973

Flordia Air National Guard 1946-1982.

Flying, "Designing The F-80." December 1948.

Francillon, Rene J., The United States Air National Guard. London: Aerospace Publishing, 1993.

Futrell, Robert Frank, The United States Air Force in Korea. New York: Duell, Sloan and Pierce, 1961.

Goldberg, Alfred, ed. A History of the United States Air Force 1907-1953, Trenton: D. Van Nostrad, 1957

Green, Bill, The First Line. Fairview: Wonderhorse, 1994.

Gross, Charles Joseph, Prelude to the Total Force: The Air National Guard 1943-1969, Washington: Office of Air Force History, 1985.

Hallion, Richard P., "P-80: Story of a Star." Air Enthusiast, November 1979-February 1980, #11. Pg. 54

Hasskarl, Robert A., "Every Inch a Fighter," Airpower Historian, July 1962.

Isham, Marty, "Fighter Inteceptor Squadrons." Interceptor. January 1979. Pg. 5ff.

Jackson, Robert, Air War Over Korea. New York: Charles Scribner's Sons, 1973.

Johnson, C. L. "How We Engineered The Lockheed Shooting Star." Aviation. July 1945.

Johnson, C. L. "Development of the Lockheed P-80A Jet Fighter Airplane." USAF Case Study, no date.

Knaack, Marcelle Size, Encyclopeda of U. S. Air Force Aircraft and Missile Systems, Vol. 1., Washington: Office of Air Force History, 1978.

Life. "War By Jet and GI." July 17, 1950, Vol. 29, #3. Pg. 27.

McLarren, Robert, "P-80 Still 'Right' After Five Years," Aviation Week, July 19, 1948, pp. 22.

Maurer Maurer, Air Force Combat Units, Washington: USAF Historical Division, Air University, Department of the Air Force, 1961.

Maurer Maurer, Combat Squadrons of the Air Force in WWII, Washington: USAF Historical Division, Air University, Department of the Air Force, 1969.

Nebraska Air National Guard 1946-1981

Oatron, Joel J. ed. Ohio Air National Guard. American Yearbook Company.

Ravenstein, Charles A. Air Force Combat Wings 1947-1977. Washington, Office of Air Force History, 1984

Robinson, Robert, USAF Europe, Vol. #1 1948-1965, Carrollton: Squadron/Signal Publications, 1990.

Robinson, Robert, USAF Europe, Vol. #2 1947-1963, Carrollton: Squadron Signal Publications, 1982

Stocker, Joseph, "Ace Air Force Stunt Team: Acrojets." Air Trails, May 1950.

30th Anniversary, 176th Tac Airlift Group, 1952-1982.

Thompson, Warren, "Shooting Stars Over Korea." Air Power, March 1985, Vol. 15, #2. Pg. 22.

Thompson, Warren, "The (Shooting) Stars of Korea." Air Enthusiast, April-July 1982, #21. Pg. 21

USAF Historical Study #81: USAF Credits for the Destruction of Enemy Aircraft: Korean War, Maxwell AFB: Air University, 1963.

Wooldridge, E. T., Jr., The P-80 Shooting Star: Evolution of a Jet Fighter, Washington: Smithsonion Institution Press, 1979

ALSO: Extractions from the individual unit history's of the mentioned Air Force and Air national Guard combat units. The majority of this material is available on 16mm microfilm through the Albert Simpson Historical Research Center, Air Force Historical Research Agency, Maxwell AFB, AL. I am indebted to these over-worked people, as well as to the staff of the Air Force Museum, Research Division, Wright Patterson AFB, OH for their support.

Additional acknowledgement goes to the following who provided photographs and sundry information in support of this project: Duane Biteman; Bob Burns; Bud Butcher; Gerald Cantwell; Dick Chard; Bill Cleveland; Job Conger/Airchive; Tom Crawford; Duncan Curtis; Larry Davis; Bob Dunnavant; Mike Fox; Vince Gordon; Ed Hodges; Marty Isham; Leo Kohn; Tony Landis; Tony LeVier; Denny Lombard; David Lucabaugh; David Menard; William O'Donnell; Merle Olmsted; Doug Olson; Lionel Paul; Richard Penrose; Dick Phillips; Ron Picciani; Steeve Seele; Jack H. Smith; Warren Thompson; Earl Watkins; and Brig. General Walter Williams.

Particular acknowledgement goes to "Mr. F-80," himself, Robert Esposito, who probably has more knowledge of the Shooting Star than anyone and has been a good friend for decades.